The Buried Life of Things

Simon Goldhill offers a fresh and exciting perspective on how the Victorians used material culture to express their sense of the past in an age of progress, especially the biblical past and the past of classical antiquity. From Pompeian skulls on a writer's desk, to religious paraphernalia in churches, new photographic images of the Holy Land and the remaking of the cityscape of Jerusalem and Britain, Goldhill explores the remarkable way in which the nineteenth century's sense of history was reinvented through things. *The Buried Life of Things* shows how new technologies changed how history was discovered and analysed, and how material objects could flare into significance in bitter controversies, and then fade into obscurity and disregard again. This book offers a new route into understanding the Victorians' complex and often bizarre attempts to use their past to express their own modernity.

SIMON GOLDHILL is Professor of Greek, Cambridge University; John Harvard Professor in Humanities and Social Sciences, Cambridge University; Director of the Cambridge Centre for Research in the Arts, Social Sciences and Humanities; Fellow of King's College, Cambridge; and Fellow of the American Academy of Arts and Sciences. His internationally award-winning books include *Jerusalem: City of Longing* (2008), *Victorian Culture and Classical Antiquity* (2011) and *Sophocles and the Language of Tragedy* (2012).

The Buried Life of Things

How Objects Made History in Nineteenth-Century Britain

SIMON GOLDHILL

CAMBRIDGE
UNIVERSITY PRESS

CAMBRIDGE
UNIVERSITY PRESS

University Printing House, Cambridge CB2 8BS, United Kingdom

Cambridge University Press is part of the University of Cambridge.

It furthers the University's mission by disseminating knowledge in the pursuit of education, learning and research at the highest international levels of excellence.

www.cambridge.org
Information on this title: www.cambridge.org/9781107087484

© Simon Goldhill 2015

First published 2015

Printed in the United Kingdom by TJ International Ltd. Padstow Cornwall

A catalogue record for this publication is available from the British Library

Library of Congress Cataloguing in Publication data
Goldhill, Simon.
The buried life of things : how objects made history in nineteenth-century
Britain / Simon Goldhill.
    pages   cm
ISBN 978-1-107-08748-4 (hardback)
1. Material culture – Great Britain – History.   2. Consumption (Economics) – Social
aspects – Great Britain – History.   I. Title.
GN585.G8G65   2014
306.4'6–dc23

2014023809

ISBN 978-1-107-08748-4 Hardback

Contents

Plates

Figures

All images are from the author's private collection unless otherwise indicated.

Introduction
The buried life of things

The Victorian drawing room is an immediately recognizable stereotype of the profusion of things: the mantelpiece with its knick-knacks, tables with their ornaments and lace, books, mirrors, sideboards, flowers, lamps, vases, work-baskets, boxes, cards … For the modern historian, such a room speaks insistently not simply of a history of taste, but also of the interconnected forces of the industrial revolution, which changed the modes of the production of things, and the imperial project, which changed the modes of the circulation of material objects and their owners. The market for things altered fundamentally in the nineteenth century.[1]

For the nineteenth-century novelist, the drawing room was a stage of moral and cultural value through its things. Mrs Gaskell's controversial best-seller *North and South* has the inequalities of industrial production as its explicit and polemical frame. When Margaret, the novel's heroine, enters the drawing room of the Thorntons, the mill owners, she has a moment to look around: 'It seemed as though no one had been in it since the day when the furniture was bagged up with as much care as if the house was to be overwhelmed with lava, and discovered a thousand years hence. The walls were pink and gold: the patterns on the carpet represented bunches of flowers on a light ground, but it was carefully covered up in the centre by a linen drugget, glazed and colourless.'[2] The tastelessness of the room is imaged through an archaeological metaphor, as if the distance Margaret feels from it makes her into a historian excavating a lost and buried culture, like Pompeii. Even the carpet is covered by a 'glazed and colourless' drugget, as if the floor-cover itself needs uncovering to be properly seen. 'Glazed and colourless' will slide easily into a metaphor of the indifference to the sufferings of others which marks out the mill-owners' unblinking response to industrial production.

The description continues: 'The whole room had a painfully spotted, spangled, speckled look about it, which impressed Margaret so unpleasantly that she was hardly conscious of the peculiar cleanliness required to keep everything so white and pure in such an atmosphere, or the trouble that must be willingly expended to secure the effect of icy, snowy discomfort.' Cleanliness may be next to godliness, but in this room cleanliness is an icy rejection of life and comfort; the decoration is there to be preserved not enjoyed as beauty. It is not hard to predict that Margaret's encounter with Mrs Thornton will not go well, and that such an iciness will be embodied in her moral attitude to the workers of the mill as well as to her son's personal life. The Thorntons' cleanliness can be set in telling contrast with Mrs Gaskell's portrayal of the Brontës' parsonage in her celebrated biography of Charlotte Brontë, as she brilliantly reclaims the shockingly coarse Brontë girls for propriety and fame: 'Everything about the place tells of the most dainty order, the most exquisite cleanliness. The door-steps are spotless; the small, old-fashioned window-panes glisten like looking-glass. Inside and outside of that house goes up into its essence, purity.'[3] This is the truly high-minded cleanliness of moral and social purity: 'spotless' as opposed to 'painfully spotted', 'dainty' and 'exquisite' as opposed to 'icy . . . discomfort'. In biography as in narrative fiction, the house and its things form the physical embodiment of the owner's moral values, an image of a cultural identity. Things, we know, tell a story.

This book is about how things become a way of telling the story of history in the nineteenth century. It is clear enough that things can be treated as fetishes, icons, objects of lust or fashion, aestheticized, ritualized, symbolically exchanged, and can transform the world through technological innovation (at least).[4] 'One universally acknowledged truth about the Victorians is that they loved their things.'[5] I have not set out here on the crazed adventure of trying to write a history of things in all their various guises and transformations and politics in the nineteenth century. Nor have I turned even to the restricted but culturally expressive genre, which goes back to antiquity, where an object like a coin or a bible is given a voice and a narrative, which allows an oblique perspective on human activity, from a material otherness, as it were – though it is certainly one way in which a thing can tell a story.[6] Nor have I set out to trace the construction of historical sites, an inventive process of genealogy and heritage that has transformed particularly the tourist experience of history from the nineteenth century until today, through a combination of texts, buildings and mementos, although the increasingly dominant intellectual field of historiography, the practice of leisured travel, and the fascination with historicized material remains will run as thematic links through each chapter of what follows.[7] Nor is there any extended analysis of how one author or one novel makes things a dynamic signifying system within their writing, reflects on commodification, or collects curiosities, although novels are quoted and discussed in every chapter.[8]

Rather, I am interested in the multiform practices whereby things become invested with historical meaning, are made to tell history, take on political, religious or intellectual significance – and consequently are intensely fought over – because of the history they are understood to embody. This book hopes to uncover this shifting life of things, as they flare into significance (and become forgotten), are excavated to reveal an extraordinary shift in understanding (and are discarded or reburied), become the object of passionate historical controversy to the point of requiring parliamentary intervention, only to pass into indifference. The relationship between the materiality of history and the stories of history turns out to be remarkably unstable and fractious.

The book begins with a single pair of unique and individual objects – identified and labelled human skulls – and explores how they became objects of display and what this display betokened within nineteenth-century culture. These skulls from Edward Bulwer Lytton's house at Knebworth in Hertfordshire, England, were dug up in Pompeii and are identified as the skulls of named figures from his celebrated novel, *The Last Days of Pompeii*: real skulls, but of fictional characters. These objects become thus a way of articulating the contested boundary between history and fiction, genres anxiously attempting to define spheres of authority, not least through the reception of Scott, Macaulay, Renan and Bulwer Lytton himself. As phrenological exhibits they bring contemporary science to the fore as a new technology of comprehending the physical world. They are still on display today at Knebworth, but, without explanation, remain objects of no more than passing exoticism or disregard to the tourists trailing through the house.

If the first chapter takes unique and even outlandish objects to explore the key arena of fiction and history as competing authoritative discourses, the second chapter takes three religious objects, each of which has some claim to paradigmatic status: a Roman mosaic discovered in Frampton, Dorset, with a Christian symbol built into it; a stone altar erected in a church in the university city of Cambridge; and a chasuble, a ritual robe, woven by a leading architect for the founder of a new religious order, established at Oxford after the crisis of the Oxford Movement. Nineteenth-century religious conflict in Britain was as intense as at any other period since the Reformation, and its violent disagreements often focused precisely on the history of the Church, in a way which modern Christian institutional thinking has largely obscured. The general questions that seemed most insistently pressing to mid-Victorian religious controversy turned precisely on critical history. Was the life of Jesus as represented in the authoritative

texts of scripture historically accurate? Should the early Church be determinative of modern religion, and, if so, how? Did the Anglican Church have
a significant history before the Reformation? Could the history pronounced
by Church authorities be reconciled with the history pronounced by modern sciences such as geology, or with modern history's sense of what
constituted adequate evidence? Each of the objects discussed in this second
chapter might seem typical of a general class of things: there is now a lot of
Roman archaeology which can be visited in Britain and seen on television;[9]
it is unlikely that any visitor or parishioner in a modern Anglican church
would find the presence of a stone altar in a church an abomination
sufficient to imprison the incumbent who allowed it; a chasuble worn for
a religious service can now be happily viewed both as an acceptable part of
the splendour of religious worship and even as an aestheticized item in a
museum.[10] Yet in each case, when Victorian religious sensibilities came into
contact with these things, spiralling historical invention, bitter theological
and political wrangling, and intricate acts of rebellious artistic representation took place. This remarkable explosion of how things mean, as history
and religion clash, is what the second chapter seeks to explore.

Chapter 3 moves from individual objects to large classes of objects, and,
in particular, the thousands of photographs of Jerusalem and the Holy Land
which were produced in the nineteenth century. The new technology of
photography engaged with the new science of archaeology to produce a new
vision of the Holy Land. As the first chapter is concerned with archaeology's
discovery of reality in things, and as the second chapter is concerned with
how nineteenth-century religion envisions the materiality of the world, so
the third chapter is concerned with biblical archaeology, its claim to determine the real of the Bible authoritatively, its ability to represent the history
of things in material form. The intense fascination with the truth of the
Bible, the strident claims of new sciences in Victorian culture, and the
commitment to the ideological expectations of the imperial project make
biblical archaeology the archetypal test case of the buried life of things in
nineteenth-century culture. Photography's claim on the real was informed
consistently by a 'biblical gaze', whereby the contemporary landscape,
buildings, people of the Middle East, as well as scripturally significant
sites, become a sort of living testimony of an ancient history, contemporary
proof of a biblical past's physical truth. The circulation of these photographs
of biblical lands was ordered into professionally produced albums, which
structured an ideologically determined itinerary to position the visitor or
viewer within a particular religious and political perspective. This political
positioning is revealed most vividly by photograph albums produced by the

Ottoman court for western consumption, which explicitly aim to produce a counter-view to the western Orientalist construction of the East as backward and old-fashioned. The Sultan wished to rewrite western history of the East by producing his own version of a resolutely modern empire. Photographs circulated, that is, as objects in a politically and religiously charged conflict over the representation of the present and the past, and photographic images of the present, as the embodiment of modernity or antiquity, became the means and matter of this conflict. Photographs as things and of things brought the Bible, history and politics into sharp contention.

Chapter 4 takes us out of the nineteenth century in that its focus is on the planning and building work of the Mandate in Jerusalem. Yet C. R. Ashbee, the civic advisor in Jerusalem who did so much to determine the early policy of the British in Palestine, was intellectually formed in the late pre-Raphaelite and early Garden City movements and heavily influenced by William Morris, the Arts and Crafts movement, and Edward Carpenter. He brought a fully articulated nineteenth-century aesthetic to Jerusalem – and with it changed the material appearance of the city. This chapter is concerned with how history is made on the ground. It traces how the Holy City's physical form was reconstructed to embody a view of the city's history. Chapter 3 traced how an image of Jerusalem and the Holy Land was produced in and by photographs; chapter 4 shows how this image in turn informed the planning policies of the imperial authorities in Jerusalem, with lasting effect. Ashbee made things tell the history that he wanted to become visible.

The final chapter develops directly from this discussion of the rebuilding of Jerusalem, and also looks back to the church politics of the second chapter, by investigating how restoration and reconstruction became central metaphors for Victorian thinking, especially but not solely with regard to material culture. Restoration and reconstruction are key expressions of how the past can be expressed in and by contemporary things. Restoration requires human agency and intent to move through the present to an idealized model of the past; reconstruction requires the rebuilding of a fragmentary or ruined present. Both are ways of embodying a material history. Both are ways of challenging the present in the name of history.

There are evident thematic and narrative links between these chapters. The Bible and classical antiquity are dominant models of the past for nineteenth-century culture and consequently provide a constant framework for understanding how history and religion take shape through things. The birth of Jesus and the composition of the New Testament in the Roman

Empire provide a necessary if combustible connection between these two genealogies. Classics – Greek and Latin – formed the basis of elite Victorian education; Christianity from the start remained obsessed with its obstreperous genesis and incremental accommodation within Greco-Roman culture – 'What has Athens to do with Jerusalem?', as Tertullian railed in the fourth century – and nineteenth-century Britain repeatedly strove to negotiate the tension between its classical learning and its Christian ideals.[11] Material culture, from archaeology to architecture to art, played a formative role in this process of accommodation. Each chapter is also concerned with how things are used to make what is invisible visible – whether it is theology, history, fiction or the truth of the self. The material and the spiritual, the physical and ideological, the real and the imaginary, come together, as the buried lives of things are narrated. This book traces how the nineteenth-century pursuit of historical truth seeks to find a grounding in physical reality. Each chapter discusses also how individuals and their cultural formation, ideological commitments, and personal foibles actively engage with the process of making things speak. The power of objects lies in their uncanny ability to make it seem that *saxa loquuntur*, as Freud famously said of Pompeii: 'The Rocks Speak'.[12] Uncovering the processes of this objectification – how objects become treated as if their meaning were not the construction of human interactions – is a running theme of this book. Each chapter also explores how things are uncovered as sites of contest and then fade into a newly buried life of obscurity (although often with strange trailing clouds of influence). *Das Ding an sich*, as Kant establishes at the fountain-head of nineteenth-century philosophy, is unknowable.

It is certainly possible to find antecedents of such questions and concerns throughout cultural history, not least in antiquity and the scriptural records themselves. But it seems to me that there is something specific to the nineteenth century about the organization of knowledge I am tracing in this book. First of all, the nineteenth century witnessed a radical and rapid change in the understanding of the material world through the swift and all-embracing reach of the sciences of geology, chemistry, physics, astronomy, archaeology. The intense rate of technological innovation, iconic of the nineteenth century's self-awareness of progress, did not merely foster such intellectual advances, however. Rather, technology was part and parcel of the contest over how the material world should be understood to reveal history. So, as we will see in chapter 3, the innovative technology of the steamship brought more and more Europeans to test their new technology of photography in the Holy Land, to produce images which contributed to the new science of archaeology, which was itself seeking to show that the

Bible was grounded in reality, against the challenge of geology's and critical history's different understandings of the past. What is more, the Empire and the nation state, specifically nineteenth-century contexts, provide unparalleled frameworks not just for the stories of identity that things can tell, but also for the very material possibilities for revealing the buried life of things: it is the shifting geography of nineteenth-century empires too that brings so many Westerners to explore the Holy Land, or which makes the story of Roman Britain a freshly significant genealogy. The combination of new material sciences, new technology, and the new political and social opportunities to exploit things, creates a nexus of forces specific to nineteenth-century culture.

Nineteenth-century material sciences quickly came up hard against inherited textual authorities. Geology and Bishop Ussher could not both be right about the dating of the earth, although there were awkward attempts to ameliorate the evident clash. Could the flood recounted in Genesis have taken place over the whole world but left no trace in the physical record? If Jerusalem was a glorious city of gold, why did it look like a small, backward, dirty Middle Eastern hill-top town without a decent water supply? Again and again this book tells the stories of travellers whose journeys brought them face to face with a material reality that challenged their imagination and their expectations of the world formed through what they had read and been taught. Textual authorities about things had been significantly challenged. In the wake of the French Revolution, institutional power too in the nineteenth century was repeatedly threatened by revolutions of authority, and fought back accordingly.[13] My question of how things come to matter for history has to be seen within this broad and specifically nineteenth-century cultural narrative of unstable political identities and shifting strategies of representation.

What follows are necessarily essays towards a history of how things tell the past in nineteenth-century culture: a full account would be prohibitively long and beyond the scope of a single scholar. The book is intended rather to explore significant and telling examples of a fundamental nineteenth-century cultural phenomenon and to provide paradigms of the potential of what might be called an interdisciplinary approach to such a phenomenon: it treats high and low texts, texts of very different types, from novels to treatises to poems to graffiti and inscriptions; it discusses art, architecture, archaeology, clothes, technologies, gestures of self-presentation – the full gamut of verbal and material culture. The time-frame is what we keep calling the long nineteenth century, from the French Revolution through to the First World War. The range of subjects is also larger than is often seen in a short monograph, with evident consequences for the possibility of including certain sorts of historical detail: the footnotes and more than usually extensive bibliography are designed to direct the interested reader towards further background discussion, where it is particularly relevant and has informed my analysis, and thereby to maintain the focus of the book.

The first chapter is developed from its first outing in *Representations* 119 (2012), and materials from the fourth were also used in *From Plunder to Preservation*, edited by Peter Mandler and Astrid Swenson (British Academy, 2013); the final chapter will appear, I hope, in shorter form in a forthcoming book co-written with Jim Secord, Clare Pettitt and Peter Mandler. The scope of the book, however, is partly a product of having had the good fortune to work as the principal investigator in two inspirational and supportive interdisciplinary research groups over the last decade, 'Abandoning the past in an age of progress', a fifteen-person team funded for five years by the Leverhulme Trust, and 'The Bible and Antiquity in Nineteenth-Century Culture', an eleven-person team funded for five years by the European Research Council. It is a pleasure to be able to thank my colleagues from both teams for much help and criticism over many years, especially, for this book, Claire Pettitt, Peter Mandler, Jim Secord, Astrid Swenson, Scott Mandelbrote, Michael Ledger-Lomas, Gareth Atkins, Brian Murray and Kate Nichols. For intense theoretical conversations, I couldn't have been more fortunate in having Miriam Leonard, Brooke Holmes and Constanze Guthenke as interlocutors and friends. Several chapters or parts of chapters have been tried out on audiences in Princeton, Berkeley, Chicago, London, and I thank my hosts and audiences there. Other debts are too numerous to list here.

1 | A writer's things

Edward Bulwer Lytton and the archaeological gaze

Knebworth House is the seat of the Lytton family. The original red-brick Elizabethan manor was extensively redesigned in the mid-Victorian period by its most celebrated owner, Edward Bulwer Lytton, who continued the work started by his mother, in a high Gothic style, complete with turrets, gargoyles and a decorated hall with minstrel gallery, armour and an inscription of welcome around the wall just beneath the embossed and chandeliered ceiling – creating out of the actual Elizabethan house a building that looks more like an Elizabethan house should look for a successful historical novelist of the nineteenth century.[1] The interior was in turn redecorated again in 1905, to lighten the wood and to bring more openness into its sepulchral gloom, under the ownership of Edward's son, Robert Bulwer Lytton, who was a popular poet under the pen-name Owen Meredith. The work was undertaken by Sir Edwin Lutyens, already the most distinguished of modern British architects, the designer of New Delhi – where Robert Bulwer Lytton had been Viceroy of India. Edwin Lutyens was also Robert Bulwer Lytton's son-in-law, although, by the time of the commission, the marriage, opposed by the parents when first proposed, had already collapsed. The house itself encapsulates a history of Victorian architectural politics, and the engagement of that politics in the history of Empire and, more surprisingly, in a history of (familial) literary endeavour, as the building expresses the changing image of its owner's public self-presentation.

Inside the house, as is the way with such stately homes today, there is a series of small exhibitions, one of which focuses on the most famous Bulwer Lytton, Edward, who wrote not only *The Last Days of Pompeii*, one of the best-selling Victorian novels which founded the genre of toga fiction – more than 200 novels about the Roman Empire were published in the eighty years following – but also a string of best-selling novels in his long and hugely successful career as a novelist, politician (though he was removed from office after a funding scandal), and widely influential figure, who prompted public scorn as well as admiration.[2]

The exhibition is intelligently composed, even if it cannot wholly escape a tinge of the hagiographic. It duly records that Bulwer Lytton was responsible for phrases such as 'the pen is mightier than the sword', and 'It was a dark and stormy night'; it collects wonderful examples of versions of *The Last Days of Pompeii*; and it decorously refers to his violent and abusive relationship with his wife, Rosina, acted out in a blaze of recriminatory publicity from them both, and includes some of the scandalous, prurient and outraged pamphlets circulated at the time that Edward forcibly committed Rosina to a lunatic asylum for speaking against him at a political husting. The hagiography could easily be paralleled from contemporary sources. The *Encyclopaedia Britannica* in 1859 declared that Bulwer Lytton is 'now unquestionably the greatest living novelist'. Margaret Oliphant regarded him as 'the first novelist of his time', surpassing Dickens and Thackeray.[3] The exhibition does not record the equal and opposite reaction of intense hatred that Bulwer inspired as a person and as a writer. Kingsley dismissed him as 'a self-sustained, self-glorifying hot house flunkey'.[4] Thackeray, in a long campaign of disdain, vilified him as 'bloated with vanity, meanness and ostentatious exaltation of self'[5] and christened him the 'Knebworth Apollo'.[6] Bad reviews and personal violence seem only to have increased his sales.

There is one tiny part of the exhibition in a case on the landing that almost no-one looks at with any attention today. This is a pity, because it actually provides an extraordinary glimpse of Victorian display that goes back to Bulwer's time, and indeed the identification labels are still rather curly Victorian paper slips in a distinctive nineteenth-century hand. It is also a pity because what this exhibition puts on display is quite remarkable. Inside the standard, large, upright display cabinet is a smaller Victorian glass case, designed to sit on a desk. There are two skulls in it, which are labelled as the skull of Arbaces and the skull of Calenus. That is, the visitor is presented with the bodily remains of two of the leading characters of *The Last Days of Pompeii*.

Being faced by these skulls is a decidedly weird and macabre moment that bursts through the piety of the shrine of the house with a shock of laughter and confusion. The bones of literary inventions? How can the skulls of characters from a novel be on display – or how can they still be on display without explanation? How did they arrive there? Who put them in a glass cabinet in Bulwer's home? And, above all, what does this display tell us about the interplay of fiction and science, and about the construction of archaeology, in the nineteenth century?

In exploring these immediate questions, this chapter will bring together three particular contemporary critical concerns, which are all too often allowed to develop separately. The first concerns things and their display within Victorian culture of the spectacle. How objects become conceptualized within particular regimes of knowledge and perception at different cultural moments has become a particular concern of literary critics and cultural historians, where both materials (such as glass) or the representation of specific objects within novels or other writings (such as Peggoty's work-box) have been analysed with some flair – and at its most abstract level the discussion has been (over)dignified as 'thing theory'.[7] The display of objects reifies them and frames them most directly within regimes of knowledge. The skull – whether held by Hamlet, on a pole in a colonial jungle adventure, in a Gothic mansion's vaults, or in the hands of a medical scientist – brings a set of contextualized associations, which are being radically reorganized in the nineteenth century, as we will see, by phrenology, medical science and the sciences of racial theory, especially anthropology, nationalist history, and museology. The skulls of Arbaces and Calenus turn out to embody a specific turning point in the history of the exhibition of bodily remains. One claim of this chapter will be that Bulwer's skulls epitomize an important era of transition in the period between 1830 and 1860 in thinking about display and the body.

The second critical issue concerns the self-presentation of writers through their houses, as a set for the performance of their celebrity. In the nineteenth century, thanks as much to the massively increased circulation of written materials as to the changing cultural values of Victorian society, writers became superstars in a way previously unattested. One consequence of this was that writers' houses became sites of pilgrimage.[8] As the inner self was felt by literary pilgrims to have been moulded by the intense emotional experience of reading, so the place which had moulded the self of the author was a lure to a further wondering imaginative embrace, a further contact with the reality which, it seemed, must have been formative for the author, who had been so influential for the reader. So, too, writers used their houses as part of the arsenal of self-presentation.[9] At the most direct level, Sir Walter Scott self-consciously created Abbotsford, his baronial pile, as an expression of his willed literary persona. Its Romantic, Gothic and baronial image promoted and projected an image of the author. His house was a version of his work, as one with his work, to be read through his work – and his work through the house, home of the author, seat of his creative genius.[10] And it was designed to be maintained, as it has been, as a museum of the author. At a less direct level, as I mentioned in the introduction, Elizabeth Gaskell's biography of Charlotte Brontë was instrumental in constructing not just a lasting idea of the author, but also a picture of the author as essentially located in and formed by the house and environs in which she lived.[11] So Bulwer Lytton was acutely aware of how an author's physical surroundings were part of the persona of the successful writer, and, as we will see, the skulls of Arbaces and Calenus not only are some of the writer's things, by which his public life as a writer takes external shape, but also mark a turning point in how a writer's writing space becomes part of a public imagination.

The third major area of debate is the history of archaeology. Archaeology was developing rapidly as a discipline, and played a major role in the arguments between philology, biblical criticism, and their claims on the reality of ancient history.[12] This background narrative, which is now becoming well known, has broad implications also for the status of excavated and displayed objects. With the growing impact of archaeology, the regime of knowledge within which an exhibited skull is recognized inevitably changes. Pompeii had been the most stunning archaeological discovery of the eighteenth century, much as Troy was for the nineteenth. Bulwer Lytton was shown around Pompeii by Sir William Gell, the leading publisher of the excavation. The display of the skulls of Arbaces and Calenus mark also a juncture in the history of archaeology, not in terms of the growth of the discipline itself, so much as in terms of the interface between the disciplinarization of the field and its public recognition.

While these three areas are each the subject of intense contemporary scholarly interest, it is far less common to see how they necessarily interrelate (although archaeology has self-consciously become more aware of its necessary engagement with the theories of materiality that also inform 'thing theory').[13] Bulwer Lytton's exhibition of the skulls of characters from his novel cannot be appreciated, I will argue, without seeing their place within the space articulated by the interlocking and changing ideas of the display of (bodily) objects, the self-presentation of the writer, and the history of archaeology – together. What is more, the bizarreness of this particular display will turn out to be a sign and a symptom of its position at a specific turning point in these three histories and their interaction. By placing Bulwer's skulls in a comparison with Scott's and Freud's displays of heads, we will see their place in a nineteenth-century narrative of how a writer's things express the self, a moment touched by the history of nationalism, science and race. Finally, just as Knebworth House now comes layered in most contemporary visitors' imagination by a history of its use as a backdrop for pop concerts and films (two different versions of England, one self-consciously modern, one self-consciously nostalgic, a strange calque on Bulwer's own faux Gothic nostalgia and trendiness), so the skulls today, when not bafflingly mute to the visitor, come layered with a *loss* of the frames that made sense of Bulwer's exhibition of them. A memorial of what has passed away . . .

* * *

Let us begin with the story of how the skulls arrived at Knebworth. The two skulls were both excavated in Pompeii, and were presented to Bulwer in 1856 by John Auldjo (1805–86).[14] The two labels within the glass box, part of the display, and now curled with age, are the dedication, a hand-written address slip, from John Auldjo to Bulwer of Park Lane; and an identification of the skull of Arbaces with a quotation from *The Last Days of Pompeii*; both are written in the hand of Auldjo. John Auldjo was a friend of Bulwer's from Cambridge student days. They remained in contact throughout their lives, albeit sporadically, it seems, by letter. Only a handful now survives, but they are warm in tone, and Bulwer added a note to the bunch of seven letters which he preserved at Knebworth, that Auldjo was a 'good fellow'.[15] In 1836, he dedicated the third edition of his silver-fork novel *Devereux* to Auldjo, with what appears to be genuine affection and regard, a gesture which moved Auldjo, still in Italy, greatly. Auldjo also arranged for an Italian translation of *Last Days*. Auldjo was a serious intellectual figure, who was elected a fellow of the Geological Society and the Royal Society, and who was a member of the Royal Geographical Society. He first came to public attention as an author with a stirring account of an ascent of Mont Blanc, which he illustrated with his own sketches.[16] He then moved to Naples, while he prepared a book on Vesuvius, in which he surveyed the volcano, and produced accounts of its eruptions over the previous 200 years, complete with a multi-coloured map of all the modern lava flows.[17] He went on to publish a journal of a trip to Constantinople and the Greek Islands.[18] Auldjo was, in short, a well-respected man of science, a published surveyor and traveller, whose reputation depended on empirical and accurate observation.

In Naples, Auldjo was a particular friend of Sir William Gell, who published the most definitive and influential guide to the excavations of Pompeii, and to whom *Last Days* is dedicated. Gell always calls him 'Mont Blanc Auldjo', and, as his work progressed, for Gell Auldjo became 'the wet-nurse of the volcano' and finally 'the High Priest of Vesuvius'.[19] Auldjo accompanied Gell in giving Sir Walter Scott a tour of Pompeii – an event recorded in one of Bulwer's footnotes in *Last Days*: 'When Sir Walter Scott visited Pompeii with Sir William Gell, almost his only remark was the exclamation, "The City of the Dead! – The City of the Dead!".' – a note added to explain Bulwer's use of the phrase, 'City of the Dead', to describe the dawn torpor of Pompeii, surveyed by Arbaces, as an anticipation of the future of the city.[20] It seems typical of the relationship of Bulwer and Auldjo, as much as Bulwer's sense of a good story, that Scott's expedition is slimmed down to only its most famous members and to a single memorable comment. Gell's letters to the Society of Dilettanti certainly reveal a more engaged and engaging stay.[21]

Auldjo and Bulwer spent time together in Pompeii, and Auldjo's expertise on the volcano has an evident impact on the descriptions in *Last Days*. More tellingly, it seems that one of the most celebrated scenes in the book was suggested to Bulwer by Auldjo. Bulwer could not work out how he would enable his hero and heroine to escape from the eruption. Auldjo suggested that a blind girl – Nydia – who would not be inconvenienced by the enveloping darkness of the ash cloud, could guide them out.[22] Bulwer acknowledged the help of his friend, anonymously, in the introduction to *Last Days*.[23] Regrettably, Auldjo's notebooks and diary from his earlier years do not reveal anything of his relationship with Bulwer, though there are some nice sketches of his Italian houses, amid a tedious obsession with the details of the weather, church attendance, and his dinner, especially when it involved veal cutlets.[24] He also took joints of veal with him on the ascent of Mont Blanc.[25]

Auldjo returned to London to live in Noel House, Kensington. A financial disaster in 1856, the details of which are now impossible to uncover, led him into severe difficulties and he was forced to sell up the house and its contents. He left for Europe. When Auldjo was forced to leave Noel House, he saved only a few prized possessions. Among them were the skulls of Arbaces and Calenus, which had returned with him from Pompeii, where they had been excavated. The precise date or circumstances of the excavation are not recorded, but it is worth noting that it is not at all usual to dig up and carry away body parts – as opposed to other treasures – from Pompeii. The standard and frequent contemporary discussions focus on the casts of bodies that were made *in situ* and there are no bones from Pompeii on display in European museums. These skulls are exceptional. Auldjo sent these treasures to Bulwer with a letter which covers his obvious distress at his financial misfortune with a charming elegance: 'I know they will be taken and probably remain undisturbed for ages at Knebworth, where, perhaps, they may be found by Macaulay's New Zealander, when Knebworth House will be visited as one of the shrines of England.' The skulls from the city of the dead evoke a celebrated image of the passing of time and the fall of a city from Macaulay, as Auldjo is forced to leave the ruins of his London life. He imagines Knebworth as a shrine of England, and his skulls as if a relic of the shrine. And that indeed is how they are displayed.

Auldjo had written to Bulwer back in 1836 about how *Last Days* had changed visitors' perceptions of Pompeii:

Will it not gratify you to know that people begin to ask for Ione's house – and that there are disputes about which was Julia's room in Diomed's villa – Pompeii was truly a city of the dead – there were no familiar spirits hovering over its remains – but now – you have made poetical its very air – you have created a new feeling in its visitors. In the dusk, wandering through its deserted streets, the rapt antiquarian startles at the rustling of the olive leaves and fancies he sees the shade of Arbaces the Egyptian beneath the luxuriant festoons, or the peasant girl tramps her way home, singing her evening song, pictures to himself Nydia, feeling her way through the forum and crying, 'come, buy my flowers'.[26]

Auldjo playfully recalls the visit of Walter Scott: Pompeii was truly a city of the dead, as he had called it, before Bulwer's novel had revivified it. Now visitors see the record of his story, and recall in their imaginations his version of history. The visitor is called an 'antiquarian' (a figure close to Scott's heart), and it is antiquity itself that has been fashioned by Bulwer's vision. Even Murray's *Guide* now quoted from *Last Days*. The novel filled and structured the imagination of visitors to Pompeii.

Shelley had already written these famous lines in his ode to Naples:

I stood within the city disinterred,
And heard the autumnal leaves like light footfalls
Of spirits passing through the streets; and heard
The Mountain's slumbering voice at intervals
Thrill through those roofless halls.

What was a Romantic, deserted landscape for Shelley, has become now peopled, not just a landscape with figures, but a landscape with named characters.

Bulwer himself had set up this expectation in the most marked fashion at the end of *Last Days*. On the last pages of the novel, Bulwer writes that (542–3): 'In the house of Diomed, in the subterranean vaults, twenty skeletons (one of a babe) were discovered in one spot by the door. . . . The sand, consolidated by damps, had taken the forms of the skeletons as in a cast; and the traveller may yet see the impression of a female neck and bosom of young and round proportions – the trace of the fated Julia!' (As Jensen's story 'Gradiva' is motivated by the erotic imprint of a foot, so here the erotic imprint of a neck and breast stirs the story of Bulwer. The fetishization of the body part takes on a new twist with this erotics of the archaeological trace, from cold ash to warm flesh, a reverse of the ineluctable mortality of biblical language.) 'In the garden was found a skeleton with a key by its bony hand, and near it a bag of coins. This is believed to be the master of the house – the unfortunate Diomed, who had probably sought to escape by the garden . . .' (the word 'probably', a coy critical caution, shows the imagination at work . . .). 'As the excavators cleared on through the mass of ruin, they found the skeleton of a man literally severed in two by a prostrate column . . . Still after a lapse of ages, the traveller may survey that airy hall within whose cunning galleries and elaborate chambers once thought, reasoned, dreamed, and sinned the soul of Arbaces the Egyptian' (543–4).[27] The final hours of each of his characters, climaxing with Arbaces, are given the final stamp of authenticity by the excavation of their bodies in modernity. The 'cunning galleries' of Arbaces' house, the physical embodiment of his cunning mind, is the visible, architectural frame for his destroyed form: to destroy the threat of Arbaces, the narrative has not just to kill him but to smash him in half, and bury him. The physical remains of Pompeii are taken, by a particular twist of the Barthesian reality effect, as the archaeological proof of the authenticity of the novel's narrative. The story takes shape as Bulwer looks at the remains of Pompeii, and the remains survive to assure the reader of the truth of the tale.

What's more, Bulwer adds a long endnote to this page. A significant majority of serious novels written in the nineteenth century, which take antiquity as their subject, have learned footnotes that give sources or archaeological details. *Last Days* has footnotes in the text and also longer endnotes for further explication of his evidence. He explains that (553) 'At present (1834) there have been about three hundred and fifty or four hundred skeletons discovered at Pompeii . . . The skeletons which, reanimated for a while, the reader has seen play their brief parts upon the stage, under the names of Burbo, Calenus, Diomed, Julia and Arbaces, were found exactly as described in the text.' Bulwer uses the scholarly apparatus of the endnote to reconfirm that he has been precise in the description of the remains of his characters. He overlaps fiction and archaeological science so that his novel is but the reanimation of the skeletons that are excavated, just as the excavations are the demonstration of the novel's claim on our imagination as truth. Auldjo's description of the visitors at Pompeii is playing out Bulwer's discourse of archaeologized verisimilitude. The tourist will, as Bulwer demands, see in and on the ground the physical signs of Bulwer's Pompeii.

* * *

The skulls of Arbaces and Calenus, it seems, were identifiable from the narrative of their death, and Auldjo with his friend Gell could easily find them, no doubt. But there is another reason why these two skulls are chosen.

For these are the only two heads in the novel which are given a full, physiognomic description. So, the description of the discovery of the skeleton split in two by the column continues (543–4): 'the skull was of so striking a conformation, so boldly marked in its intellectual, as well as its worse physical developments, that it excited the constant speculation of every itinerant believer in the theories of Spurzheim who has gazed upon that ruined palace of the mind'. Spurzheim's physiognomical system was particularly well known for his development of phrenology, and his celebrated model of a whitened head marked out with the sites of the faculties of mind was widely circulated.[28] Phrenology had been one of the hottest topics in the 1820s, passionately supported by its gurus and sharply criticized by both churchmen and scientists alike. After a stinging review in the *Edinburgh Review*, Spurzheim had visited Edinburgh to lecture, stayed seven months, and by 1826 Edinburgh was gripped by 'phrenological mania'. Phrenology was even more popular in America, where the essays of George Combe – a scientist from Edinburgh who also lectured in America – sold 200,000 copies.[29] (Both Poe and Whitman were strongly influenced by the claims of Combe and Spurzheim.[30]) Spurzheim had died in 1832 shortly before Bulwer's visit to Pompeii, which stimulated the writing of the novel in 1834. Fully 3,000 people attended Spurzheim's funeral in Boston, Massachusetts, where he had been lecturing to large crowds. On his death, Spurzheim's skull (as well as his heart and brain) was preserved for display, and his skull was the subject of much phrenological triumphalism. It was in Boston too in 1834 that Henry Tuckerman wrote a review of *Last Days* for the short-lived and meagrely circulated *Annals of Phrenology* triumphantly claiming Bulwer as an adherent of the new and still beleaguered science.[31] Bulwer uses the science of phrenology – and encourages his readers to do the same – to capture the conflicted personality of Arbaces, on which he lavished many pages in the book. For the author, it seems, as for the characters in the novel, Arbaces was a deeply uncomfortable mix of powerfully attractive intelligence and more gross, physical appetites and ambitions. This unsettling characterization is expressed in a physiognomy that works through a discourse of race and morality that underpins the whole novel. His body announces this conceptual danger immediately (16):

His skin, dark and bronzed, betrayed his Eastern origin; and his features had something Greek in their outline (especially in the chin, the lip and the brow), save that the nose was raised and aquiline; and the bones, hard and visible, forbade that fleshy and waving contour which on the Grecian physiognomy preserved even in manhood the round and beautiful curves of youth.

This physiognomy needs careful reading to make it 'betray' its otherwise potentially concealed origin; by a casual glance, he could be taken for Greek – ever the physical ideal, especially in the nineteenth century –though the nose and bone structure are not fully Hellenic. What's more, 'a deep, thoughtful and half-melancholic calm seemed unalterably fixed in [his dark eyes'] majestic and commanding gaze. His step and mien were peculiarly sedate and lofty': he has the presence and the seriousness of a born ruler. Even his status as an outsider is not clearly denigrating: 'something foreign in the fashion and sober hues of his sweeping garments added to the impressive effect of his quiet countenance and stately form' (16). Foreignness in Arbaces adds to his impressiveness, his stateliness. Arbaces' physicality is dangerous because, unlike the Romans, who in the book are corrupt, physically and morally, his otherness is close to a Greek appearance; it impresses and commands attention. Arbaces is seductive, and his threat is not merely that he leads men and women astray, but also that he looks like a real leader. In the novel, Arbaces manipulates others through spectacle, deception, and false promises: his body emblematizes his power. Arbaces, the manipulator of spectacle, becomes a spectacle of Knebworth, his body still an image to conjure with.

Calenus, the second named skull, is also described, but he is a much more straightforward and less threatening villain: 'His shaven skull was so low and narrow in front as nearly to approach to the conformation of that of an African savage, save only towards the temples, where, in that organ styled acquisitiveness by the pupils of a science modern in name, but best practically known (as their sculpture teaches us) amongst the ancients, two huge and almost preternatural protuberances yet more distorted the unshapely head.' Needless to say, once Bulwer Lytton has put flesh on this skull 'none could behold [him] without repugnance and few without terror and distrust' (46–7). Greek sculpture reveals to us the ideal of physical form: the Greeks stand at the head of this racialized hierarchy of bodies. Next come the Egyptians, at least in the supreme and supremely dangerous form of Arbaces, a middle ground of nearly looking Greek, and nearly being wonderfully intelligent and nearly being an excellent leader, but in each area corrupting the ideal with deformity and evil. Beneath him, come the Romans, who are corrupt, fat, lecherous, or haggard, pale and thin: within the narrative economy, they deserve their fate at Pompeii. Below even them, the African savage stands as the opposition of all civilized form. Again it is 'modern science' (that is, Victorian science) that allows the reader (and author) to descry the physical grounding of the character flaws of Calenus. In his organ of 'acquisitiveness', there are two distorting lumps, 'almost preternatural' – that is, found in nature but so monstrous as to question the boundaries of normality – which further corrupt the already corrupt shape of his head. 'Acquisitiveness' is the eighth faculty in Spurzheim's phreno-logical system (the 'science modern in name'), which with syncretism typical both of phrenological writing and of Bulwer's intellectualism, is brought into contrast with a broad, culturally privileged classicism, tinged with a racialized nationalism. (Combe's *System of Phrenology* (1822) had already compared Egyptian and Greek representations of the body in favour, inevitably, of the classical Greek models.) Calenus' skull reveals his horrific personality, for which only the African savage can provide any sort of template – a template which is set in its place by the idealism of classicism, embodied in the perfection of ancient sculpture.

By 1834, when Bulwer was writing, physiognomics was no longer the hot topic of the salons that it had been in the 1820s, although 'the opinion that phrenology was a "good thing", socially speaking, was to be taken from innumerable journals'.[32] What has been called the most influential book of the period – which far outsold Darwin and Chambers, and was far more heatedly debated than either, after, at least, it was published in huge numbers in a very cheap edition – namely, George Combe's *Essay on the Constitution of Man* (1827) – had sections on phrenology, as one would expect from a man who had so vigorously defended phrenology through the 1820s.[33] Phrenology had been strongly attacked as a science, but it had found a niche in materialist theories, which gave it a potentially radical political frisson; or, less controversially, 'phrenologists appear[ed] to be the most strenuous advocates for putting society on an improved footing'.[34] Bulwer is both drawing on the cachet of phrenology and distancing himself from it, when he describes the excitement of 'every itinerant believer in the theories of Spurzheim'. The expression 'itinerant believers' might recall the disreputable hawkers of phrenology through the fairs and markets; there is a certain sniffiness in Bulwer's phrasing, further marked in his return to classical sculpture as the truly best guide to a face. But as the description goes on, he is also using Spurzheim's theories to add a patina of scientific interest to the portrayal, and is allowing the technical vocabulary of phre-nology a more authoritative role. Bulwer, as ever, wants to have his cake and eat it: and provides a fascinating example of the hesitation *and* glamour with which science enters the popular public sphere.

There is, however, also a religious matrix connected to this racialized nationalist physiognomics. Roman religion falls into the well-known image of a naïve paganism, dedicated to ritual sacrifice (a cruelty that finds fullest expression in the gladiatorial games) and a lack of love or grace or intellectual honesty. This representation of paganism is standard in a string of historical novels and religious tracts that deal with the spread of early Christianity in the Roman Empire.[35] But Arbaces, just as his body looks close enough to the Greek ideal to be unsettling, has a dangerously seductive version of the history of religion: like the modern scholar Martin Bernal *avant la lettre*, who polemically found African origins for our privileged Greek ideas, he claims that 'Egypt . . . is the mother of Athens. Her tutelary Minerva is our deity; and her founder, Cecrops, was the fugitive of Egyptian Sais.'[36] Claiming Egypt as the mother of Greece – his blood as the origin from where the Greekness of the hero, Glaucus, comes – confuses the genetics of nationality. Arbaces even claims that Christian theology is just a pale recollection of Egyptian thought: 'the believers of Galilee are but the unconscious repeaters of one of the superstitions of the Nile' (141). What will become a commonplace of comparative mythology later in the century is sufficiently worrying even to its author that Bulwer adds a defensive footnote: 'The believer will draw from this vague co-incidence a very differ-ent corollary from that of the Egyptian.' It seems as if Bulwer is concerned that he may have made Arbaces too convincing, or as if he is worried that Arbaces' voice might be mistaken for the author's. Perhaps he was right to be worried. Robert Taylor, a significant influence on Darwin, was impris-oned in the 1830s on a charge of blasphemy in part for tracing scriptural ideas to Egyptian sources. He defiantly scrawled 'Everything of Christianity is of Egyptian origin' on the walls of Oakham Gaol.[37]

More surprisingly, the Christian characters in the novel are either a wild adolescent, like Ione's brother, who veers between Arbaces and the Christian Church – and is killed well before the end of the book, with Bulwer's familiar narrative solution for a difficult character – or the equally awkward and harsh Christian leader Olinthus who is 'sanguine and impet-uous', 'fierce and intolerant' in his denunciations of Pompeian society (308, 350). He too dies in the conflagration of the volcanic eruption, falsely celebrating the end of days. The volcanic eruption frees him from his impending doom in the arena to die in the conflagration instead – and thus denies him the chance of the crown of martyrdom. A dead Christian, but no saint . . . Rather, it is Glaukus, the Greek hero, who is left to convert to Christianity later in Greece, bringing together the Greek and Christian ideals. The only traditional saintly Christian is met but briefly in passing, like a ghost in the woods, as he stalks past Pompeii on his way to another history. Bulwer's particular version of Christianity needs a classical back-ground, or, more precisely, needs to base itself on the cultural privilege and idealism of Hellenism, and to link the Glory That Was Greece with the

Glory of the Lord. The beautiful Greeks become beautiful Christians – and almost everyone else is burnt or crushed to death. The aesthetic privilege of Athens is seamlessly and genealogically linked with a firmly genial Christianity, though the narrative closure in geniality, like so much Victorian Christian expansionism, depends on a barely concealed violence. The bodies of the figures of the novel represent their religious agendas – in service of Bulwer's own image of the development of early Christianity.

Charles Leland is the first visitor I have found to comment on the display of the skulls at Knebworth. Leland was an American journalist, best known to his contemporaries for some comic ballads, but who also contributed significantly to folklore research, and had a long and surprisingly influential engagement with paganism and witchcraft. His *Memoirs*, even within the genre of memoirs, are distinctive for their self-serving name-dropping. He visited Bulwer, a childhood hero of his, at Knebworth in 1870, and, in line with their shared interest in the occult, was offered – but declined – the opportunity to sleep with Bulwer's crystal ball under his pillow. (The crystal ball, on its stand, is on the top shelf now of the same exhibition cabinet in Knebworth containing the case of skulls.) But it is only in passing that Leland mentions seeing the skull of Arbaces.[38] He does not mention whether it was in a display case; nor does he mention the skull of Calenus. But it might be Leland's comment which is the source for later stories of Bulwer writing with the skull of Arbaces constantly on his desk.[39] The image of the skull on the desk as a *memento mori* is familiar from Renaissance art onwards, and it takes on extra power in Gothic literature. Leland comments only in passing on the skull; but it must have been labelled or discussed to be identified by the visitor, and, if it was, as later writers suggest, on Bulwer's desk, cased or otherwise, it is highly unlikely that the skull was placed on 'the writer's desk' casually by Bulwer, who was always deeply aware of his self-presentation. If, as seems likely, the skulls were already in their case with the labels of Auldjo, then only Arbaces' skull is explicitly identified, and Leland may simply not have known or asked for the identity of the second skull. The only contemporary evidence for the display is Leland's unhelpful remark. The exhibition may, of course, have been later, as part of the memorialization of Bulwer's life (in which his son and his grandson, his particularly generous biographer, played an integral role). Interestingly, no visitor comments that there were two skulls, or names the less memorable figure, Calenus. What does seem clear, however, is that Bulwer himself used the skulls in constructing and projecting his own image as a writer, a cultural icon.

* * *

We are now in a position to understand more fully why Bulwer has these skulls on display at Knebworth. It is also the display of an ideological construction of the body's truth. They are labelled with precise names, picking up a precise discourse, so that we can see the physiognomics of savagery, the dangers of false religion, the truth of racial nationalism. These are the horrid, cracked skulls of punished and threatening false leaders. Look on these and see transgression, see thus who you should be, under the skin, and thus in the real! *The Last Days of Pompeii* uses archaeology as a science of truth to ground its story of Pompeii in the real, and returns to the excavation in Pompeii to find both the foundation and authorization, or even authentication, of its own truth. The real of the excavation, two named skulls, are returned to the author for display as signs of the reality of the story, not necessarily of the literal and detailed truth of the story, but of the ideological underpinnings that structure the story's narrative and its journey towards a Hellenized Christianity.

In this cabinet, we can see the integral complicity of science – not just archaeology, but also physiognomics, art history, phrenology – with a national, racial, religious discourse – and *performed* in the spectacle of display. When readers found Bulwer intellectually stimulating or even profound, *and* when readers ranted at his superficiality and pseudo-philosophical posturing, in both cases it is a response in part precisely to such manipulation of the ideas of the moment. This display is a precisely located transitional moment. It may echo the old tradition of the cabinet of curiosities as it may also echo the religious display of relics (though for an Anglican like Bulwer Lytton, this would have smacked too redolently of Catholic superstition). But it is the *scientific* frame that makes Bulwer's display trendy in 1856. Following Spurzheim, there were scholars beginning to describe, annotate and collect skulls in a new way.[40] John Hunter, an eighteenth-century antiquarian, had put together a collection of skulls in Kensington, a collection of curiosities, named individuals, and examples of natural history; Samuel Morton in Philadelphia, and Joseph Hyrts in Vienna in the mid-nineteenth century, however, constructed systematic collections of skulls along phrenological lines to demonstrate social and national truths. The Knebworth display thus appears at a crucial transitional moment in the development of science and the styles of exhibition. It may be thought to look back towards the display of individual named skulls as a curiosity of celebrity, but also forward to a collection like the very different museum of Pitt Rivers. The Pitt Rivers Museum in Oxford was founded in the 1880s, and is only one of a string of major scientific collections of skeletons and skulls in the last quarter of the nineteenth century. These collections were attempts at a systematic exploration and exhibition of racial typology and national difference, as well as marking individual corruptions and distortions of type. By the 1880s – when both science and the history of exhibitions had advanced so far from the 1830s – there was a fully developed cultural expectation of how to see in such bones the truth of the history of man. It is this developing nexus of scientific ideas, which reached an apogee in the 1880s, that Bulwer aims to activate twenty-five years (and more) earlier.[41]

These skulls reveal history to the viewer, a history tied up with archaeology's ability to uncover the truth of early Christianity, not just as a religious system grounded in the real of history (a paradigmatic mid-Victorian obsession), but also an Anglican Christianity defined in and against both the threat of the East and the promotion of a national identity (from the man who wrote *England and the English* amongst other discussions of national character and its basis in history, from novels such as *Harold, the Last of the Saxons* or *The Last of the Barons* to his lectures such as *Outlines of the Early History of the East*). The skulls, brought back from Italy to England, stand not just for the story of *Last Days of Pompeii*, nor just for the racial, national, religious ideology that the book encapsulates, but also for the need publicly to display the narrative as a gesture of self-identification, buttressed by the claims of modern science as a regime of knowledge. Here we see how the status of the object on display is interwoven with the self-presentation of the author and with the history of archaeology in the service of a religious and racial story of national identity.

The significance of this juncture in the broad history of display can be made more precise, however, by a brief comparison with Sir Walter Scott and with Sigmund Freud, at either ends of the nineteenth century. Both Scott and Freud were obsessed with archaeology; both used their desks as display areas, for things recovered by archaeology, and both used their writer's space as a self-conscious theatre of self-expression. Walter Scott's Abbotsford, as we have already indicated, was a house built to express a literary persona. Central to that persona was the figure of the antiquary. Scott was celebrated for his recovery of the lost linguistic and cultural world of the ballad, and was directly involved in the discovery of the physical remains of an old Scotland in and around Edinburgh. He also gently mocked his own antiquarian interests in *The Antiquary*.[42] Scott draws himself as author close to the Antiquary – a 'self-posturing' which may be 'tongue in cheek',[43] but which also artfully and humorously mixes the roles of fiction writer, historian and mocked antiquary. This historical fiction revels in failed or misleading stories of the past, or, better still, in the *pleasure* of historical imagination, the joy in the stories and objects of the past, even when they are destined for mockery or failure. The narrative of the book itself ambles along from site to site (the Roman fort which turns out to be modern, the spooky mines, the stately homes, the sublime view), happy in its own digressive touring. And the description of the Antiquary's house is uncannily – or precisely – echoed in published descriptions of Scott's own house with its collection of historical memorabilia.

There is a string of accounts of pilgrimages to Abbotsford, headed by Washington Irving's visit of 1816, when Scott was alive and in residence. Irving describes Scott's display, lovingly collected and exhibited by its owner, and his account[44] is echoed by later writers who itemize the list of curiosities more fully:

> In the library: Napoleon's blotting paper and pen-tray taken from his carriage after Waterloo; Queen Mary's seal and a piece of her dress; Prince Charlie's quaigh and a lock of his hair; Helen MacGregor's brooch; Flora Macdonald's pocket book; Rob Roy's purse; locks of Nelson's and Wellington's hair.[45]

Scott's things are connected to his passion for national history, but collected, displayed and discussed as if they were in a cabinet of curiosities. The objects are each linked to a historical figure and have significance first and foremost for that connection with a famous man or woman. None is expanded into a story, or seeks to tell more than its metonymic relation to greatness. Just as with a cloth used to wipe Jesus' brow, the dress fragment of Queen Mary is only more than a rag in that it once touched a queen. No surprise, then, that the word 'reliquary' is used of the collection: as if, indeed, they were (religious) relics, not of a Gospel but of a history of the British Isles.[46] But Scott's antiquarianism looked quite out of date already by the middle of the century, when the science of history and archaeology had taken over the way objects were to be catalogued, discussed and made to reveal a history. Scott was foundational for the historical fiction which Bulwer excelled at, but the version of history that his writer's things displayed is quite different from Bulwer's.

Consequently, when Scott puts a skull on display, it seems a very different sort of thing from Bulwer's, as Irving describes it:

> Before dismissing the theme of the relics from the Abbey, I will mention another, illustrative of Scott's varied humors. This was a human skull, which had probably belonged of yore to one of those jovial friars . . .
>
> This skull he had caused to be cleaned and varnished, and placed it on a chest of drawers in his chamber, immediately opposite his bed; where I have seen it, grinning most dismally. It was an object of great awe and horror to the superstitious

housemaids; and Scott used to amuse himself with their apprehensions. Sometimes, in changing his dress, he would leave his neck-cloth coiled round it like a turban, and none of the 'lasses' dared to remove it. It was a matter of great wonder and speculation among them that the laird should have such an 'awsome fancy for an auld girning skull.'[47]

This skull has no name, and is casually referred back ('probably') to the monks of Melrose Abbey. It is, however, little more or less than a death's head, a *memento mori*, used to frighten the silly maidservants, part of Scott's humorous and self-deprecating take on the past. Unlike Bulwer's skulls, Scott's relic opens no national, racial, historical lesson. It can be handled and dressed up: it is not kept in a glass case: it can be touched, and not merely looked at ('do not touch the exhibits' is a sign of museum culture). Auldjo's signage and his letter may be gently and self-consciously wry, but Scott's skull is a source of boisterous joking and dressing up: a stage prop on the set of his self-presentation.

Scott also had plaster casts of two other skulls on display, however. The entrance hall to Abbotsford is a bizarre *bricolage*. It has on one wall Scott's relics from the field of Waterloo; on another, statues of saints copied from Melrose Abbey. On the mantelpiece are two models of skulls, those of Robert the Bruce, and Guardsman Shaw, a boxer who had fought as a Life Guard at the battle of Waterloo. Like his other mementos, these models of heads are metonymic memorials of national history, military exploits of manliness to stir the soul. The skulls are named, but unlike Bulwer's relics, have no physiognomic narrative, and a quite different sense of national history attached. They are curios of Scott's cabinet – awaiting Scott, the antiquarian host, to give their story to us, the visitors.

Freud's study, recreated in London as late as 1938, is Victorian not just in the date of its inception, but also in its love of the clutter of things. Freud worked surrounded by figurines, pots and other objects from archaeological digs, and would occasionally use such recovered things in the analysis of patients to clarify his theories of buried memory. Recent critics have brilliantly outlined Freud's use of the metaphor of archaeology in his scientific writing, whereby he compared 'clearing away the pathogenic psychical material layer by layer', to 'the technique of excavating a buried city'.[48] Paradigmatically, he was fascinated by Jensen's story 'Gradiva', which is about an archaeologist travelling to Pompeii, and suffering from a delusion that a girl from the city of the dead has come to life. After writing his essay, Freud visited Rome and bought a copy of the Gradiva frieze, which he included in his study's collection. Already in 1901 he owned a fragment of a Pompeian wall-painting. As with Scott and Bulwer, Pompeii played a significant role in Freud's imagination as a model of the past, the excavation of truth, the discovery of buried reality. His copy of the Gradiva frieze, layered with the significance of his analysis of the Jensen story about delusion and desire, and its involvement with the search for the buried life in the mind, becomes an uncanny icon of the role of the past and the fetish of the object in psychoanalysis. Freud's scene of writing is an archaeological space.

Freud's collecting has been finely analysed too,[49] and there are only two points that I wish to emphasize. First, his collection mixes Egyptian and Greek and Roman and Indian and Chinese objects, without apparent concern for the national, racial history which underlies Bulwer's exhibition of the skulls of the Egyptians. For all Freud's engagement with classical Greece, he was also committed to a pursuit of the pre-history to which archaeology gave access, and to a *universalizing* account of human development. The Gradiva frieze is invested with a complex of memories and stories and intellectual positions, cued by Jensen's tale and Freud's analysis of it, but the majority of the objects in his collection are *types* of votive offerings, dedicated figurines, or other small pots and urns made for ritual. His archaeological gaze should probably be connected intimately to his complex religious feelings which gave rise to *Moses and Monotheism*, just as his passion for classical Greece cannot be separated wholly from the complicity between Philhellenism and German nationalism[50] – and Freud had good reason to reflect on racial and physiognomic stereotypes in fiercely anti-Semitic Vienna;[51] but Freud's things do not give rise to the sort of religious and nationalist narrative that Bulwer revels in, any more than his collecting is like Scott's antiquarianism. The history Freud's collection reveals is quite different from Bulwer's or Scott's. Following the universalizing tendencies of contemporary evolutionary biology and history, and in contrast to the growing Aryanism of Germanic culture – or, perhaps, better, located in the matrix defined by such extreme models of cultural understanding – Freud's things do bring together science, history and fiction, as do Bulwer's and Scott's, but both the way in which the objects represent history, and the history represented, betoken regimes of knowledge unavailable to Scott or Bulwer.

Secondly, Freud's collection and the history it reveals are part and parcel of the development of the science of archaeology, which made huge progress in the seventy-five years after Bulwer received Auldjo's gift. The field had become a professional discipline, where it had been peopled previously to a large degree by committed amateurs and local historians.[52] By 1900, Scott's antiquary was not just a figure of fun, but deeply outmoded – as was a gentleman excavator like Auldjo. Where Bulwer had to demonstrate his concern that a reader might think he supported his villain's version of the Egyptian or Eastern influence on Christianity, such views were a commonplace of the new, anthropologically inflected comparative religion – which produced different murderous complicities between science and racism and nationalism. Most simply put, where Scott's displays look back to the cabinet of curiosities, the antiquarian collections of a previous century, Freud's display mimics in small scale the new museums, with their investment in the new sciences dedicated to uncovering the past.

So Freud too did, of course, own a skull on a skeleton when a medical student – he bought it with two other students for his studies and they each wrote their names on it.[53] This skull is an anonymous object for learning anatomy in the most general way, and was discarded by the mature Freud (there is no record of a skeleton in his house when he was a psychoanalyst, though his prosthesis used after the operation for cancer of the mouth still sits in a cupboard: part of an artificial, manufactured part of Freud's skull, another sign of the medicalized head). Instead, Freud, above the couch on which his patients lay and in the room around them, collected heads – a head of a goddess, a death mask from Roman Egypt, classical sculptured busts, Egyptian wigged heads. These heads are emblematic of Freud's sense of history, of his sense of art, and his desire to create a specific space for the psychoanalytic session. The physiognomics that excited Bulwer as a science never quite leaves popular culture, but the changing metaphors of the head (as the 'head shrinkers' become professionalized), and Freud's universalizing archaeology of the mind, find external form in the anonymous heads, from many different cultures and styles, displayed as an artistic collection all around the office.

Bulwer's display of skulls marks, then, a transitional moment, between the antiquarian collecting of things as tokens of great men or prodigies, the trivial made significant as synecdoches of grandeur, and the new museology and archaeological science of the end of the Victorian era (and beyond). The skulls of Arbaces and Calenus are framed by contemporary science. Yet, the quirkiness of the skulls' connection to specific (fictional) individuals looks back towards the cabinet of curiosities: a modern exhibition of skulls would need many examples, graded to reveal their characteristics. The skulls are like relics, but re-framed by a telling modernism.

From Scott to Bulwer to Freud, then, there is a history to be articulated about a writer's things as gestures of self-presentation – the construction of an image of the scene of writing as an icon of the writer – and the engagement of this constructed image with a history of archaeology as the science of recovered and displayed things, and the type of historical narrative such displays are designed to cue. Bulwer appropriates Scott, the master of historical fiction, to his project via the writer's trip to Pompeii; Freud appropriates Jensen to his project via the story of the delusional fiction of history in Pompeii. No surprise that writers are competitive with the past, but that both Freud and Bulwer use an archaeological metaphor for their acts of appropriation is doubly pointed not just because archaeology is a science designed to make a possession of the past, but also because, especially in the nineteenth century, archaeology is integrally linked to an imperialist agenda. Each writer's display of his things is also part of an agonistic self-presentation, troped by archaeology. There are, no doubt, other writers and other types of display that could nuance this broad account of change over the century: Carlyle kept a finger recovered from the Civil War battle site of Naseby on his writing desk; Haggard possessed a copy of the Sherd of Amenartas, a rune-covered pot-sherd, which sets off the archaeologist Holly on his adventures in Haggard's famous novel *She*. And the contrasts I have developed here are articulated pointedly to emphasize a structure of difference, where continuities also exist (not least in the lure of the reality of objects to ground historical narrative, a shared nineteenth-century empiricism). But from this discussion of the transitional cultural place of Bulwer's skulls, there are three further conclusions we should draw about the exhibition at Knebworth.

First, we should not forget how perverse the display of *fictional* characters' bones is. There is an extraordinarily wilful manipulation of levels of fiction and reality both in Bulwer's novel, and then in its reception by his friend Auldjo. They move seamlessly between the archaeological record and the fiction of the novel, playing different levels against each other: the novel moves between its detailed description of houses, as if on a guided tour of a fully reconstructed site to the almost surreal world of imagined Egyptian rites and the ins and outs of a love story. It turns back to the archaeological record to ground its story in the real, and sees the story as the re-animation of the physical remains. This is made material in the book, with its different strata of narrative, footnotes and endnotes surrounding and supporting the tale with a battery of scholarship and empirical, factual demonstration. This historical revivification is then performed by Auldjo, the guide to Pompeii, seeing and encouraging the recognition of Bulwer's characters and places on the ground, and celebrating how Pompeii becomes the city of the *Last Days*, newly 'disburied'. Then the real skulls of the realized fictional characters, taken from Pompeii, are put on display at Knebworth, as Pompeii comes home to its author. What sort of a gift is this? A friend and reader's knowing and complicit return to the writer of a sign of his fictional mastery over the real of history . . . This interplay of levels of fact and fiction does not merely shift between present and past with a characteristically Victorian historical self-consciousness, but also stretches the boundaries of the genre of realism in a way which articulates an acutely sophisticated narrative self-reflection not often predicated of the historical fiction of the 1830s. There is a real performance, a flamboyance, in the exchange between Auldjo and Bulwer: part of the self-presentation of the author is his staging of these real fictional things for our gaze and attention. The knowing playfulness of this exchange must be factored into the overdetermined meaning of the skulls' display.

Second, this particular display is articulated through a cultural construction of the body, or more exactly, through an assertion, supported by science, that there is a level of reality in the bones beneath the skin, and in the physiognomy of a person, as part of a national identity. It is this ability to see in a particular skull the generalities of race and religion, education and character, that allows the skulls to be exhibited like this without being simply a quirky joke or a megalomaniac folly. Perhaps this is one essence of why bodies are put on display: for the moment of self-definition against the form of the other – made other by the logic of spectacle. Exhibitions grant permission to look, to stare, and thus to see what is normally not made so visible – whether it is naked flesh, the distorted body, the monsters of nature, or the ideology of the self. Here perhaps we should recognize the complicit desire of the spectator, given its head by the glass-fronted exhibition of skulls.

Third and finally, it is worth underlining how the novel enters the public domain. *Last Days* was immediately and consistently successful: it circulated very widely as a three-volume and then one-volume novel; it was widely reviewed and discussed, and had an immense influence on the genre of historical fiction. Bulwer had already been looking at paintings of destructions of cities, often with a biblical timbre, before he started writing. The characters of *Last Days* quickly entered the visual repertoire; and there were also dramatic representations of the book on stage (as now there are films, comic books and so forth – many of which are on display at Knebworth). But Auldjo's gift and its display seems an unparalleled example of how the world of words interacts with material culture. Here we see the conceptualization and manipulation of the materiality of archaeological and physiognomic objectivity in service of an image of early Christianity formulated for a middle-of-the-road, Anglican perspective, keen to maintain a classical privilege in its religion. This exhibition wants you to look a very particular way.

* * *

Very few people today offer anything but the most cursory glance at the cabinet on the landing, and, without any explanation of the display, there is now, for most of us, nothing to see but the baffling sight of two skulls, with hard-to-read labels. A further label, also written by pen in an old-fashioned hand, outside the case, identifies the skulls as the skulls of Arbaces and Calenus, a bare identification, which does not acknowledge the sheer perversity of the exhibition (or provide much guidance for the perplexed). There is, I suspect, for very few spectators indeed any recognition of the ideological frames embodied in Bulwer's case of skulls – nor could the structures of complicity I have outlined be in place for a visitor of today. In contrast to the playfulness and overdetermined frameworks of signification I have been describing, the display of skulls today seems radically underdetermined – in a way which it would be too glib to see as just another turn in an object's openness or excess of meaning. The contrast between then and now is as vivid as the transition between then and now is hard to trace with precision: when did these skulls get re-buried in obscurity? What the parade of baffled contemporary tourists indicates is not just the disappearance of Bulwer Lytton, the figure and the prose, from the popular imagination and memory, but also the gap between modern and Victorian performances of cultural identity – the different place of fiction, the history of Christianity, the awareness of the Roman Empire, the place of phrenology and physiognomics, the politics of nationalist or racial affiliation. And such gaps are, as ever, telling – in both directions, about us and them. For a future cultural historian, perhaps our contemporary practice of using a stately home like Knebworth as a stage set for concerts, films, conferences, weddings, jousts, vintage car rallies, picnics, and slow-paced tours of a lost domestic style – the gamut of the commercialized heritage industry – will seem as disturbingly expressive of our society's attitude to the past as Bulwer's skulls: what there is to be seen in the cabinet at Knebworth, now and in the nineteenth century, is a changing sense of (our) historical self-placement in the world.[54]

2 | When things matter

Religion and the physical world

'The word is so full of a number of things', wrote Robert Louis Stevenson, 'I'm sure we should all be as happy as kings'.[1] Stevenson was writing a happy thought for children, but the image captures something iconic about Victorian life. In the wake of the industrial revolution and with the massive flow of goods from the growing imperial economy, nineteenth-century houses, or at least middle-class and upper-class houses, more than ever before became full of things.[2] The overflowing abundance of material possessions signals more than the taste of the era. It is at the centre of the economy; it defines public space with new arenas for purchase and sale; it fills the imagination as well as the walls and surfaces of rooms. So, whereas in the 1960s Shakespeare's birthplace at Stratford-upon-Avon was displayed to the public as an authentic reconstruction with bare, empty whitewashed walls, and a minimum of simple wooden furniture, in the 1890s it was also on show as an authentic reconstruction, but with desks, and busts, and pictures on the wall, and bookshelves and ornaments, and mirrors and books. The image of the national poet in his physical surroundings is materially formed in the image of contemporary society. Freud's office, where we ended the journey of the last chapter, may have been a unique stage for the modernity of psychoanalysis, but in its profusion of stuff it is archetypally Victorian.

This chapter looks at one specific juncture in this changing history of materiality. Since its inception, Christianity has had an insistently vexed relation to the material world. On the one hand, it parades a rejection of physicality as the grounding of spirituality. To give up all possessions and follow Jesus, to mortify the flesh, to fast with the aim of recovering an Edenic state, to reject the material world of pomp and pride, are the familiar mantras of the pursuit of an inward journey of the soul, the longings of a love for God that turns away from this world in imitation of Jesus Christ. On the other hand, the very rejection of physicality places a huge emphasis upon the body and its possessions. Simeon Stylites sat unceasingly on a forty-foot high pillar for forty years as a gesture of the imitation of the sufferings of Christ and in rejection of this world, but description after description of the saint dwells obsessively on his physicality: the rotting flesh of his wounds, the smell of his putrefying body, the exact quantities of food ingested. His very presence created a cult of the holy man, with a building complex and local economy flourishing around the pillar. The rejected world came to Simeon, and he performed his role for them accordingly.[3]

The institutions of the Church not only became very wealthy, of course, but also created masterpieces of material art centred around the cathedral and the network of parish churches. The Vatican's luxurious and hoarded prosperity and the spectacular politics of the Renaissance Popes may have been the bugbear of Anglican polemics, but Trollope's accounts of the Protestant clergy's mercantile wrangling over Church income are equally rebarbative – and knowingly so – to the paraded religious ideals of poverty and disregard of materiality. The physicality of the body, the materiality of things, and the material concerns for wealth and status constitute different but overlapping anxieties at the heart of Christian thinking.[4]

The nineteenth century witnessed the most ferocious and pervasive struggles over the role of religion in British society since the Reformation. From the 1830s onwards, the increasingly popular and vociferous evangelical demand for revival based on direct contact with the Bible and the crucified Christ clashed with the Oxford Movement's intellectualized and scholarly return to a pre-Reformation Christianity, which was quickly embroiled in a fierce anti-Catholic resistance.[5] The Broad Church found itself under attack from non-conformist, High Church, and agnostic and atheist challenges to faith. The Anglican Church's established role in politics and in the fabric of the country was intently debated, in the formal institutions of power and learning as well as in the informal arenas of culture, art and social life. The engagement of Christians across the Empire in missionary work was matched by principled and often equally health-damaging work among the urban poor of the newly industrialized cities of Britain.[6] Religious faith remained an anxious, passionate, engrossing process of self-definition throughout the century. Public, political flashpoints – the Gorham trial, the Colenso case, the so-called papal aggression followed by the return of Cardinal Wiseman as Catholic archbishop, the Maynooth grant, Catholic and Jewish emancipation – were debated in Parliament and the papers, and fought over on the streets, with as much fervour as the Reform Acts or the military expeditions of the imperial project. This religious ferment forms a horizon of expectation throughout this book, and a particularly significant context for this chapter's enquiries.

Yet there are two further specific technological and intellectual developments that frame this chapter's concerns. First, there was an extraordinary political will – and corresponding influx of money – directed towards the building of new churches and the material reconstruction of older churches. Restoration as a practice and idea is the subject of the last chapter of this book, but it is worth saying here already that in the early decades of the nineteenth century, over twenty million pounds – a truly huge expenditure – was lavished on new churches, pump-primed by an initial grant by Parliament; and the combination of new building techniques and the conceptual drive of the Gothic revival significantly changed the visual appearance of England's cities and rural parishes.[7] Any question about the material fabric of religion is played out in this climate of rapid, enacted potential.

Second, archaeology and critical history – which play a determining role in each chapter of this book – changed the intellectual conceptualization of liturgy and performance. The evidence for the early or primitive Church was subject to searching scrutiny by scholars and theologians, who were engaged in a battle over the status and authority of early Christian texts for contemporary religion. As Ernest Renan testified – and he was himself an iconic figure of the new scrutiny – 'My faith has been destroyed by historical criticism, not by scholasticism nor by philosophy.'[8] If the earliest texts were closest to Jesus and the apostles, then they could be taken as most authoritative – but which were to be trusted and what did they determine for modern practice and belief? The more sharply and convincingly the authenticity of scripture was damaged by uncertainty, the more stridently counter-arguments made claims for biblical truth. As we will see in the next chapter in detail, biblical archaeology in particular became a battleground of competing authoritative, scientific postures of faith and doubt. Arguments about the things of religion – the Church's material fabric – could become so heated precisely because of how such things seemed to embody or stage or question a historical genealogy of contemporary commitments – commitments that the participants in such arguments cared about with all their souls.

From the extraordinary abundance of nineteenth-century sacred objects, I have chosen to look at just three interrelated moments when new technological, cultural, intellectual projects flared into violent disagreements about how things tell history. These moments have been selected not because they are typical – indeed each could be seen as surprisingly bizarre – but because they tellingly reveal the faultlines in the self-confident and exuberant materiality of Victorian society. I will begin by exploring an outlandish attempt to prove through archaeological and historical analysis that Christianity began in Gloucester and was imported from England to Rome; then I will investigate how a movement that started with an undergraduate society in Cambridge led to a bitterly contested and unworkable

Act of Parliament which attempted to regulate the very fabric of Christian worship in England. Finally and most briefly, I will try to understand how a single chasuble, an item of religious dress, was made to make a political, theological and aesthetic gesture of rebellion against that Act of Parliament. Together, these three investigations pose a question of how religious things came to matter so much in the nineteenth century.

I Roman stones: 'Rome derives its Christianity from Britain, not Britain from Rome'

Back in September 1796, Samuel Lysons was excavating at Frampton in the county of Dorset in the west of England. Lysons was a plumpish, bewigged lawyer, antiquary and artist, with a passion for the Roman remains of Britain, who went on to become keeper of the records at the Tower of London.[9] He was a well-connected and already distinguished figure, who was a friend of Sir Joseph Banks and Horace Walpole, and the dig was about to be visited by the Royal Family, which was staying in full splendour nearby. Lysons had already been introduced to the Prince of Wales, and remained a friend of Princess Elizabeth, the Prince's sister, in particular and helped her with her china collection, we are told, over many years. Because of his excellent connections, twenty-two soldiers from the Royal Lancashire Regiment of Fencibles had been deployed to help the dig, and the combination of royal patronage and the spectacle of so big a project made the site an instant tourist attraction.

Lysons went on in 1813–17 to publish the discoveries he had made at Frampton and elsewhere in one of the great works of early British archaeology, his *Reliquiae Britannico-Romanae*, a three-volume folio set of beautiful hand-tinted lithographs with detailed descriptions of each site and find, including site plans. The Prince Regent, its dedicatee, and Napoleon were presented with copies. Individual prints of the new mosaics also sold very well. 'He did not belong to the eighteenth century. He was a forerunner of the moderns', writes his biographer.[10] Such a judgment may be true in that, unlike many of his contemporaries and, indeed, unlike many later enthusiasts, he approached Roman sites with care, attention and a scientific interest in measurement, dating and comparison, and he published his results accordingly.[11] But the gentleman artist – 'My dear Antiquary', as the painter Sir Thomas Lawrence addressed him[12] – would look very out of date as a hero of science by the end of the nineteenth century. More importantly, perhaps, the motives and passions that made the Frampton dig worthy of a visit by the Royal family changed significantly as the nineteenth century progressed, as did the contested relationship between material remains and history. Not least – and this is the subject of this chapter – the changing and tempestuous religious debates of the nineteenth century had a profound effect on the development not just of Roman archaeology, but also of how things could tell history.

The indication of Roman remains at Frampton had been revealed by a plough more than two years earlier, but it was Lysons' work that brought the site to the fore of the public's imagination. Lysons uncovered wonderful mosaic pavements and the outlines of a villa, all of which are known now solely from Lysons' drawings (in some cases based on a local artist's sketches), since the remains themselves were covered over or destroyed – a disregard which is a sign of a different, earlier attitude to the materials of the ancient past. (Bulwer's disburied skulls may be cased now in obscurity; but these mosaics were physically reburied.) The mosaics contained mythological images, including Bellerophon, Bacchus and Venus;[13] a scene of Neptune, with two crude Latin verse inscriptions; and, most excitingly, a *chi-rho* symbol, the standard representation of the first letters of the word 'Christ' as a sign of Christian affirmation. Lysons felt that the *chi-rho* had been added after the mosaic's first construction (which later archaeologists disproved), but was secure in dating the building: 'Of course the work was of the time of Constantine or later', he wrote to Joseph Banks[14] – and the Frampton villa is indeed now still standardly dated to the fourth century.

These discoveries at Frampton spoke to two insistent contemporary intellectual concerns, each of which had deep cultural roots. First, the villa was part of a new picture of Roman Britain, which was emerging in the early years of the nineteenth century. The previous paucity of evidence of Roman life, due to lack of systematic archaeological exploration, had raised questions of how civilized and how pervasive the Roman presence in Britain had been. The revelation of expensive properties with fine arts, especially in the south of the country, made it certain for the first time that there was a wealthy and cultured community at this boundary of the Empire. As several modern scholars have outlined, the British Empire grew with a constantly anxious look towards the Roman Empire as a paradigm and historical antecedent.[15] In particular, a narrative of national identity was being forged, which stressed that 'imperial domination enabled the civilizing of the colonized and assisted political control'.[16] Thus the British in India, say, were fulfilling a duty of imposing civilized values, as Rome had in Britain. Britain under Roman rule significantly changed from when Julius Caesar first saw it: 'the face of the island was strangely altered from that

which it presented when visited by Caesar. Well inhabited and well cultivated, it was divided like a network by innumerable roads [linking] a
multitude of flourishing cities and towns.'[17] Lysons was digging on the
estate of a wealthy, landed British gentleman and uncovered the villa of a
wealthy, landed Roman gentleman: the connections to be drawn were easily
available.[18] Yet a deeper identity – a racial or national essence – survived the
power of assimilation or domination. Both novels and history text-books
throughout the nineteenth century stressed the special combination of
Teutonic, northern strengths that bonded with Roman order and technology to create the unique British race.[19] History, and genealogical history
especially, needed to explain how and why 'the world is a world for the
Saxon race',[20] and the portrayal of Roman Britain was central to this long
narrative of the formation of a national identity.

The second debate to which Lysons' discovery made a telling contribution was the role of Christianity in this early history of Britain. As we will see
shortly in far more detail, the clash between the Anglican and Roman
Catholic Church highlighted the genealogy of Christian dogma. Catholics
repeatedly emphasized the apostolic succession, the unbroken line of
authority from Peter, the first bishop, through to contemporary bishops
and the Pope. This constituted a historical claim of considerable power: the
Catholic Church was built on the rock which was inaugurated by Jesus
himself. Protestants in turn sought to find a foundation for their beliefs in a
pre-Reformation era to counteract these claims. When Augustine came to
England in the sixth century to convert the inhabitants, what did he find?
Were there already Christians here, and if so, were they not the original,
pre-Roman Catholic Christians of the island? Did not an Anglicanism – or a
'British Christianity' – predate the arrival of the missionaries from Rome?
Evidence of early Christianity in England was a powerful card to play in
such arguments, and Lysons' *chi-rho* at Frampton was a tempting discovery,
made dangerous by the evident fact that it was fully incorporated into a set
of pagan mythological images (as were the subsequently discovered
Christian markings). Lysons himself seems to have been quite sanguine
about the uncertain syncretism of fourth-century culture, but his discovery
would bear long-lasting fruit of a more polemic and bizarre form.

A key player in the story is Lysons' own nephew, also called Samuel
Lysons. Like his uncle, the young Samuel Lysons was a local historian, but
he had few of the older man's celebrated attainments. He graduated from
Oxford with a third class degree in Classics, and took up a living in
Gloucestershire, inherited from his father. He was particularly vexed by
the publication in 1852 of *The Celt, the Roman and the Saxon* by Thomas

Wright. This volume was 'a history of the early inhabitants of Britain, down to the conversion of the Anglo-Saxons to Christianity', as its subtitle proclaimed. Wright's conclusion self-consciously set his findings against the dominant Anglican historiography of the day:

We seem driven by these circumstances to the unavoidable conclusion that Christianity was not established in Roman Britain, although it is a conclusion totally at variance with the preconceived notion into which we have been led by the ecclesiastical historians.[21]

Wright recorded the overwhelming weight of evidence indicating the Romans' continuing pagan worship; he dismissed Tertullian's famous declaration that Christianity stretched 'from India to Britain' as mere rhetorical exaggeration; he scorned the stories that Joseph of Arimathea had come to Glastonbury as mere legends. He was fully aware that the medieval chronicles, which made such claims for the presence of Christian saints in England, were thoroughly unreliable. But even Wright was worried by the single piece of evidence to set against this powerful case for the persistence of pagan religion in Britain:

One solitary memorial of the religion of Christianity, however, has been found, and that under very remarkable circumstances. On the principal tessellated pavement in the Roman villa at Frampton in Dorsetshire the Christian monogram (the *X* and *P*) is found in the midst of figures and emblems all of which are pagan.[22]

Wright is unconvinced, however, that Lysons' discovery makes any difference, and simply imagines the owner of the villa to have been a wealthy man with a taste for philosophy and literature, sufficiently tolerant 'to surround himself with the memorials of all systems'.[23] For Wright, the Frampton pavement is not a sign of early Christianity in Britain, but of an eclectic and cultivated tourist of world religions. Wright's argument is aimed firmly and with sharp intent at the established narrative of 'ecclesiastical historians', that is, at the formation of the cultural, national and religious identity of the dominant Anglican historiography.

The younger Lysons' response took a variety of increasingly bizarre forms, which, even more bizarrely, have had a continuing impact on religious history. He gave a lecture, first of all, which was published in 1860 as a small book entitled *The Romans of Gloucestershire*, in which he outlines his astonishing theory that Gloucester is the true original home of Christianity. 'It may perhaps surprise you', he begins with the insouciance of the convinced enthusiast, 'to hear that Gloucester was one of the first towns in England in which the faith of Christ was professed; it may astonish you to hear it suggested that St Paul himself preached on the streets of Gloucester.'[24] For Lysons, his uncle's discovery of the Frampton pavement was itself an act of a divine plan which he is now to fulfil: 'There seems to have been some remarkable design of Providence in leaving to the present age the discovery of things which have been kept hidden from the eyes of previous generations.'[25] Lysons could not be content with the simpler task of demonstrating that the presence of Christian symbols in Roman sites indicates the presence of Christianity in Roman Britain: he wants to demonstrate the most aggressive and extreme Anglican foundational story that, as he passionately concludes his lecture, 'Rome derives its Christianity from Britain, not Britain from Rome.'[26]

So how does Lysons argue this improbable historical case? He offers two interlocking arguments based on classical sources, which together are designed to support the significance of the Frampton pavement as the physical proof of England's early Christianity. First, he turns to Martial, the first-century Roman epigrammatist from Spain, who wrote a poem to one Claudia, who is heralded as a very cultured lady, despite coming from British stock, and who, in another poem, is married joyfully to a man called Aulus Pudens, a centurion and friend of Martial's (if that Claudia is indeed the same figure).[27] This classical source is then brought next to a passage in 2 Timothy, which salutes 'you and Pudens, and Linus, and Claudia, and all the brethren'.[28] Now, although both Claudia and Pudens are far from rare names it is assumed that the figures referred to in Martial and in the New Testament are the same people, and that Claudia was a Christian, and Pudens became one. Indeed, argues Lysons, adding a further card to the house, when St Paul in *The Letter to the Philippians* (4.22) sends greetings from 'all the saints, especially those who are of Caesar's household', who else could be indicated but Claudia and Pudens?[29] There is a small problem in that an inscription found in Chichester in the eighteenth century demonstrates that one Pudens, under the authority of Cogidubnus, dedicated a temple to the pagan gods Neptune and Minerva. But, assuming (as ever) that this is the same Pudens, it is clear that Pudens must have been converted later to Christianity by Claudia, and, indeed, 'doubtless she made it a condition of her marriage'.[30] To add to the mix, it could be – it is argued – that Claudia went to Rome either as the daughter of Caractacus, the Welsh rebel, or, more probably, as a relative, possibly the daughter, of Tiberius Claudius Cogidubnus, a British client king – which would explain the name Claudia, her presence in Rome, and her status that allowed her to marry a Roman citizen – as well as the excitement on the excavation of the inscription proving a direct connection between the royal Cogidubnus and one Pudens.

This identification of the Claudia and Pudens of Martial and the Claudia and Pudens of the New Testament, however shaky it may seem not least in terms of relative dates, had been asserted in the sixteenth century by the great historian of British antiquity, William Camden, on the authority of no less a divine than the Archbishop of Canterbury, and great manuscript collector, Matthew Parker; it had been picked up and approved by Archbishop James Ussher in the seventeenth century, and, a few years before Lysons' pamphlet, had been the subject of a book by John Williams, archdeacon of Cardigan, who also wrote a book on the religious antiquities of Wales.[31] He was happy to claim Claudia as a British Princess and a Christian heroine as part of his general interest in Welsh saints. Williams himself may have read William Lisle Bowles' pamphlet on Pudens and Claudia, where the same arguments and same proof texts appear. Bowles was canon of Salisbury Cathedral. R.W. Morgan in 1861, in a book dedicated to Connop Thirlwall, Bishop of St David's, made the same case at book length. In making Claudia and Pudens Christians, Lysons was following a small tradition, and found support precisely in the writings of ecclesiastical historians in the counties around Gloucestershire. As late as 1897, the church of St Llonio in Llandinam, Wales – which had been restored by Street in 1865 – was fitted with three fine, new stained glass windows which portray Claudia marrying Pudens, St Paul preaching to Caractacus, and the mysterious St Pudentiana.[32] The West Country origins of Christianity and its journey to Rome are enshrined in the fabric of the church, a history, manufactured from fragments of material traces, now re-told through a new material embodiment.

Bizarrely, Cardinal Wiseman, who was so involved with the polemics between Catholics and Protestants in Britain, not least through his popular novel on early Christianity in Rome, *Fabiola*, took St Pudentiana for his episcopal title and accepted his cardinal's hat in the church of St Pudenziana in Rome. In *Fabiola*, he asserts that St Peter lived in Pudens' house in Rome. This house of Pudens is now the Church of St Pudentiana, 'the most ancient church in the world', he continues, and, most mischievously of all, he had argued that St Peter's Chair at Rome, the physical sign of the apostolic succession on which the Catholic Church rested its authority, was not merely authentically ancient (as had been impugned by Lady Morgan), but was a senatorial curule chair given to Peter by Pudens. As the Anglicans attempted to construct an English, Anglican ancient history, their key witness had already been suborned to Rome.[33]

Four years after his lecture, in 1864, the younger Samuel Lysons made an archaeological discovery of his own. At Chedworth Wood in Gloucestershire, where a Roman villa had been found, Lysons discovered 'two distinct instances of the Christian monogram, carved in the stone forming the under part of the foundation of the steps leading into the corridor'.[34] Near the same spot were uncovered two stone candlesticks 'one of which is said to have on it a cross'.[35] This led one John William Grover, rector of Hitcham in Buckinghamshire and a civil engineer who worked on railways in England and Central America, to write in strong support of Lysons' attack against Thomas Wright. The villa could be shown to be old because nearby there was a bath with the letters ARVIRI on it – indicating a reference to Arviragus, a client king under Claudius, said to be the father of Boudicca. Boudicca married a man called Prasiatagus. In the villa, a sculpted stone with the letters PRASIATA was excavated: 'singularly confirming history'.[36] The ancient chroniclers, whose authority was much doubted, called Arviragus a Christian, converted by Joseph of Arimathea. 'This story has been regarded as a mere fable', commented the civil engineer, 'but this interesting discovery at Chedworth seems to indicate its truth.'[37] It was only a failure of systematic archaeology that had prevented more instances of Christian self-announcement being discovered in Roman Britain, but the few that did exist refuted Wright conclusively. The pavement at Frampton should be celebrated, Grover concluded triumphantly, as 'the most ancient Roman record of Christianity, not in Britain alone, but in the whole of Europe – outside the catacombs'.[38] The mosaic in Dorsetshire told the true history of Roman Britain, and thus of British, Anglican history. 'Results . . . won by the spade are undeviatingly true, and carry universal conviction.'[39] Things prove history.

But the connection of Roman Britain's Christianity specifically to Gloucester needed Lysons' second argument from classical sources. In Tacitus' *Annals*, there is the following passage (xiii. 32):

Pomponia Graecina, a woman of noble family, who was married to Aulus Plautius – whose ovation after the British campaign I recorded earlier – was now accused of foreign superstition. She was left to the jurisdiction of her husband. Following the ancient custom, he held the trial, which was to determine his wife's fate and reputation, before a family council, which declared her innocent. Pomponia was a woman destined for a long life and continuous grief. After Julia, the daughter of Drusus, had been murdered by the treachery of Messalina, she survived for forty years, dressed in perpetual mourning and lost in perpetual sorrow – and a constancy unpunished under the empire of Claudius became later a title to glory.

This brief paragraph is all that is known about Pomponia Graecina – that she was accused of foreign superstition, tried and acquitted through an already arcane institution of a family council, and after her acquittal, lived in a symbolic state of continuous mourning for her murdered relative. The fact that she survived for forty years making such a political spectacle of herself is what makes her newsworthy to Tacitus' cynical recording of imperial power games and their suppression of all principled opposition.

Yet Pomponia Graecina is the linchpin of Lysons' story. The steps of Lysons' argument are each fraught with difficulty but asserted with enthusiastic certainty. The 'foreign superstition' of which Pomponia is accused must be Christianity (although there were many proscribed cults at the time). She lived in mourning all her life not as a political statement, as Tacitus declared, but because to be acquitted she must have denied or concealed her Christianity, a gesture which she regretted all her life and demonstrated by her conspicuous grief.[40] But she travelled with her husband, Aulus Plautius, to Britain (although there is no evidence of such a trip and little even of the expectation that a noble Roman woman would travel with her husband on a military campaign to the borders of the Empire). Aulus Plautius campaigned in the south-west of the country; and as the name Gloucester indicates the presence of a Roman camp, it can safely be assumed that Aulus Plautius set up a headquarters at Gloucester where his wife, a Christian, would certainly have preached her religion to the locals. What is more, Claudia would have met her in Rome, and been converted by her, and so Claudia, Pudens and Pomponia could all be placed in Gloucester at the very start of Christianity. Thus 'The Christian religion was professed by Pomponia, Claudia &c, in Gloucester, in the year 46, or only eleven years after Our Saviour's crucifixion.'[41] Gloucester should celebrate its honoured place in the history of early Christianity.

Lysons was not alone in identifying Pomponia Graecina as a key early Christian, although his attempt both to make her the sponsor of Claudia and to bring her to Gloucester and to preach Christianity on Aulus Plautius' campaign, is a vivid demonstration of how much creative imagination is necessary to construct a narrative that goes beyond Tacitus' paragraph. The more austere and respected theologians Conybeare and Howson, in what had already become by 1860 its seventh edition, a standard commentary on the Epistles of Paul, had claimed Pomponia for Christianity with no further evidence than Tacitus; Lewin, an Oxford lawyer who wrote the textbook of trust law, made the same assertion in his *Life and Epistles of St Paul* of 1851, a volume popular enough to go into its fifth edition in 1890, and also argued that Claudia came as Cogidubnus' daughter to Rome and would have been made the ward of Pomponia. Henry's popular history of Britain from the late eighteenth century made the identification too, but from the 1850s onwards Pomponia's Christian belief becomes – remarkably – a battlecry of the ecclesiastical historians, and a tale lovingly disseminated by the burgeoning world of Christian historical novels.

Lysons himself further spread the story a year after his lecture was published with his novel *Claudia and Pudens: or, the Early Christians in Gloucester* (1861), a thoroughly second-rate fiction that combines a sickly love story with some naïve religious preaching and toga action.[42] Mrs Jerome Mercier picked up the same story twenty years later in her *By the King and Queen: A Story of the Dawn of Religion in Britain* (1886), a novel republished in 1898 and 1901. Mrs Mercier embodies the Sunday reading despised by Henry James (or the Silly Lady Novelists of George Eliot's scorn). She wrote a good deal for younger readers, and reveals the agenda involved in such story telling with absolute directness. In the same year as she published *By the King and* Queen, she also published a book for girls called *Our Mother Church* – the theory, as it were, behind the novel. She gently rebukes her young reader for not appreciating that 'Our English Church goes straight back to the Apostles' time', and that 'the Christian Church in this land is as old as Christianity, or very nearly so'.[43] Pomponia's Christianity is designed to bolster the authority of Anglican history against Catholic longevity.

Yet Pomponia also plays starring roles as a gentle, inspiring, dignified and committed Christian in a string of far grander novels through to the First World War. The figure of a noble, female Christian, amid the fleshpots of imperial Rome, whose husband was a military leader instrumental in the Roman civilization of Britain, was just too productive a stereotype for late Victorian religious and historical thinking. So Frederic Farrar, Dean of Canterbury, and hugely popular novelist as well as major Broad Church leader, brings Pomponia into his lurid exposure of the court of Nero, *Darkness and Dawn* (1892), not only as the protector of Claudia, daughter of Caractacus, but also as the icon whose introduction of the Gospel into the court converts Britannicus, his sister, Octavia, the Empress, and a host of slaves. Farrar knows his Tacitus very well and every element of the single paragraph is fully dramatized. She is a 'paragon of faithful friendship' because of her forty years' mourning, and her constant grief becomes a paradigmatic Victorian restraint: 'though she smiled but rarely, the beauty of Pomponia was exquisite from her look of serenity and contentment'.[44] Farrar dramatizes the trial of Pomponia as a set piece with considerable flair: he stages it as a test of Christianity in the familial and public sphere – in a way which draws on the contemporary litigiousness of church politics, which Farrar knew all too well. Similarly, A. J. Church, the popular and popularizing teacher of classical antiquity, gives Pomponia a starring role in his account of Nero's world.[45] Most strikingly of all, she appears as the adoptive mother of Ligia, the heroine of Henryk Sienkiewicz's novel *Quo Vadis* (1896), which significantly contributed to his Nobel Prize for Literature in 1905. She is, as ever, the lodestone and icon of the Christianity that pervades the novel as the counterweight to Neronian corruption. Pomponia was, for the novelists, good to think with: in the name of historical truth she enabled the promotion of Victorian stereotypes of Christian values within the household – the mother and wife as haven of morality – and combined such domestic virtues with the more public politics of such a role, as Christianity entered the imperial framework. The nineteenth-century image of Rome needed its early Christian heroine.

Yet what I find even more fascinating is how this novelistic image of Pomponia is traced and bolstered by historians and theologians writing in a more academic environment. Ernest Renan calls her 'the first of the great world's saints'.[46] With a misplaced national fervour, Pritchard and, more cautiously, Williams attempt to add her to a roster of *Welsh* saints, because of the potential connection with the family of Caractacus and the trip to the West Country. John Ruskin cites Henry, the eighteenth-century historian, to show Pomponia's 'innocence of . . . manners', and, when it comes to the beautiful Claudia and Pomponia as the holy women who brought Christianity to England, he states unequivocally that 'of their existence, and the place and manner of it, there is no doubt'.[47] There is a roll-call of minor historians and theologians, who gave well-received lectures and published respectable volumes which all cited the same passage of Tacitus, and which all duly and cautiously declared Pomponia a Christian and a Christian icon. Conybeare catches the ideology of these arguments perfectly: 'It would be hard to imagine a series of evidences more *morally* convincing.'[48] The identification of Pomponia as a Christian is right because it *ought* to be right. It is nonetheless something of a shock to find that the great Lutheran Church historian, Adolf von Harnack, also decides on the same evidence that 'We may therefore consider the Christian standing of Pomponia Graecina as established.'[49] As late as 2004, Peter Lampe in a handbook on Christians in Rome carefully supports Pomponia's Christian identity.[50]

There were barely any dissenting voices to this idealized image of an early female Christian at the centre of Roman authority in the years immediately following the crucifixion. William Lindsay Alexander, a classicist and theologian, twisted himself in knots to fit the story into an evangelical idealism.[51] He denies Pomponia is Christian, but only on the grounds that her husband accepted her defence. For this to happen, she must have denied her Christianity, but as a paradigm of early belief, she could not have denied her own commitment, and therefore she couldn't have been Christian . . . The strain in his own ideological commitments here is evident. One scholar alone, John Allen Giles, stands out for his hard-nosed dismissal of the weakness of the historical case for Pomponia's Christianity. His critique, however, was published in 1847, early in this history, and Giles gave every opportunity for his authority to be dismissed by ecclesiastically minded historians.[52] Giles had never wished to enter the Church, but had been forced into orders by his parents. He was compelled by Wilberforce, the bishop of Oxford, to suppress his arguments for the late dating of the Gospels – and then rebelliously published the correspondence on the case anyway. He was finally prosecuted and sentenced to a year in prison for falsifying parish records while conducting a marriage out of hours. One of the girls to whom he taught typography wished to marry in secret and he was helping her out; but his uncontrolled attempts to influence witnesses and obscure the facts of the case counted against him, and his congregation was keen to get rid of so awkward an incumbent. Giles was a maverick and an outsider, and it is thus no surprise that his critical comments on Pomponia were simply ignored.

The pavement at Frampton with its *chi-rho* told a story of early Christianity in England; the older Lysons himself, its excavator and drawer, seemed to favour the idea that, when Constantine in the fourth century had declared Christianity to be a licit religion, the opportunity for a public display of some Christian affiliation became available in England as elsewhere in the Empire, amid the shifting syncretism and prevalent paganism of the era. But this simple and plausible narrative was inadequate for a contested and rumbustious Anglican historiography, intent as it was on finding a deep genealogy for its institutional structure as a commitment as much to a national and cultural identity as to a religious history. The younger Lysons led the way, hunting down further physical and thus irrefutable examples of Christian self-identification and proposing a radical history of early Christianity, locating it in Gloucester only eleven years after the crucifixion. The creative search for secure textual evidence to help explain the ancient physical remains produced figures who took on a life of their own, as Claudia, Pudens and, above all, Pomponia Graecina strode across the terrain of ancient Britain and ancient Rome in the imagination of novelists and the reconstructions of academics. The fourth-century material object itself became a footnote to another history. The initial excitement of the discovery at Frampton at the beginning of the nineteenth century prompted a visit from the whole Royal Family. By the end of the nineteenth century, however, archaeological excitement had gone elsewhere (as we will see in subsequent chapters), and the modern physical loss of the pavement excited little if any attention. The fourth century became caught in the violent and undermining arguments about the authenticity of saints' lives and the uncertainties of institutionalized early Christianity. The lure of Nero and the corruptions of the imperial court proved too strong to keep the image of a possible semi-Christian in the Constantinean era in Dorset at the cutting edge of the contest of public imagination. The historical potential of the Frampton pavement was reburied. It was no longer a thing that mattered in the public imagination of religious history.

II Stone that heralds Rome: 'The restoration of churches is the restoration of popery'

Royalty visited the Round Church in Cambridge, too. On 5 February 1844, Queen Victoria and Prince Albert visited the newly restored Church of the Holy Sepulchre, known as the Round Church, in Cambridge.[53] The Queen contributed to the restoration fund, which was followed by a donation from her husband a few days later. The architect for the restoration was Anthony Salvin, who was a widely respected architect of the new school that saw the restoration of old churches as part of the restoration of the Church of England itself, but the group that spearheaded the campaign for the work was the Cambridge Camden Society.[54] The restoration itself will be discussed in the final chapter of this book – but suffice to say here that it was a drastic rebuilding which created a church of the Victorian imagination. The Cambridge Camden Society, however, although it survived only seven years, played a formative role in the religious battles that ran for the next sixty years.

The Cambridge Camden Society had been formed by two undergraduates at Trinity College, Cambridge – John Mason Neale and Edward Jacob Boyce – who spent their first vacation together in 1837 visiting churches. They were joined quickly by Benjamin Webb, another Trinity undergraduate, and soon a small nucleus of young men formed an ecclesiological society which in 1839 took the name the Camden Society, adding Cambridge to the title to distinguish it from the Camden Society in

London. Alexander Beresford Hope was one of the earliest non-students to join. It had the necessary senior support of Thomas Thorp, tutor at Trinity. Like so many boyish societies of the era, it began by arguing over rules for itself (a fine would be levied 'on all members who did not visit some specified Church within four miles of S. Mary's Church *weekly*').[55] But it quickly became remarkably influential. By 1841, it had 300 members; by 1843, its membership included '2 archbishops, 16 bishops, 31 Peers and M.P.s, 7 Deans and Chancellors of Dioceses, 21 Archdeacons and Rural Deans, 16 architects, and over 700 ordinary members'.[56] This remarkable roll call of the great and good not only indicates the class and religious background of the society's membership but also makes its rapid demise all the more spectacular.

The Cambridge Camden Society was dedicated to the promotion and regulation of ecclesiological principles in the Church of England. It reviewed new buildings – sometimes with such biting fervour that petty scandals of rebuttal and accusations of intolerable rudeness erupted – and ran campaigns against elements of liturgy, architecture and the fabric of churches of which it disapproved. It was in the vanguard of the Gothic revival, arguing fervidly for an idealism of medieval construction. Its magazine, the *Ecclesiologist*, declared ecclesiology a 'science' and evaluated ritual, decoration and church buildings according to dogmatic rules and principles – along with publishing historical and antiquarian investigations into all aspects of the materiality of the Church of England. Although there were those who thought the society excessively self-promoting, there can be little doubt that it made an extraordinary impact in a short time, with an expanding library of drawings and models, an extensive network of like-minded researchers and a journal to disseminate its views more widely.

Its strident campaign against pews and galleries in churches shows how the Cambridge Camden Society's principles entwined historical, aesthetic, political and theological concerns. In the eighteenth century, it was usual to have closed pews in churches, with high walls or curtains, which allowed richer families to sit in secluded isolation from the rest of the congregation. The gallery similarly raised some congregants into a separate arena. These closed pews became a particular focus of the Cambridge Camden Society's disdain for the religious values of the past, which restoration set out to purify and reinvigorate for modernity. 'For what is the HISTORY OF PUES', wrote Neale characteristically, 'but the history of the intrusion of human pride, and selfishness, and indolence into the worship of God.'[57] This historicism is readily politicized:

Their galleries or pavements, their dark chancels, their dismal recesses, their pews with fireplaces and easy chairs, must not be molested for they are historical. Historical indeed! but of what? Historical of carelessness and coldness, of disregard for that better past, which all of us must reverence. Historical of a state of society which would reserve even Heaven for the rich and great, while bidding the poor to worship at a distance and beneath their footstool.[58]

Edward Middleton Barry, the architect who completed his father's design for the Houses of Parliament, with fine scorn and sarcasm offers an argument that is religious and aesthetic, for sure, but also crucially challenges the idea that historical value is a given. For him, the work of restoration is also a political and revolutionary gesture, turning back the corruption of the past, as it has been institutionalized and embodied in its church architecture. The paradox of a backward-looking antiquarian aesthetic as an innovative strategy of modernity does not fit simply within a whiggish Protestant teleological account of progress. Yet despite a brief flurry of opposition, and the occasional second-rate novel, the Cambridge Camden Society's campaign was successfully instrumental in the removal of almost all closed pews from English churches.[59]

The exceptions which survived the society's zeal show how the pace of change could vary locally across the country and how different smaller communities reacted to the proclaimed progress of Victorian society. So, the church of Holy Trinity at Stratford, where Shakespeare is buried and thus a site of national pilgrimage, actually introduced square box pews, a gallery and a 'three-decker' pulpit as late as 1839.[60] The guide-book was delighted and throughout the 1850s declared, 'On entry, it is immediately apparent the hand of discriminating taste has been at work' . . . 'In the nave whatever was ugly and inappropriate has been removed, open seats substituted.' The church is now 'free from disgust and vexation attendant upon the view of a neglected and dingy edifice'.[61] The pews were not removed in the name of restoration until 1886.

Yet it was the Society's great success of the Round Church at Cambridge that turned out to lead directly to the Society's closure and its removal to London and reformation as the Ecclesiological (late Cambridge Camden) Society, where it continued to run, although without the overheated excitement of its earlier years, until the *Ecclesiologist* and the society folded in 1868. It is the sudden storm over the Round Church that I wish first to focus on here.

The Round Church repair work was necessary because there had been a collapse of part of the church, but the restoration project was undertaken by the Cambridge Camden Society with a paradigmatic fanfare of self-promotion. The scheme was announced as '*in Cambridge*, our workshop and training school for future church restorers, and *to the world* our example of what can be done and how'.[62] The Queen's visit appeared to set the seal on the society's aims of renewing the church through a campaign of restoration. It was a considerable shock, therefore, when shortly after the Queen's visit, the incumbent, R. R. Faulkner, very publicly opposed the consecration of the building. He wrote to *The Times* on 7 August accusing the designers of introducing 'abominations of popery' into the Anglican Church, and followed this broadside with a further pamphlet.

He decided to take to court the church wardens who had allowed into his church what he so hated. He was supported by a truly thundering leader in *The Times*: the plans of the Cambridge Camden Society will speedily provoke 'disgust and apprehension, when it is perceived to what offensive extremes they too carry their desire of innovations, under the plea of revivals of ancient images'.[63] *The Times* recognized that public perception here is paramount, as it manipulated such perceptions: 'It is not enough that an objectionable practice is in itself insignificant or can even be so explained as apparently to savour nothing of Romanism; the appearance of it, the tendency that is supposed to bear in that direction, is quite sufficient to make the disputed point a matter of grave displeasure and vital offence'[64] – that is, the object in the church may be of little matter, and could even be explained as innocent, but if it is merely thought to have tendencies towards Rome, that is enough to justify 'grave displeasure and vital offence'. With such dodgy and aggressive arguments from on high, it is easy to see how the dispute could swiftly veer into violent disagreement in an uncontrolled manner. Although Faulkner failed in the Consistory Court, he appealed to the higher church institution of the Court of the Arches, where in 1845 Sir Herbert Jenner Fust found in his favour.[65] The offending materials were 'thrown out ignominiously into the Churchyard'.[66]

What was it that had so upset Faulkner? It was not the wholesale redesign of the old building to an imagined model of a pre-Reformation church, although this could be thought to represent a turn towards Catholicism. It was rather the presence of a stone altar and credence table in the church. These were in his eyes the 'most pernicious and soul-destroying heresies' and he declared himself 'fully resolved to use every means to remove these abominable pieces of superstition and Popery from my church'.[67] It was the altar about which the argument flared most stridently.

There was both a general case and a specific one. The general case was, in a nutshell, as the evangelical Francis Close entitled one of his many pamphlets, that 'The Restoration of Churches is the Restoration of Popery'. Indeed, the subtitle of this pamphlet declares that this assertion is to be 'proved and illustrated from the authenticated publications of the Cambridge Camden Society'. For Close and many other evangelicals as well as many Broad Church theologians, the restoration movement was extremely worrying. Although its stated aims of renewing the Church of England were evidently admirable, there was a deep-seated anxiety that this renewal was really and secretly an attempt to re-introduce a form of Roman Catholicism.[68] What was so upsetting was not that the architecture of the Gothic revival seemed to wish to take Britain back before the Reformation – although the iconic position of the Catholic Pugin and his publications in this movement was taken as a sign of its dangerous tendencies[69] – so much as the fact that interest in reviving ancient forms of worship seemed system- atically to seek to re-establish forms and practices of worship which were associated with the Roman Church.

So facing East during communion so that the congregation could not see the sacrament, or kneeling at the altar during the sacramental service, or even putting candlesticks or flowers on the altar could be taken as clear signs of a popish bent. Similarly, wearing a chasuble or alb were demonstrable indications of an attempt to invest the officiant with unsuitably priestly qualities. Officiants at a church service who appeared to their aggressive and unwilling congregants to be tainted by such ritualism could find themselves followed home by an angry mob and publicly chastised by the church authorities, most notoriously at St Barnabas, Pimlico, and at St George-in- the-East in the East End of London. As we will see shortly, candles and altars and chasubles remained so heated a topic that eventually by the 1870s the government felt moved to pass an Act of Parliament to regulate Christian worship. As the Oxford Movement was seen to inaugurate a move towards Rome, which reached a climax of anger and disappointment when Newman did indeed join the Catholic Church, so the restorationists of the Cambridge Camden Society were seen as harbingers of a Catholic plot to change the Church from within. Accusations of insidious antiquarianism and perfidy flew: '*Such Churches* are palpably *unfit for* all the circumstances of modern worship ... we want *Protestant Churches, not Popish Mass-houses*', screamed Francis Close in typical and typographical hysteria.[70]

The more specific argument, however, was what the law case depended on, and it concerned primarily the altar.[71] Faulkner, the complainant about the Round Church, was actually resident at Havering, where there was a stone altar, and Francis Close, his most vocal supporter, had himself set up stone altars at his own church in Cheltenham,[72] but this did not stop the material of the altar becoming part of the public argument, although the rubrics of the church to which Falkner appealed and the case which the Court of the Arches upheld was only that the altar should be moveable. The altar at the Round Church, it was claimed – falsely, in fact – was not moveable. But the ground for the outburst of emotion had been prepared in Cambridge for some months by a long-running pamphlet war.

As ever, the details of this argument are petty and were debated with a fervour which is difficult to appreciate from afar. In 1842, the classicist and moderate evangelical Anglican James Scholefield preached a sermon before the university on the subject of the Christian altar in which he took to task those who would erect stone altars rather than movable wooden communion tables. The implication was that by constructing an object that was clearly an altar – stone and fixed – the eucharist was a form of sacrifice, since sacrifices happened at altars, and that the officiant was a sacrificing priest. This was of a piece not just with the status of the priest in Roman Catholicism as opposed to Anglicanism, but also promoted a view of the true presence of the body and blood of Christ at the communion which was at odds with Anglican orthodoxy.[73]

Scholefield's argument was opposed and restated by a flurry of warring pamphlets and sermons.[74] The *Ecclesiologist* had already reported that even the use of the word 'altar' could lead to complaint: 'the word *Altar* is always used in publications of the Cambridge Camden Society, instead of *Communion-Table*, as it is called in the rubrick and canons of our Church'.[75] In response to Scholefield and his supporters, it was quickly pointed out with strident scholarly apparatus that the words 'altar' and 'table' (as in 'God's Table') were used interchangeably in the Hebrew and Greek Scriptures. But this did not stop the anxiety. 'Priesthood, and sacrifice and altar are terms so inseparably related to each other that the denial of one is a denial of all, and the proof of fitness of either leads to the admission of the others.'[76] Charles Warren, the vicar of Over, a village near Cambridge, felt that Scholefield's argument attacked his very office: 'Professor Scholefield has attacked the chief power and privilege of the Christian Priesthood.'[77] As late as 1874, when, as we will shortly see, the conflict was exacerbated by the Public Worship Regulation Act, the leading ritualist John Dykes (whose middle name, wonderfully for a ritualist, is Bacchus), was responding vehemently to the same case: 'I *do* teach that the Lord's Table is an Altar', 'The very word "Altar" suggests reverence; the word "Table" does not'; 'if I am not a priest, then what am I?'[78]

Sir Herbert Jenner Fust, 'after maturely weighing the subject',[79] refused to confirm the sentence of the lower court on the grounds that the altar was not demonstrably movable. It was duly moved out. This 'humiliating specta-cle'[80] was, however, only the first of a series of conflicts about the religious politics of the Cambridge Camden Society that year. Concerned religious leaders resigned, and in 1845, faced by mounting controversy, the Committee decided to disband the Society – which led to a further flurry of public letters and internal wrangling, before the society moved to London and a less antagonistic and publicly controversial role.

The irony remained that the decision to put the altar in the Round Church in this form had not even been made by the Cambridge Camden Society. The architect, Salvin, offered a donation of £50 for the purpose, had made the decision and created the design by himself.[81] Nor, it was sug-gested, had Faulkner initially been outraged by the altar (and certainly not when the Queen and Prince Albert were ceremoniously admiring the beauty of the Church). The altar became an object of intense debate because it focused a series of theological and political questions that seemed to go to the heart of Anglicanism as a religion of national culture. The material form of the altar became the alibi for deep-seated, religiously motivated conflicts. The thing mattered because of how it seemed to embody a range of invisible principles about how the non-material and material world interacted, about how the actual body and blood of Christ were to be conceptualized and how the mediating role of the priest in making visible God's presence in the world was to be understood. How material should religion be, and how should religion be material? 'Material phenomena are both the types and instruments of real things unseen', as Newman put it in the *Apologia Pro Vita Sua*.[82] It didn't much matter that Faulkner and Close regularly officiated in holy services at a stone altar when they bitterly, publicly, aggressively opposed the stone altar at the Round Church. This was neither cognitive dissonance nor hypocrisy, but a function of how the object itself became the sign of a set of ideological positions, and thus objectified as a physical encapsulation of those positions. That's how this thing came to matter.

III Aaron's dress: 'a tinselled show, with processions of gorgeous banners, decorated crosses and women and young girls'

Restoration as an architectural movement and a principle continued to grow, and, although opposition to it became more articulate and sophisti-cated, as we will discuss in the final chapter of this book, some 7,000 of

England's 10,000 parish churches, as well as its major cathedrals, experienced varying degrees of rebuilding and redesign over the next sixty years, according to principles set in place to a significant degree by members of the Cambridge Camden Society. Within churches, however, by the 1860s the spread of High Church ritualism, the threat of which had been part and parcel of the opposition to the altar in the Round Church, had become increasingly evident to a broader public and increasingly a subject of distrust and alienation.[83] There were occasional riots against ritualists, repeated protests and the atmosphere of antagonism between rival groups of worshippers has been beautifully caught by Chadwick's description of St George-in-the-East in London:

The best days witnessed pew doors banging or feet scraping or hissing or syncopated responses. The worst days witnessed gleeful rows of boys shooting with peas from the gallery, fireworks, flaming speeches from tub orators during services, bleating as of goats, spitting on the choir-boys, a pair of hounds howling gin-silly round the nave, cushions hurled at the altar, orange-peel and butter, kicking or hustling of clergy. One of the altar carpets was crammed into a stove and pew no 16 in the south aisle was used as a privy.[84]

Thomas Arnold had scornfully dismissed the Oxford Movement's tendencies to ritualism as the 'fanaticism of mere foolery. A dress, a ritual, a name, a ceremony – the superstition of a priesthood, without its power.'[85] Arnold is precise in the categories which had become so contentious: how to dress, what ritual to observe, what the names for religious things were, how ceremonial a service should be – all tied to the position of the religious leader, with the hostility towards Catholicism's idea of a sacrificing priest. But for the Dean of Canterbury in 1863 any move towards ritualism was also 'a step in the deterioration of the national character', and consequently needed a national solution.[86] Yet the potential psychological deformation of austere hostility towards any 'gorgeously conducted service' had already been mercilessly staged by Anthony Trollope in *Barchester Towers* (1857) where for horrid Mr Slope 'aversion [to Puseyites] is carried to things outward as well as inward. His gall rises at a new church with a high-pitched roof; a full-breasted black silk waistcoat is with him a symbol of Satan; and a profane jest-book would not, in his view, more foully desecrate the Church seat of a Christian, than a book of prayer printed with red letters, and ornamented with a cross on its back.'[87] Things upset Slope. A pitched roof – a demand of the restorationists – and a full-breasted waistcoat – the paraded sartorial style of the ritualist – culminate in his imagination in the medieval style of adding illuminated first letters to a psalter or prayer book, even in the simplest form of a bare colour, coupled with the display of a cross, itself a potentially popish gesture – which, for the resolutely low Anglican, makes such a prayer book more foul an object than a book of scurrilous jokes. The material text of holy scripture needs, it seems, rigorous policing.

These parodies and vitriolic scorn reveal the posturing of extreme responses for and against a High Church ritualism over twenty years. Yet the threat and lure of ritualism was felt to be sufficiently pressing in the 1870s that evangelicals, led by Lord Shaftesbury, could join forces with the Broad Church leaders of the institutional centre of the Church, led by Archibald Tait, the Archbishop of Canterbury, together with support from non-conformists like Charles Spurgeon, to develop a national, legal response against such High Church practice.[88] The Public Worship Regulation Act was brought before Parliament by Archbishop Tait in 1874. The passing of the Act depended on particularly complex political infighting, manipulated in particular by the then Prime Minister, Disraeli, in part at least as a conscious attack on his old enemy Gladstone, who had long harboured Tractarian sympathies. 'The debate in parliament stirred deep passions.'[89] The Queen herself was in support of the Act, however, and it seemed at first blush finally to be a compromised but effective triumph against ritualism. Now, by law, if a church officiant was accused of facing eastward during the sacramental service, mixing wine and water at the communion table, having candle-sticks on the communion table (except for necessary light), using incense, wearing elaborate robes, kneeling during the communion service, or using wafer bread, his congregants could complain to the bishop, who could forward the complaint to a new court headed by the retired judge of the divorce court, Lord Penzance, who could order the offending clergyman to desist from such activity, and then, if necessary, punish the miscreant with imprisonment, if he continued to disobey the authorities in contempt of court.

Such a political decision – for the state to regulate religious practice, and through a judge rather than through the bishops – prompted an extended outcry. For some, of course, it was a vindication of their fears that ritualism meant popery, and constituted a justified state response to what was seen largely as upper-class, educated men imposing their views on an unwilling congregation: 'They are seeking to revive the very worst abuses of mediaeval times under the specious plea of liberty for the Church. They are seeking to crush and trample on all consciences but their own.'[90] The confessional was a huge source of sexual, familial and religious anxiety.[91] Others went so far as to suggest that the compromises that had allowed the Act's passing were a step too far of appeasement: ritualism 'begets and nourishes infidelity'; it is no more than 'a gilded bauble, a tinselled show, with processions of gorgeous banners, decorated crosses and women and young girls', but the procedures of the new Act gave so much leeway that this author announces he has left the Church of England altogether in protest.[92] But the hostile reaction to the Act was similarly powerful and varied and extremely vocal.

There was a wholesale rejection of the suitability of a lawyer, and a divorce lawyer at that, to pronounce on matters of complicated religious regulation. Most gently, it was suggested that if church authorities could have been appointed to judge church matters, the Act would have been acceptable: 'It would have had Scripture for its authority, apostolic usage and primitive practice for its precedent.'[93] More aggressively, it was argued that the new court had no authority over spiritual matters and that a campaign of civic disobedience was required.[94] Contrary to the accusations, the aim of the ritualists was loudly proclaimed to be no more than an attempt 'to restore the Church of England in her beauty, and in her ritual, to what she was *before the Reformation*';[95] or, more precisely, to follow the desire of the Reformation itself: 'What the Ritualists sought to do was precisely what the framers of our existing Prayer Book sought to do: to restore primitive usage.'[96] Roman Catholics were determined to have none of this invention of a pre-Reformation uniquely British Church: 'It is in vain that Anglicans appeal to "Beda" and the "British Church" ... historically speaking, there are two parties and two parties only – the Catholicism of Rome, and the Protestantism of the Reformation.'[97] R. W. Church had written a long historical exposition of how the state could not properly interfere with church matters as a critical response to the Gorham Trial in 1850, when Erastianism had become such a heated political topic. Tellingly, he republished it now with only the briefest of re-introductions.[98] For many in the Church, the row about ritualism became reframed as a debate about disestablishmentarianism: should the Church maintain a complete separation from state interference on religious matters?

The Act duly led to a string of prosecutions as the Ritualists stood their ground. Most famously, Sidney Faithorn Green, incumbent of St John the Evangelist in Miles Platting near Manchester, was arrested in 1881, after much theological remonstration and legal wrangling, and imprisoned for his continuing ritualist practice. He was kept in gaol for twenty months, his property was sold to cover his costs, his wife and four children were turned out of house and home onto the street (although in reality maintained financially by his supporters). But the image of a pious and beloved clergyman put in prison for such a length of time proved too damaging. Figure 2.1

shows Arthur Tooth in jail – and the contrast between his pious demeanour and the bars of prison seems to be designed to lead the viewer's sympathy towards a concern about the good sense of the Act in practice. Denison – a ritualist 'in principle, wholly; in practice, as I have seen my way to revive and restore'[99] – Mackonochie, Dykes, Neale were all churchmen who maintained respect, despite the heated atmosphere of suspicion, accusation and proclamation, and even when forced to resign.[100]

The Act was largely considered by church and laity then and by historians today to have been a total failure in the attempt to control ritualism, and many of the activities or styles of worship that caused such offence in the 1870s are now both usual and acceptable in Anglican churches across England. When Archbishop Benson in 1890 was called finally to sort out the issue of candle-sticks and the like, his decision of limited support for ritual freedom was based on a full history of English Christianity typical of the Anglican historiography so despised by Newman. He cited twenty-three authorities from the Council of Hatfield in AD 680, and, along with Reformers like Cranmer and Tyndale, fathers of the Church such as Basil and Chrysostom, as well as the Clementine liturgy. Although the Act was not subject to a full governmental review until 1906 and not repealed until the 1960s, Benson's judgment effectively ended its authority. The *Guardian* understood the historical significance of Benson's opinion and expressed it with exemplary clarity: 'The Church of England of the present is historically one with the Church of England of the past ... She was not a creation of Henry VIII or Edward VI.'[101] The Ritualist claim of a restored continuity with the past as a justification for innovations in contemporary practice was upheld.

So, when the Church of Holy Trinity at Stratford-upon-Avon, Shakespeare's church, was again being remodelled, in 1889, three years after the pews had been removed, the floor was excavated, and a very large old altar slab of Purbeck marble was discovered. It had been buried during the violence of the Reformation and its aftermath. This stone altar slab was promptly re-used as the *mensa* of the new high altar. It caused and, as far as I am aware, causes no traceable anxiety at all. As the nineteenth century was reaching its close, the historical significance of a stone altar had faded to indifference, even and especially in this church imbued for its pilgrims with a special significance for English national identity. What had been a material sign of a radical break with the past is now celebrated as a display of continuity with it. How things change ...

Archbishop Benson himself noted how strange this change felt and what a sign of the times it was. After visiting St Jude's, Kensington on Sunday

Figure 2.1 *The Reverend Arthur Tooth in Prison, Vanity Fair* (1877). Leslie Ward, 'Spy' the artist, was amused and excited to draw Tooth from life in the jail.

8 March 1891, he wrote in his diary: 'But how curious the change in the notion of Divine Service. Here is an <u>Evangelical</u> congregation and minister – cross on altar, and a white cloth with lace border always remaining on it and a piscine and a surplice choir – any one of these things would have been deadly popery (except in Cathedrals the choir) – <u>since I came of age</u>.'[102] His emphasis on the fact that this is an evangelical church which normally would have bitterly opposed such ritual, and that the change had happened

since he himself had turned twenty-one, is paradigmatic of the self-awareness of the rapidness of this religious development, and the sense of historical time it encapsulated.

This narrative of how the Church together with government attempted to control ritualism, and failed, could undoubtedly be explored in much more detail, as its ins and outs engaged so many religious figures in such complex negotiations and such overheated public and private exchanges.[103] But enough has been said, I hope, to frame adequately the third religious thing I wish finally and briefly to discuss in this chapter, the marvellous chasuble pictured in Plates 1 and 2, made probably by G. F. Bodley, for Watts and Company.[104] It was manufactured for the Society of St John the Evangelist in about 1882, precisely while Sidney Green was languishing in prison for wearing such vestments. George Frederick Bodley is best known as an architect of the Gothic revival. In 1874 with two other prominent architects, George Gilbert Scott and Thomas Garner, he founded the ecclesiastical and domestic fittings and furnishings firm, Watts and Company. In the year in which the Public Worship Regulation Act was passed, to found a company dedicated to the production of the vestments, religious fittings, and other materials banned under the new law was a gesture of pronounced political resistance. Each of the three architects was already fashionable, successful, and a well-known advocate of restorationist principles, however, and the firm had, in fact, no trouble from the law (a safe enough rebellion, it turned out, and financially savvy). The Society of St John the Evangelist was founded in 1865 in Oxford, a monastic order of the sort promoted by the Oxford Movement – an outrage to muscular and highly-sexed family Anglicans like Charles Kingsley – and perhaps deserving the title of the first such institution in England since the Reformation;[105] the chasuble, whose floral designs indicate strikingly its genesis in the aesthetic environs of Morris and the pre-Raphaelites, was commissioned for one of the Society's founders, Richard Meux Benson. It would be hard to imagine an article more pointedly and wholeheartedly calculated to stand in opposition to the contemporary antagonism to ritualism: a banned priestly vestment for a member of a celibate monastic order, decorated with a full panoply of modern Morris-influenced imagery, in the name of a return to pre-Reformation culture.

Yet it remains a remarkable piece. On the back, there is an image of the crucified Jesus, with gently drooping head and relaxed, unemaciated, barely bloody body. This is not the tortured flesh and twisted, anguished form beloved of Spanish medieval and Renaissance sculpture, say. What is most remarkable about the image, however, is that the cross itself is depicted as a flourishing palm tree with branches and leaves, and around the foot of the cross are not the skulls, sniffing dogs, gambling soldiers and weeping women of medieval iconography but a luxurious garden of sunflowers and other plants. This is not the grim Golgotha, Hill of the Skull, the desert of mourning. There are in the Christian tradition occasional images of trees where the branches form a cross. In Christ Church, Jerusalem, the first Anglican Church in the Holy City, founded in the 1840s by the first Anglo-Prussian bishop, Michael Alexander, there is above the altar a stained-glass window with a tree whose branches form a cross swathed in flowers. But there is no Jesus on it, and this church is explicitly designed for the conversion of the Jews and has an inscription in Hebrew on the altar below the window. Even when the crucifixion is imagined in a green and pleasant landscape with flowers, as a handful of medieval manuscripts depict, the cross itself is always bare and simple wood. At Easter some churches may decorate a bare cross with flowers to symbolize the living Jesus (Victorian sentimental Easter greetings cards showed women doing this), and there are Victorian album prints and die-cuts of crosses made up of flowers or covered with flowers.[106] None also has the body of Jesus on it. But here, despite the long tradition back to Helena's discovery and display of the True Cross that crucifixion was on a bare, crude wooden cross, this cross is growing branches and flowers on it, like a flourishing tree.

The image here may be the *etz chayim*, the tree of life, forbidden to Adam after the Fall in Genesis (3.22). The tree of life in Jewish tradition is an image of Torah and learning: wisdom, says Proverbs 3.18, is a 'tree of life to those who grasp it, and those who draw near it are fortunate'. So too 'the fruit of a righteous man is the tree of life', 'a desire fulfilled is the tree of life', 'a healing tongue is the tree of life'.[107] This rich imagery from the Hebrew scriptures also underlies the Christian typological reading that sees the tree of life as fulfilled in the cross. As the tree of life represents the immaculate life before the fall, so the cross is the route back to that Edenic perfection. The Franciscan St Bonaventure's *Lignum Vitae* is a thirteenth-century meditational text that links Hebrew scriptural verses with the Gospel narratives they prefigure through the image of the tree of life. Plate 3 is a manuscript from the Cistercian Abbey at Kamp that illustrates the tree (Beinecke ms 416). The diagrammatic tree has twelve branches and twelve fruits each portraying a mystery from the life of Christ. The root of the tree quotes from Revelations (22.2), that favourite Victorian text also, 'And on both sides of the river was the tree of life, bearing twelve fruits, yielding its fruits every month: the leaves of the tree for the healing of the nations' – a text used repeatedly to link the tree of life and the cross of the crucifixion, 'the healing of the nations'. 'Every medieval diagram is an open-ended one in the manner of examples', states Mary Carruthers, 'it is an invitation to elaborate and recompose, not a prescriptive, "objective" schema.'[108] Bonaventure's text demonstrates how the tree of life becomes a potent structural device for interconnecting scriptural passages in an expanding reflection on the religious life. The flourishing tree on Bodley's chasuble suggests that the cross has indeed become a tree of life, with all the exuberant productivity of spiritual reading that such an image might provoke.

The front of the chasuble, however, gives an even more precise understanding of this image. There are four decorated panels framed and separated by a green and gold band. In each of the four panels there is the same device of twelve flowers linked into a chaplet that surrounds a central inscription that runs across the circle of interlocked stems. The inscription reads "I EASE YOU", where the four letters I, E, S, and U are picked out as larger than the others. This is a quotation from a celebrated poem by the Anglican priest and metaphysical poet, George Herbert (from *The Temple* (1633)):

JESU is in my heart, his sacred name
Is deeply carved there: but th'other week
A great affliction broke the little frame,
Ev'n all to pieces: which I went to seek:
And first I found the corner, where was *J*,
After, where *ES*, and next where *U* was graved,
When I had got these parcels, instantly
I sat me down to spell them, and perceived
That to my broken heart he was *I ease you*,
And to the whole is *J E S U*.

The poem's conceit overlaps the breaking and healing of the poet's heart with the breaking and remaking of the name of Jesus, so that the letters IESU spell 'I ease you' – as the poem performs its reconstruction at the level of the word. In the beginning was the word, Jesu (first word indeed of the poem), and the word is inscribed in the heart, the 'sacred name'; and is broken with the heart and is returned in different multiple punning forms in the process of healing. It is a sort of resurrection of the word from where the letters are individually 'graved' – the word 'grave' is to be heard, of course – a resurrection to the wholeness of Jesus, last word of the poem, now typographically marked out as individual letters and spelled out as an integral word, with the hope of ease always to be heard in it. The unbroken word JESU, first word, becomes, last word, both its letters and the word: a required double vision. On the chasuble, the different sized letters, and the way the phrase is broken by the circle of stems into the semantically chaotic I – EASEY – OU, embodies and demands the requirement of restorative reading: to find the meaning, to take one's reading back to Herbert's poem, to replay the poem's fullness from the germ of its brief and broken citation.

There is a second quotation that runs along the five green and gold bands which separate the four panels: 'I said I will go up to the palm tree. I will take hold of the boughs thereof.' This verse is from the Song of Songs, the intensely erotic poem that is often read in Christian tradition as an allegory of Christ's love for the Church. The palm tree has on it clusters of fruit (to which the woman's breasts are likened in the Song of Songs), which the man promises to grasp. Again, in Christian allegorizing interpretations – and the Song of Songs has a huge number of commentaries – to go to the palm and to grasp its fruit is seen as an image of turning to the cross to grasp the truth of the Christian message – an act to be undertaken with love. This verse from the Song of Songs seems to explain the image of the cross on the back of the chasuble. Since the Christian approaches the cross as a palm laden with fruit, so the cross has become a palm in its promise of flourishing redemption. The verse on the front of the chasuble from the Hebrew scriptures finds iconographic fulfilment in the image on the back.

Both quotations turn us, then, towards the image on the back of the chasuble. But how do the two citations on the front of the chasuble speak to each other? At one level, it might seem to suggest that the promise of ease is to be found precisely in the promise of approaching the cross as a fulfilment of the tree of life. Yet this also creates what might seem a bizarre almost typological connection between the poetry of Herbert and the poetry of the Song of Songs. The double vision of Herbert – and so much of Herbert's poetry is concerned with how to see correctly – finds itself doubled with the Song of Songs in an interwoven intertextual communication. This is a highly literary and literate work of weaving.

There is perhaps another level of semantics here too, however. Each of the four panels has twelve flowers blossoming on it. This may recall the vision of the tree of life in Revelation with its 'twelve branches and twelve fruits'. But this sort of numerology also may lead us back to the robes of the High Priest as described in Exodus. The woven garment known as the *ephod* and worn by the High Priest has the names of the twelve tribes of Israel on it. The priestly tribe of Aaron was established when Aaron's rod, alone of the twelve rods of the twelve tribes, flourished with almond blossom: each flourishing here is like Aaron's rod. And the book of Revelation again encourages a typological connection between the twelve tribes of Israel and the twelve apostles (21.9–14) – in turn symbolized by the twelve jewels on the breastplate of the High Priest, arranged in four lines like the chasuble's four panels. The twelve flowers, that is, within the ever-expanding numerological semantic profusion of allegorical or typological reading may take us not just towards the many twelves of biblical interpretation but also towards the robes of the High Priest – a gesture of claimed status for the priest of the communion which, as we have seen, is precisely a bone of contention between the Broad Church and the Ritualists.

Bodley's chasuble, then, is a remarkable thing. It weaves into its fabric an intricate pattern of cross-referenced literary and theological allusions, iconographic novelties, and gestures of doubling – back and front, ancient and modern, poetry and scripture – to create a space of semantic exploration of the role of a priest in ritual. It acts like a material gloss on another of Herbert's poems in *The Temple*, 'Aaron' whose five verses each end: 'thus are true Aarons dressed', 'Poor priest thus I am dressed', 'In him I am well dressed', 'And be in him new dressed', 'Come people; Aaron's dressed'. It is a poem which moves from the ideal of how a true Aaron – a priest – should be dressed, itself a metaphor for spiritual well-being and pastoral guidance – through self-doubt that the poet himself could ever live up to such ideals; to a recognition that through Jesus the poet/priest can be restored; to being 'well dressed' and thus, with all the weight of newness in Christian language from the new life of conversion to the good news of the Gospel, 'new dressed'; to a final performative invocation of achieved calling: 'Come people; Aaron's dressed'. To put on Bodley's chasuble is, in such terms, to dress as Aaron.

And there's the rub. To dress as Aaron is exactly what frightened Broad Church and evangelical Protestants. Not only does such a vestment insist on the priestly function of the officiant, drawing attention through its lavish imagery to the symbolic role of its wearer, but it also raises the question of the priest's body itself. The literary and artistic layering of the chasuble draws attention to the modernity of its art and its sense of a British literary tradition: it places its wearer within this milieu. The antipathy to communities such as the Society of St John the Evangelist, expressed by figures such as Charles Kingsley, focused on the dubious masculinity of the celibate male – with evident prurience about the community's homosocial bonding and its threat to sexual normality – here linked through its Pre-Raphaelite imagery to a dodgy, artistic, sexualized world. The chasuble richly adorns and sacralizes the (de)sexualized body of the celibate priest – it conceals it from gaze and draws attention to its hiddenness. The anxiety provoked by the chasuble stems not only from what such a vestment proclaims ritually but also from what it covers.

The chasuble for all its subversive stitching passed largely unnoticed in its time, worn in a small all-male ritualist monastic community, and it is now in the Elizabeth Hoare Embroidery Gallery in Liverpool Cathedral, a building whose initial design was drawn up by Bodley, who in his final years oversaw the work of the young Giles Gilbert Scott, third generation of the Scott family of Gothic revival architects, a young man who at age 22 had won the competition to build the new cathedral. (Bodley, of course, had been a pupil, colleague and friend of Giles Gilbert Scott's grandfather.) The chasuble and its setting, then and now, are part of the genealogical history of the Gothic revival in the Anglican Church. In the gallery, away from its religious service, it sits today as an aestheticized memorial of a once insistent theological fight, its boldly aggressive assertiveness rendered mute by historical forgetting.

The *chi-rho* discovered by Lysons became a found sign which produced stories that took on a life of their own, and which became woven into the historiography and fiction of the period, while the stones themselves disappeared back into the soil. The material object was significant as proof because of its incontestable materiality, but as it came to tell a story, its physical existence no longer became a source of care, while the stories it provoked multiplied and circulated, untethered to the object itself. The stone altar of the Round Church became a lightning rod for aesthetic, theological and political anxieties, loaded with invisible ideological burdens, until it too was thrown out ignominiously. The altar's material and its groundedness – its fixity – was the precise source of anxiety, but once it had been thrown out – moved – it became mere matter, left in the graveyard, and of no significance. Both the mosaic and the stone altar didn't just stop being things that mattered, but also, in a sense, stopped being things: fragmented, shattered, buried, decomposed, they lost the very presence and material objectivity that gave them power as things.

By contrast, Bodley's chasuble was manufactured in order to tell a religious story, with a sophisticated network of semantic interplays, literary allusiveness and theological and political self-positioning. To make it, to wear it, to observe ritual performed by a man in it, to see it now in an Anglican cathedral museum, where it is preserved 'for history', is to engage with this work of constructing religious meaning. In the nineteenth century it made a ritual and artistic statement about religion conceived and enacted in a historic framework, where the contested history of the Church was central to the Church's self-awareness; now, displayed, without a warm body wearing it, in a museum, the chasuble is also a reminder, a relic, of that passed time. As with Bulwer Lytton's skulls, the glass case marks the radical change in the object's cultural purchase and, in an embroidery gallery, allows its aesthetics to be separated from its theological polemic. The chasuble matters – is made to matter – within this network of competing historical forces. But it is a designedly assertive thing, however intricate and engaging its imagery seems, however much it may seem to have lost its immediate political engagement. It wants and has impact, an impact for which an invisible theology is integral to its visual effect. In Roland Barthes' terms, such religious things are therefore myths.

These three objects, Bodley's chasuble, the *chi-rho* at Frampton, the stone altar of the Round Church, demonstrate just how promiscuous this religious engagement with things is – offering intent and passionate attention, swirling stories, and rapid dismissal, followed by slow forgetting and incremental ignorance. (As Horace says of a long-gone love affair, *heu fabula quanta fiebam*: 'Oh, how big a story did I become' – and how brief a phrase recalls that now . . .) Things excite and lose contested meanings, flare into significance and fall into forgottenness, perform an assertive theological intent, and become the focus of suspicious anxiety – and, at best, end in the safe preservation of heritage, behind glass. This engaged enactment of the buried life of things is integral to the material culture of Victorian religious experience. Perhaps Bodley's chasuble, like Bulwer's skulls, displayed now as an example of embroidery, can stand as an icon for modernity's deeply restricted view of nineteenth-century historical materiality, of how religious things mattered; a deeply restricted view, that is, of the past, the glass through which the self-definitions of the present are constructed.

Imperial landscapes, the biblical gaze, and techniques of the photo album

Capturing the real in Jerusalem and the Holy Land

I How to look like a tourist

Despite what we say when we walk into a shop, we are never just looking. All viewing is a theory-laden and history-laden activity.[1] Our eyes are trained and layered with a history of images, of ideas, of ideology. Both seeing and being seen are framed by this social and intellectual placement: 'how you look', in English, can be transitive or intransitive. How you look can mean the activity of staring, glancing, squinting, stereotyping; or it can mean how you appear to others, 'how do I look?', your role as an image for others to see, how you present yourself, in terms of dress and deportment, class and nationality. Seeing oneself being seen is an integral part of the regime of the visual, an integral part of how seeing becomes a performance, a performance through which identity is enacted. The tourist abroad constitutes a particularly charged moment in this drama of the gaze: the tourist is caught between the self-consciousness of self-presentation – how one dresses, stands, stands out, culturally, nationally – and the self-conscious viewing of the other. In this chapter, I shall investigate how the nineteenth-century traveller's looking was articulated in Jerusalem and the Holy Land in two particular ways that together go to the heart of how cultural identities are performed, negotiated, denied through the history of photography and painting. First, I shall explore how what might be called 'the biblical gaze' informed the Western traveller's experience of the real. Second, I shall look at how the production of professional albums – edited collections of photographs – produced a specific political, cultural and religious contest over the nature of the real. In both cases, we will see how new technology became a dominant force in a battle over the representation of the Middle East, a technology which has not yet stopped expressing and fuelling conflict in this region.

It is well known, of course, that there is a very long tradition of the Western representation of the Holy Land and Jerusalem especially, which took a new and particular shape in the nineteenth century, with the onset of tourist travel and renewed imperialism, on the one hand, and the development of photography and new forms of printing and the distribution of images and writing, on the other.[2] Illustrated descriptions of the holy sites and of the tourist trail proliferated, from the high-end productions of David Roberts in the middle of the century – with a grand list of subscribers, hand-tinted, folio-size images, and a text by the celebrated preacher and novelist, George Croly – to the more widely circulated tour guides at the end of the century, which develop from the elegant etchings of Bartlett to the mass-produced guides of Baedeker and Murray.[3] Yet the specifically religious dimension of this imaging has not yet been fully appreciated, and there has been almost no discussion of how the profusion of images was organized – and the traveller's steps and perspective regulated and remembered – by professionally produced albums.

It has become a commonplace of the field, after the contributions of Edward Said, that the Middle East has been scarred by the Western orientalist gaze. The ideologically laden practices of Western representation of Arab lands has been defined, it is claimed, by a regime of barely concealed imperialism: the construction of the orient as a backward, tricky, exotic, dangerous place, distinctive for its glorious richness and crushing poverty, its religious extremism and noble simplicity.[4] This activity of viewing constructs a perspective that prepares and fosters a sense of the superiority of the Western subject, which in turns grounds a political and religious imperialism. As we will see, there can be no doubt that the Western photographic representation of Jerusalem and the Holy Land in some senses conforms to this stereotype of the orientalist gaze, but, it will be demonstrated, the particular formulation of this gaze through nineteenth-century Christian thinking has been systematically undervalued in the search for orientalism's colonial politics. Furthermore, this chapter will demonstrate not merely that we need a far more nuanced understanding of the motivations and practices of the artists, photographers and viewers than this broad theoretical stance allows, and also, and perhaps more importantly, that even the more critical approaches to Said's work have tended to underplay how much self-aware contestation around the construction of the real took place, especially through the photographic medium.[5] Self-awareness and ideological positioning are fully part of the aesthetics of photography from the earliest days in the Holy Land. This will be most strikingly demonstrated by my final example of an album, a magnificent set of photographs produced at the Ottoman court which reveal how the Ottoman authorities at the highest levels self-consciously attempted to manipulate the new media of photography and both recognized and worked to reverse the orientalist gaze in the name of a modern Ottoman national state.

Palestine indeed provides a particularly complex test case for the dynamics of orientalism and imperialism, one where modern political affiliations have tended shrilly to oversimplify the past. First of all, Palestine in the nineteenth century was not a Western colony, like India or many African territories, nor invaded and taken over like Egypt or Algeria, but part of the Ottoman Empire, ruled from Istanbul, once a Christian city, a second Rome, the capital of the Christian East, now overbuilt by an Islamic empire ruled by Turks, whom Hourani strikingly calls 'the Romans of the Muslim world'.[6] The region was administered by different local Ottoman centres of authority, and thus had no political or social integrity as a country, despite its figuration in the Western imagination as the Holy Land. The Arab population, like the Jewish and Christian, was subject to the Sublime Porte and had diffuse affiliations – to extended family, tribe, and, for at least a few upper-class leaders as the twentieth century progressed, to incipient nationalist ideals, though even this sense of identity was contested until well into the twentieth century.[7] The relationship between Ottoman rulers and the Arab inhabitants of the region, despite shared Islamic religious affiliations, regularly flared into resentment, and, especially with the Bedouin tribes, rarely demonstrated a centralist control.[8] Different, competing Western powers had interests in the region, and interactions of the Western authorities and the Ottoman world were thus always mediated – triangulated – through a consciousness of competition with other Western powers. There was no direct relation of Western colonizer and Eastern colonized. Such Western interests were expressed consequently not in direct imperialism primarily, but in competition over the right to protect pilgrims; in competitive building programmes in national style; and in political influence with the Sultan, most notably with the German involvement with the railways and, later, with British involvement with oil pipelines.[9]

Throughout the nineteenth century, this Western engagement was most dramatically enacted in military support or intervention according to wider international political policies concerning the state of the Ottoman Empire (the 'sick man of Europe'), especially with regard to the expanding and militant Russian empire. Both Montefiore's housing development (*Mishkenot Sha-ananim*) and the Russian Compound were built outside the walls of Jerusalem because of negotiations with the Sublime Porte following and in the light of the Crimean War.[10] The population of the region, what's more, was to Western and local eyes remarkably polyglot and varied. Jerusalem, for example, ruled by an Ottoman administration, had from 1840 onwards an absolute majority of Jewish inhabitants, mostly poor Eastern Jews, but, as the century advanced, with an increasing percentage of differently dressed Western Jews, who spoke Yiddish rather than Arabic or Ladino. There was also a substantial Arab population, but here too difference was strikingly evident – between, say, the few dominant upper-class Palestinian families, and the Bedouin tribseman or Felahin in the fields. There was also a divided Christian population – where Armenian and Greek Orthodox Christians were almost as alien to Western Christian visitors as the Arab and Jewish population.

Above all, however, and in sharp contrast with India or Africa, and despite all the complexity of local affiliations and nationalities, Palestine was for Western eyes the Holy Land. It was invested with a spiritual and moral fervour that was unparalleled in orientalist and imperialist attitudes elsewhere. The Holy Land played a determinative role in the West's self-image of the growth of civilization. It was an integral element in the narrative of Christianity that undergirded the imperial project. It is in this context that the Archbishop of York, speaking to the Palestine Exploration Fund in 1875, could declare ringingly to applause that the society was interested in Palestine because 'Palestine is ours'.[11] Palestine is ours because it is the home and source of Christianity and its values. What I have called the biblical gaze needs to be comprehended within this particular formation. The geography of the Holy Land could never be simply a picturesque landscape, but was always invested with the deep significance of the land that nourished the Judaeo-Christian tradition, the land where Jesus walked and talked. The Western visitor to the Holy Land was always viewing both a strangely other place, and the homeland from which the West's deepest and most cherished values grew and where they found their origination and most authentic expression. The biblical gaze was a strategic way of bridging this tension within such a positioning of the historical subject.

There are two further major elements of historical background that need to be emphasized at the outset of this discussion of how the real is imagined and imaged by the visitor to the Holy Land. The first concerns technology and tourism. The invention of the steamboat changed the Holy Land forever. In the nineteenth century, for the first time, tourism to Palestine became a relatively easy prospect, in terms of cost, time and safety; and the number of tourists rapidly expanded, not least with the activities of Thomas Cook.[12] Jerusalem and the Holy Land were deeply embedded in the Western imagination. The Biblical injunctions not to forget Zion and the concomitant desire to return from exile gave rise to centuries of literature and art, representing the city as a glorious and profound endpoint of the journey of life, or as a model for the perfection of heavenly or earthly existence.[13] But now many individuals could come into direct visual contact with the region.

This resulted in a huge explosion of books and articles about visiting Jerusalem and other religious sites (itself part of the technological and political innovation of new printing and circulation methods). More than 2,000 book-length accounts were produced in just the first seventy-five years of the nineteenth century – more than the previous fifteen hundred years put together.[14] One result of this was that every traveller's mind was informed by pre-reading and by the circulation of images. So Harriet Martineau's celebrated three-volume account of her eight-month trip in the East (1848) paradigmatically records her experience of 'these places [which] had been so familiar to my mind's eye from my youth up': 'with all this before my eyes, my mind was with the past. It seemed as if the past were more truly before me than what I saw.'[15] For Martineau, her imagination, her mind's eye, has been trained since she was young to envision the biblical past, so now she sees 'vast spaces of time' in the present landscape, and, what's more, she sees this past as more real – 'more truly before me' – than the present scene. 'Here was the ground chosen by David, and levelled by Solomon to receive the Temple.'[16]

A. W. Kinglake's wonderfully witty *Eothen* (1844) by contrast suggests a more wry and detached view of such historicizing: 'There are people who can visit an interesting locality and follow up continuously the exact train of thought that ought to be suggested by the historical associations ... I am not thus docile: it is only by snatches, and for a few moments together, that I can really associate a place with its proper history.'[17] The fey man-about-town – Kinglake's persona – finds it hard to concentrate on 'proper' historical associations (and indeed he seems more interested in meeting girls than in a religious experience in Bethlehem). He gently mocks the pious tourist with 'the many geographical surprises that will puzzle the "Bible Christian"'.[18] His assumption is that the 'Bible Christian' will be disoriented by the gaps between the present and the historical imagination, when the resistant real of the landscape challenges the expectations formed by the Bible and how it has been taught.

This sense of the insistent and troubling real is vividly displayed by Mrs Mott in 1865 in a book illustrated by Bedford's photographs (which we will discuss shortly). Unlike Martineau and Kinglake, Mrs Mott neither became famous, nor did her work circulate widely, but, perhaps because of its very ordinariness, it beautifully exemplifies the gestures of disappointment that become prevalent in the genre: 'I should like to have been alone at Bethlehem ... I should have recalled Jacob and Rachel, or my favourite Ruth clinging so fondly and faithfully to the aged Naomi and gleaning in the fields of Boaz ... But, alas! Here as elsewhere, the holiest thoughts are rudely crushed by the things that be.'[19] Her grammar – 'I should like to have', 'I should have . . .' – marks the longing for religious experience that is recorded only in the crushing gap between expectation and reality. *Things*, things that be, get in the way.

Thus by the end of the Victorian period, it had become such a cliché within this literature to record surprise and disappointment in seeing the real Jerusalem – so small and ugly in comparison to its glorious depiction in art and literature – that it also became an anticipated cliché of experience to be disappointed. Stephen Graham, typically, was fully prepared for the dislocation of unfulfilment: 'friends told me that I was sure to be disappointed, that everyone going there nursed high hopes which were destined to remain unfulfilled . . . the banality and sordidness of the everyday scenes would be a great shock to me'.[20] Yet – and quite untypically – Graham's response is to transcend the anticipated disappointment by a new revelling in the real, as he travels incognito with poor Russian pilgrims, and dresses with such convincing poverty that he is shunned by his unrecognizing fellow Englishmen with disdain. In order to be able to look at the Holy Land without the trained eye of expected disappointment, Graham now has to look and act the part of the real, impoverished and pious pilgrim.

In the latter half of the nineteenth century, thousands of people from England, for the first time since the Crusades, came into contact with the insistently real heat, disease, smell and sights of Jerusalem. It was no longer possible to depict Jerusalem as it had been depicted in Renaissance art, a city of the imagination. Or rather, the imagination had to take a detour through the real in a different way. It is within this context that photography becomes a particularly significant medium. Alongside travelogues, illustrated bibles, models, panoramas, novels, operas, shows in Britain which displayed images and stagings of the Holy Land, photographic images circulated widely, particularly in the last quarter of the century, preparing visitors' expectations of the Holy Land, acting as mementos after trips, exchanged between family members and friends; filling the imagination with images of reality. The experience of the real was constantly mediated – anticipated, formed, overdetermined – by the medium of photography, and the commentary that went with it. The steamboat, the camera and the increased circulation of print, as linked technological innovations, changed the nineteenth-century experience of the real of the Holy Land.

The second major element of historical background I wish to underline is the invention and practice of archaeology as a scientific discipline, and, with it, the mapping of biblical Palestine.[21] Edward Robinson is usually taken as the founder of Biblical Archaeology, and his attempts to locate the real of the biblical texts in the real of the land had a profound effect on how the city and countryside could be viewed. Biblical archaeology became a best-selling and much reported genre. Where travellers used to arrive clutching just their bibles, they now arrived clutching their Bibles and modern survey equipment. From Captain Warren digging the Temple Tunnels to Mark Sykes drawing up the map of the Middle East, archaeology and politics combined to change how Jerusalem could be, should be seen.

The challenge to the authority and historical truth of the Bible mounted by nineteenth-century critical scholarship prompted archaeologists to seek for material evidence of the truth of scripture. As biblical criticism challenged what should be thought to be real in the scripture (as opposed to the mythical, legendary and false), so archaeological science claimed to uncover the real which proved the truth of scripture. In the rhetoric of this intensely felt and bitterly argued controversy, 'the exact place where', 'the real objects', 'the very stones that', were taken as brute facts to set against the speculation of critical enquiry. James Fergusson, the most influential architectural historian of his era, who engaged broadly in cultural debates especially through discussions of the architecture and archaeology of the East, reveals the desire that motivates this project of biblical archaeology with unsettling directness: 'There is scarcely a fact or an expression in the whole book [the Bible] that is not made clearer by the knowledge we have already derived, or hope hereafter to obtain, from the discoveries in this long-buried land; and they promise to supply us with exactly what we wanted to understand and realise what we there find written.'[22] Archaeology's finds have helped clarify almost every aspect of the Bible – but this hyperbolic description of how archaeology has bolstered the facts of scripture immediately becomes a hope for the future – as if such finds could only prove and clarify (and not challenge or throw doubts). Indeed, archaeology promises to reveal 'what we wanted' – both what we lacked and what we *desired* – in order both to understand and, more shockingly, to 'realise' scripture. What modern archaeologists fear as a methodological crisis – that you can only find what you want to find – is for Fergusson a happy rather than a vicious circle, a positive promise. Archaeology not only clarifies and helps understand, but finally *realizes* holy writ. Archaeology makes the Bible real.

As geology had turned the physical nature of the earth into evidence that challenged the Bible's chronology and thus its authority, so biblical geography and biblical archaeology set out to rediscover the truth of the Bible in the physical soil of the Holy Land. Tellingly, the first serious Ordnance Survey maps of Jerusalem were drawn up as maps of Jerusalem *at the time of Jesus*. Illustrated bibles reproduced archaeological evidence, with photographs of religious sites today. The real of Jerusalem could be proved now only by archaeology's science. As much as art history provided an essential discursive frame for the traveller to Italy's cities, archaeology became embedded in the intellectual expectations of a visitor to Victorian Jerusalem. Pilgrims for centuries had wept and wondered at the Holy Places; now the ground trodden by the figures of biblical times needed to be uncovered by archaeology, to be recovered for authentic religious experience. Photography provided an essential tool of authentication for this science of authority.[23]

This passion for the real of archaeology also fed back into biblical representations in high art. Exhibition reviews regularly commented on the degree to which the images of the biblical world could be said to be accurate according to the most up-to-date archaeological discoveries. So, to take but one example, Poynter's *The Visit of the Queen of Sheba to King Solomon* (1890) was very widely discussed as Poynter's masterpiece, and praised for its 'archaeological accuracy',[24] its research and scholarship. Poynter was close friends with Layard, and Layard's discoveries at Nineveh, consulted at the British Museum, informed the depiction of the palace of Solomon. It was criticized in exactly the same terms: 'A work which above all is archaeological must be unimpeachable in all respects, and we should be glad to learn on what authority the painter grounds his belief that this variety of marble [*giallo antico*, or yellow-veined marble] was in use in Judaea at the time of Solomon.'[25] Paintings of classical antiquity were evaluated within the same matrix (as were stage sets and costumes). Within this regime, photographs of objects, along with visits to museums, became a familiar part of the painter's toolbox, providing a new access to the archaeology of the past which was to inform an artistic vision of the biblical past.

Technology (the steam boat bringing tourists into contact with the realities of another culture) and new regimes of knowledge, especially archaeology – aimed precisely at authoritative access to the realities of the Holy Land and its history – overlap in the new machinery of photography.[26] Images of the Holy Land are central to the nineteenth-century history of photography – many of the earliest photographers travelled in the East, and many of the first sets of images to be widely circulated were of biblical subjects. In turn, the new science fundamentally alters how Jerusalem and Palestine are represented in the nineteenth century. Where John Murray's first handbook for travellers in the Holy Land recommended the Bible as the best guide for Palestine, in 1876 the Baedeker tellingly could declare in reverse that 'Palestine is the best guide to the Bible'. That is, the reality of Palestine, its landscapes, people, physical impact, will direct a reading of

Scripture – reading the Bible is now *grounded* in the real – and photography as a practice played an integral role in this new authorization of the word from the facts on the ground.[27]

It is fascinating that the earliest photographers journeyed with artists, and they both made images of the same view.[28] Indeed, many early photographers also doubled as painters. So, Frederick Goupil-Fesquet, probably the first photographer to enter Palestine, travelled in 1839 with the painter Horace Vernet. Goupil-Fesquet also drew and painted. But soon a radical divide opened between painters and photographers. 'The absolute truthfulness which is inseparable from a photograph'[29] was set in opposition to the artistic vision, where 'taste and imagination inevitably modelled reality'.[30] Salzman, whose photographic album of Jerusalem offered not only scenes but also close-ups of architectural details, offered his images as 'conclusive, brute facts'.[31] As Frith boasted, the 'truthfulness' of the camera is 'unimpeachable'.[32] The English were particularly taken with the new medium: 53 English photographers in the Holy Land are attested in the Victorian period (with France next with 15, then the Americans with 11).[33] The circulation of photographs offered to put into the hands of a large public the reality of Jerusalem without the need for visiting, and without the veils of a writer's prose or a painter's brush. Photographs, according to the earliest artists, offered a unique and unimpeachable claim on the real.[34] The pictures painted by artists may have been more or less realistic – committed, that is, to the genre of realism, more or less successfully – but within the rhetoric of early photography, a rhetoric that has never fully passed away, the camera was taken to offer a direct impress of the real itself, without mediation. It is tempting to think that so much early photography takes place in the Holy Land precisely because in the nineteenth century, thanks to the critical challenges to the Bible, there was no other geography where the real mattered quite so much and was invested with quite such polemical authority.

II The biblical gaze

But it is not hard to show that this claim on reality was deeply mediated by a vision of its own. Many photographers were sent out by governmental agencies. The Royal Engineer expeditions of 1864 and 1868, which were so important to the imperial mapping project, were accompanied by McDonald who kept a photographic record of the projects. The record itself becomes part of the scientific exploration and thus the representational control of the region, which led towards political control.[35] One of the greatest collections of photographs was formed by the American Colony, the well-known religious commune of Swedish and American Christians. They produced huge numbers of pictures, but their commercial sale of a restricted group of scenes helped create a repertoire of generic images, which in turn were circulated by tourists back at home, preparing the next travellers for what – how – to see. The scenes that were taken by almost all of the nineteenth-century photographers were, of course, highly selective, and recognizably generic. Religious buildings were of obvious interest (not only because the static nature of buildings chimed with the limitations of the early technology) and the solid materiality of what was imaged made a strong case for the camera's power to capture the physical world authoritatively.[36] Landscapes were carefully framed according to a Biblical perspective. Rocky scenes with a single shepherd and some lambs echoed the language of Scripture and the artistic tradition, where the literalization of the 'Lamb' of God and the 'Shepherd of the People' was pervasive. The reality of the photograph's careful scenography allowed the viewer to see continuity between the biblical past and contemporary Palestine, creating a religious experience of immediacy, a recognition or determination of the imagination come to life – 'for real'. The selection of buildings and scenes created a vision of a biblical landscape.

A powerfully mediated Christian view of Palestine was already firmly in place in nineteenth-century travel writing. Paradigmatically, Chateaubriand wrote of seeing Jews on his trip to Jerusalem. This passage is paradigmatic not least because it is quoted by Conder – a Protestant Englishman of science quoting a Catholic French man of letters – and indeed by a string of further English encyclopedias and travel articles: it was felt clearly to capture a vivid and telling visual injunction.[37] Here is how Chateaubriand instructs Christian travellers to see contemporary Jews by the so-called wailing wall:

> to be struck by supernatural astonishment, you must view [the Jews] at Jerusalem; you must behold these rightful masters of Judaea living as slaves and strangers in their own country; you must behold them expecting under all oppressions a king who is to deliver them. Crushed by the Cross that condemns them, skulking near the Temple, of which not one stone is left upon another, they continue in their deplorable infatuation.[38]

This paragraph summarizes the religious gaze perfectly. The aim is 'supernatural astonishment' – an awestruck recognition of religious significance. What is to be seen is a fully embodied Christian history, where the Jews are placed in their past as 'the rightful masters of Judaea' – an Old Testament biblical inheritance – but now brought low by a destruction which is both the product of the Roman Empire's force as described by Josephus – 'slaves and strangers in their own country' – and a proof of a New Testament promise: 'crushed by the Cross that condemns them'. The correct moral attitude to such a sight is rigorously demanded. The Jews foolishly await their Messiah; theirs is a 'deplorable infatuation' – an expectation close to madness. They resist the conversion offered by Christian missions, one archetypal form of travel to Palestine, a resistance 'under all oppressions' – an expression which firmly implies the contemporary Ottoman Empire's regime and its predecessors. The proof of this account is offered in passing. The Jews skulk by their Temple of which 'not one stone is left upon another'. This is, of course, a citation of the Gospel – unmarked here as a self-evident truth – and it provides the authorization for the historical connections Chateaubriand asks his viewers to observe. To look is to look with eyes formed by a biblical vision, to see a religious, transcendent reality. Photography brought the reality of Palestine into this perspective.

Figure 3.1 gives a good sense of this dynamic. It is a picture taken by the celebrated Bonfils studio in Beirut, from around 1870. It gives a striking introduction to the strategies of *biblical* representation in photography. The image depicts Capharnaum, in Galilee, where Jesus preached at the beginning of his ministry. Foregrounded are the ruins of the synagogue, the very stones of the pillars through which Jesus strode (as archaeology determines). The ruins put us in touch with the reality of the Bible as the photograph puts us in touch with the reality of the ruins. So the scattered pillars are the insistent focus of the image. In the background, a coarse field stretching back towards the fading hills of Galilee, there are two contrasting figures. On one stone sits an Arab youth in a characteristic headdress and carrying a shepherd's stick. He stands in for the continuity of the past in the locale, the sort of simple shepherd to whom Jesus spoke most clearly (as the homilies would have it). This makes sure that the classical pillars are correctly located in a Middle Eastern context, and provide us with an icon of the witness to Jesus, as if this youth is in a line with 'the shepherds watching in their fields'. This has to be marked as a Middle Eastern not a Greek set of pillars, however classical they may seem. But standing, and picked out by his dark robes against the fading background, is a monk or, less probably, an orthodox priest, dressed in a simple habit, with a skull-cap, with a long white beard, and he seems to be carrying a walking stick or switch. He stands in for an image of the Christianity to emerge from this site: not the grandeur of a papal ceremony or the intellectualism of

3.1 Capharnaum, a picture taken by the Bonfils Studio. According to the Gospels, Capharnaum was the home town of the apostles Simon Peter, Andrew, James and John.

theological debate, but a single religious figure in a field, a minister reflecting on the site of Jesus' ministry. Even if this figure looks somewhat archaic or even Eastern, especially to a Victorian Anglican, nonetheless he provides a model, a silent injunction, for the tourist's religious experience: a different type of witness to the tradition of scripture. At very least, the two spectators in the picture, the two witnesses, with their apparently different perspectives, pose the question of 'with what eyes will you look on this place of Jesus' work?' Matthew 11.23 predicts the destruction of Capharnaum, because of its sins, despite the miracles that were performed there. Capharnaum is an icon of the morality integral to the landscape of ruin. The simple monk and the simple shepherd bear witness to a town's moral downfall. This photograph, that is, both represents a biblical site, now in ruins, and also positions the viewer in a historical and religious frame. We are asked to see the real as determined by archaeological science and captured by photographic science, but the conclusive brute facts are also

3.2 Capharnaum, from *Earthly Footsteps of the Man of Galilee*, ed. John Vincent, James Lee and Robert Bain.

given a historical frame, a different sense of reality by the shepherd and the priest. The synagogue may be ruined but Christianity marches on: the synagogue *must* be ruined as a sign of Christianity marching on. Christian supersessionist teleology is what is to be seen in this landscape. This is, thus, in all senses a biblical landscape. Our vision may have a historical layering, but here the viewer is being asked to place himself self-consciously within a Christian tradition, to share that vision.

Figure 3.2 offers a revealing contrast. It is also of the ruins of Capharnaum, from approximately the same vantage point. But this image, from an American published album we will look at later, offers a far less complexly layered image, which allows us to see the powerful rhetoric of Bonfils all the more clearly. Without the figure of the boy and the priest, this second picture depicts a classicizing ruin. As such, it certainly still is capable of evoking the history of the site, and it can conjure the viewer's associations through the title alone. Yet it has none of the positionality of the Bonfils image, the construction of the subject position which is provided by the different figures of the priest and the boy, the shepherd and the shepherd of men, nor can it articulate the precise sense of religious history that the priest as descendant of Jesus' mission and shepherd boy as potent symbol of it can express. It stands more closely in line with the familiar aesthetic of classical ruins or biblical buildings: the landscape without figures lacks the figuration Bonfils' image provides.

Regrettably, we have no direct record of the motivations of either photographer; nor, as far as I am aware, do we have any recorded responses to these precise images, although as we will see later, we do have some extremely directive remarks on how to read such images attached to them. The contrast between them, however, shows the work of construction – the posing – within the Bonfils image, which offers the cue to interpretation. And, as we have seen, a biblical hermeneutic, a horizon of expectation formed by a theological perspective, is expected both by those that strive to find a religiously informed historical intensity in such a scene and those that gently mock it. The long history of the training in how to view a biblical landscape is the frame for the work of such images.

A simple title, however, shows all the more strikingly how the photographers can manipulate the expectations of such a biblical gaze. Figure 3.3, from a decade or so later also by the Bonfils studio, at first sight appears to be a pastoral, agricultural scene from any part of Palestine. Four figures are cutting wheat in a field with small hand scythes, a fifth bearded man sits and watches. In the foreground, a bearded, turbaned man with a pipe addresses a woman, who is holding a sheaf of wheat, and seems to be smiling, barely, towards the camera. This could be a snapshot of everyday rural life, a tourist image of the other at work. It is, however, explicitly titled 'Ruth and Boaz'. That is, the title makes of the picture a *tableau vivant* of a celebrated biblical story, which, as Mrs Mott already has indicated, was a particular favourite of female reflections on the values of the Bible. Not only did Ruth and Naomi provide a model of female devotion, beloved of Victorian values, and a story of conversion, equally privileged as a Christian narrative, but also and more particularly, Ruth and Naomi provided a hinge between the Jewish world of the Hebrew bible and the story of Christianity by providing the *fons et origo* of the Davidic line which, as the opening of the Gospel of Luke itemizes, is the genealogy of Jesus.[39]

In a standard *tableau vivant*, actors represent a scene or characters from the past. Mrs Hamilton's 'Attitudes', for example, encouraged Mr Hamilton's guests to stare at his beautiful wife in a series of more or less

3.3 Ruth and Boaz, Bonfils Studio.

revealing poses under the guise of representing celebrated figures of the past. In the living panoramas that were part of the spectacular show-world of London, pygmies, say, were put on display as themselves, exotica from abroad to be stared at as specimens.[40] A photograph of Don Quixote in his study is plainly an actor in a studio setting dressed to illustrate a novel, much as a Shakespearian actor might be posed to illustrate a performance or a character.[41] In Figure 3.3, however, the viewer is asked to see in the real of the photographed, contemporary scene a sort of allegory or icon of the biblical past. These are not 'Ruth and Boaz' themselves, nor actors repre-senting 'Ruth and Boaz'. Rather the realism of the photographic medium allows us to see in the present of Palestine a deep continuity with the biblical past. The presence of the pipe might strike us as an insistent reminder of the modern, but the picture's title insists that we look past the pipe into a different temporality, where the current mundane world is thus layered with the type of the past, and the everyday becomes a sign of a religious continuity.

So, George Adam Smith, an influential minister of the Free Church of Scotland, whose *Historical Geography of the Holy Land* went to twenty-five editions, encouraged the elision between biblical texts and contemporary countryside, between the image of the Holy Land in the mind and the Holy Land to be visited: 'You see the landscapes described by Old Testament writers exactly as you will see them today.'[42] The slippage in his use of tenses is eloquent. What is to be seen is – exactly – a landscape described by the Bible. Roland Barthes famously writes on how photography uncannily stages the 'there-then becoming the here-now'. The biblical gaze gives this dynamic an especial poignancy and ideological weight, as the there-then and here-now are mediated by a theological fervour for presence. The denial of modernity to the orient has been articulated by modern critics as a politics of superiority: here, however, we can see a more complex temporality, where the apparent agelessness (despite the pipe) of the pastoral scene is in service of a biblical gaze which demands a religious recognition of continuity and type. The antiquity of this present is not an indication of backwardness but a sign of its privileged source.

The story of Ruth and Boaz leads to the foundation of the house of David, which leads to the birth of Jesus (at least so the genealogy of the Gospel of Luke would have it). These first three photographs thus also form part of the same biblical gaze. The connection between the Old and New Testament (as the Christian tradition terms it), embodied in typology, in prophecy, and, for most of the Christians I have been discussing, in history, means that the scholars and travellers perceived a continuum between the different periods of archaeological sites or historical memorials that they viewed. Although the Hebrew Bible and the Gospels were often subject to separate attack in nineteenth-century critical scholarship, the defence of the veracity of the texts through archaeology and through the realism of photography allowed itself to celebrate the continuity of the biblical, providential world, not just in sites like the Temple where Harriet Martineau's recognition of the Temple of David and Solomon can meld effortlessly in her travelogue into Jesus' overturning of the money-changers' tables and into the prophecy of the new dispensation of Christianity in and through the destruction of the Temple, but also in sites like Capharnaum, where the history evoked by the image is taken to include the deep biblical past. Just as each challenge to the veracity of the biblical texts from critical scholarship challenged the edifice of religious faith, so each act of verification, each recognition of the real, each perception of the link of past and present, contributes to the wholeness of the truth. Photography's real entails the biblical real.

3.4 Shepherd's Sling, American Colony Studio, a picture taken by Lars Larsen, one of the Swedish community of the Colony, described also by Selma Lagerlöf, also from Sweden, the first female winner of the Nobel Prize for literature.

Within such a perspective, these biblically charged pictures may not even need a title. Figure 3.4 is an untitled and beautifully composed photograph from the American Colony studio in Jerusalem. This image, for any literate viewer, can hardly fail to recall the young David, facing his Goliath. Untitled and carefully aestheticized, this image becomes a site for the Christian imagination to express itself, to find in the present an echo, a framing, a recognition and (self-)confirmation of the past. In all of these images, the realism of photography is put in service of a carefully constructed perspective that encourages the viewer to find the biblical past, his or her continuity with that past – and the realism in turn authorizes the religious gaze as seeing what is really there, the truth. Realism is always a profoundly ideological mode of representation.

The Prince of Wales was sent on a tour of the East in 1861 not long after the death of his father, explicitly as a training exercise in diplomacy, as much as a version of the educational value of a Grand Tour. Accompanying the Prince were Dean Stanley (somewhat against his will) and the photographer Francis Bedford. Stanley was already famous for his published travels in the Middle East as well as a trusted leading Anglican churchman.[43] Bedford was already England's most respected photographer of landscapes. On their return, Bedford's pictures were displayed in London and then sold in albums of different sizes or as individual prints, with brilliant critical and financial success.[44] It was one of the defining collections of a generation's visual imagination of the Holy Land. The Prince kept a diary, and Dean Stanley published his sermons on the trip. Stanley encourages the Prince (and his wider audience) to understand and participate in the biblical gaze. How, he wonders, are they to view this desolate land whose glory has passed away. One should never say 'There is nothing to see', declares Stanley, rather 'it is by thinking of what has been here, by making the most of the things we do see in order to bring before our minds the things we do not see, that a visit to the Holy Land becomes a really religious lesson.'[45] Religious lessons are won by bringing to our mind the things we do not see: that is how 'to make the most' of what we do actually see. The disappointment of the real is turned to an experience of religious value by seeing the unseen.

As they approach Jerusalem, this need for a biblical gaze is reinforced with more passion and the explicit ideological underpinnings of a religious perspective:

We are not pilgrims: we are not crusaders. But we should not be Christians – we should not be Englishmen – we should not, I had almost said, be reasonable beings, if, believing what we do about the events that took place here, we could see Jerusalem and the Holy Land as we would see any other town or any other country. Even if it were only for the thought of the interest which thousands in former ages have taken in what we shall see – if only for the thought that we shall now be seeing what thousands have longed to see and not seen – if only for the thought of the feeling which our visit to these spots awakens in the hearts of thousands far away in our own dear homes in England : – we cannot but gather up some good feelings, some more than merely passing pleasure, from these sacred scenes; and can we forbear to add, that there is, besides and above all this, the thought that we may possibly be thus brought more nearly into communion with that Divine Friend and Saviour, whose blessed feet, eighteen hundred years ago, walked this land, through whose words and acts in this country every one of us, at some time of his life or other, has been consoled and instructed, and hopes at last to be saved?[46]

Stanley's language epitomizes the historical and religious layerings of this biblical perspective. It is telling of Stanley's particular Anglicanism that he immediately denies being a crusader or a pilgrim (he knows his audience) and it is amusingly typical that his tricolon climactically rises from Christian, to Englishman to reasonable being. It is almost a condition of the reasonableness Stanley embodies to react to Jerusalem with a unique set of feelings. Partly it is because of the sheer power of expectation that so many – from pilgrims to Crusaders – have invested in the sight and site of the Holy City. Partly it depends on 'believing what we do' about the Passion – the embracing complicity of a community's religious commitments. Partly it is the knowledge that in reaching Jerusalem they are fulfilling aims that many before them have failed to achieve – the self-awareness and self-congratulation of the traveller at a hard-won destination – explicitly here related back to the Prince's subjects in dear England (the use of the word 'dear' for images of the architecture and institutions of home is one of the most pervasive emotive clichés of Victorian travel writing). But above all, claims Stanley in his climactic ending, it is because here in Jerusalem there is the chance of a unique communion with Jesus, whose feet had touched this selfsame soil. The religious hope of salvation undergirds how Jerusalem should be viewed and experienced.

Stanley's sermons go hand in hand with the public circulation of Bedford's images. They provide the normative, public commentary to the pictures. The Prince's more political and less organized reflections remained private. For him, the most poignant of visits and the most poignant of Bedford's photographs were the sites of Syria where Christians had been massacred, and where there was no memorial beyond the landscape's emptiness – a more modern geo-political religious history. The traveller to the Holy Land was well prepared before arrival, and zealously reminded after return, as to what was at stake in the desolate views, rural scenes and unmarked ruins. 'Stanley accumulates, with pictorial vividness, the wealth of historical associations, both sacred and profane, which gather around the Holy Land . . . Stanley may almost be said to have re-discovered Palestine by the force and freshness, the local colour, the truth and detail of the impressions which he realised for himself and conveyed to his readers.'[47] The Holy Land required a biblical gaze to be seen, properly, in its historical and religious significance. The real needed its detour through the unseen.

The year after the Prince's trip, the Queen's Bible was published. This was a lavishly produced edition of the Old and New Testaments, with commentary, two volumes of massive size and weight, bound in beautiful, embossed red leather, with thick, highest-quality paper, and fastened with bronze clasps.[48] It was a limited edition of 170 copies, priced terrifyingly at 50 guineas, and was designed for and exhibited at the Great Exhibition at South Kensington in 1862. The commentary, especially for the later books of the Old Testament and for the New Testament, is largely no more than lists of parallel passages or very brief linguistic comments on the translation. But the longer explicatory notes especially on Genesis reveal its mid-Victorian concerns. On Genesis 8.17 the editor, Gilbert McCallum, begins: 'The testimony of the Bible is infallible; but its statements cannot be antagonistic to the facts of science' (a statement that could lead into problems with miracle stories later on), and on Genesis 1.14, the appointment of the sun and moon to regulate the seasons, the editor notes that this almost certainly does not mean that the sun was created after light (Genesis 1.3), but quotes Whewell's theorizing on light as a potential answer to anyone who would see a problem with such an ordering of things. Both volumes are illustrated with photographs by Frith. Genesis has images only of Hebron, Exodus has a full range of Egyptian archaeological sites and brooding images of the Sinai desert, carefully distinguishing between the erroneous early Christian identification of Mount Sinai and the true site of the revelation. The Psalms have images of Jerusalem and the Cedars of Lebanon, Acts cityscapes of Damascus. All show biblical landscapes and ruins. Most strikingly perhaps, there is one image – and only one – which has no claim to be a biblical illustration. Amid the verses of Luke 21 nestles a fine shot of the new English Church in Jerusalem, consecrated in 1849 by the Anglo-Prussian Bishop in Jerusalem – a potent symbol of the British, Anglican, commitment to imperial and missionary expansion in the Holy Land, and thus a particularly fitting and politically poignant illustration for the Bible of Queen Victoria, on show at the Great Exhibition.

Suitably enough, in the next year, 1863, Thomas Jones Barker completed and exhibited his famous picture *The Secret of England's Greatness*, which depicts Queen Victoria at Windsor presenting a Bible to a kneeling and exotic African king.[49] The Queen's Bible is a luxury item from the very highest levels of society, and as such it shows the degree to which photography and photographic images of the Holy Land were authorized within a privileged discourse as support for and a guide to reading the Bible. The newspaper advertisement for the volumes carried an endorsement from Dean Stanley (of course), testifying to the photographs' embodiment of the real of the Holy Land. From the Queen down, it seems, photographs had become instrumental in constructing the image of the real of the Bible.

Many other types of image also circulated in profusion, of course. Images of local people, except for typological shepherds, however, were of much more restricted scope. Exotic portraits of 'Oriental Families', with an evident interest in oriental costume, inherently contrast with familiar family portraits from European bourgeois albums; equally common are scenes of 'backward' labour – ancient styles of threshing, say, or weaving from a pre-industrial age, or potters at a simple wheel – and street scenes with exotically dressed Bedouins and Turks, always with room for a camel or two. It would be easy to categorize and criticize the exoticism of these portraits as both loving and dismissive in the paradigmatic gesture of the Victorian encounter with the domesticity and splendour of the East. 'Eastern costume is one of the blunders of a luxurious but half-civilized state of society', reflected Frith, sniffily.[50] He also had his picture taken dressed as a Turk, a photographic equivalent of the celebrated portraits of David Roberts or Lord Byron in eastern robes and turban – a performance of dressing down as much as dressing up, a reflex of orientalism; playing the other, as it were.[51]

Figure 3.5 is exemplary of such portraits of local colour, a posed representation of non-industrial, 'half-civilized' labour. Yet this image is also brought into a socio-religious perspective by the careful supervision of the Franciscan monks – it's all a long way from the cloth factories of England with all the polemics about poverty, industrialization, and the changing city, familiar from novels as much as from political analysis and newspaper debate. The Franciscan in the frame gives religious bearings, which, as we will see shortly, are very precisely articulated in this case. Such images do testify to a state of society, which, in Victorian thinking on the development of culture, can only be a less civilized version of the West. In contrast to the 'geopiety'[52] of the landscapes and church-scapes, this easy Orientalism prepared a traveller for the otherness of the East or memorialized it as a souvenir. The photography here seems to fit well with the mix of alienation, disappointment, discomfort and intense religious experience, which runs through the Western written responses to Jerusalem. Yet even these images stand in a continuum with the more obviously religiously charged images I have been tracing as signs of the biblical gaze: in the Holy Land, with its own sense of temporality and history as the origin of Western religious values,

16. **Officina Sartoris**

3.5 Officina Sartoris, Franciscan *Album Missionis Terrae Sanctae* – a tailors' workshop.

the lack of modernity in the scenes of everyday life is also an invitation to discover the significance of the past in the present, to articulate a religious continuity, to locate oneself as a historical, religious subject.

III The album: regulating the profusion of images

So far, I have focused largely on the production of images by two main studios: Bonfils in Lebanon and the American Colony in Jerusalem. Bonfils was staffed largely by local photographers, many of whom were Armenian or Marionite Christians;[53] the American Colony supported mostly American and Swedish evangelical Protestants.[54] Both studios produced individual images, however, that circulated very widely particularly through the commercial channels of tourism – as did a wide range of other individual photographers and studios, which have begun to be extensively catalogued by modern scholars. Many such images were bought by travellers as mementos and used back in European homes as preparation for future trips as well as recollections of past visual experiences. Malek Alloula powerfully expresses one political strand of how such photographs were used, particularly in the colonies and particularly in the early twentieth century:

> Photography steps in to take up the slack and reactivates the phantasm at its lowest level. The postcard does it one better; it becomes the poor man's phantasm: for a few pennies, display racks full of dreams. The postcard is everywhere, covering all the colonial space, immediately available to the tourist, the soldier, the colonist. It is at once their poetry and their glory captured for the ages; it is also their pseudo-knowledge of the colony. It produces stereotypes in the manner of great seabirds producing guano, the fertilizer of the colonialist vision.[55]

No doubt, in the Holy Land religious piety could also provide an alibi for such cheap orientalizing and imperial recollection. In the nineteenth century, individual photographs were stuck into personal albums and diaries, for private and shared pleasure (and in some grand cases for the public display of class and status beloved of the Victorian home: the carte-de-visite in this context has also been well analysed).[56] Tauchnitz, the German publishing house, even published novels with blank interleaved pages so that travellers could add purchased photographs of the locales of the stories – a remarkable *éffet du réel* apparently closing the gap between fiction and the material shape of things, as photography strove to ground the imaginary world of the novel in (images of) a real world. Such photographic images were formed in a matrix of biblical and political perspectives, and through their circulation helped form the imaginative repertoire of their Western viewers.

By the turn of the century, however, clear lines start to emerge between different groups. The profusion of images prompted more careful and regulated collections. Christians continue to circulate the standard images of holy sites and biblical landscapes, and some photographs start to appear in illustrated bibles as authenticating illustrations of the scriptural narrative, often alongside other artwork.[57] There are some fascinating Jewish post-cards advertising the Holy Land as a place to visit and emigrate to.[58] These re-frame landscapes and street scenes not as souvenirs or preparations for the otherness of tourism, but as an image to be completed by the imagination of the viewer as a potential home, a challenge to see yourself in the image in a different way from the biblical scenes. A profusion of individual albums, often souvenirs of personal trips, have been noted by scholars as a sign of the spread of photography and of its domestication into the dynamics of display and collection within the Victorian household and its institutions of class and education.[59] Like miscellanies, which began as private scrapbooks and became a publishing success across the nineteenth century, or personal albums in which guests wrote poems or drew pictures for their host, personal albums of photographs became signs of status and taste. Lady Brassey took rather upmarket photographs and collected them in grand albums for domestic (self-)display.[60] Bishop Blyth had his own rather uninspired three albums of snaps of religious buildings interspersed with family and official portraits, a private, domestic record of his very public time in Jerusalem.[61] But in the last decades of the century specific groups also start to use the potential of the album of collected images as part of a directed ideological project, and it is on these – surprisingly undiscussed by current scholarship – that I wish to focus here.[62]

Three productions from the earlier years of the century mark the beginnings of the model of the professionally produced album and do so in quite different ways. David Roberts has already been mentioned. His three-volume publication *The Holy Land* (1842–9) is huge, unwieldy, designed as an expensive and lavish display item, and comes with a long list of wealthy and distinguished subscribers. Each image is hand-tinted, and framed by a text by the celebrated preacher and novelist George Croly, with spare but scholarly footnotes and an unornate narrative of historical and geographical description. The images are of what will become standard scenes of harbours, approaches and groves, and the trajectory follows a standard traveller's route. The book is to sit in a wealthy drawing room, and it is experienced on the one hand as an armchair tour, invoking the experience of visiting the Holy Land through its delicate and beautiful images and simple text; and, on the other, as part of the politics of display within a domestic space, announcing its owner's values and aspirations. Its image repertoire combines the biblical gaze with a traveller's curiosity for the sights of arrival and passing on the route.

Ten years later, Frith's *Egypt and Palestine* (1859) has a similar scale (although in only two volumes). But now the images are all photographs. Each has a brief and often rather idiosyncratic commentary by Frith himself. Although the subjects are similar to those of Roberts, there is no apparent order to the pictures, which skip from country to country and site to site. Nor is there any coherent agenda to the commentary, which lacks the religious or scholarly authority of Croly. There is a revelling in the sheer brilliance of the technical virtuosity of the camera's work, with striking perspectives, angles and viewing points – often several images of the same site. This too is an extremely expensive and difficult-to-manage book. It occupies a similar space to Roberts – designed for display, exhibiting its own lavishness and skill, and encouraging a fragmented, aestheticized experience of a biblically tinged landscape from a wealthy Western drawing room.

A mere seven years later in 1865 the Ordnance Survey publication of Jerusalem marks a watershed in the mapping and representation of the city.[63] The four volumes are no easier to use in terms of their bulk, but the strategy of representation is markedly different. As one might expect from the genre, this book proclaims its scientific organization. The photographs are divided into careful and explicit categories, 'interior of the Haram', 'exterior of the Haram', 'Citadel', 'Church of the Holy Sepulchre'; 'views within the city', 'views exterior to the city walls', 'the environs', 'panorama'. The categories themselves make a map, starting inside the city's monuments, moving to the streets, beyond the walls, the neighbourhood, and, finally, the panorama of the whole, each area carefully marked out as such. The photographs are largely by McDonald and are very fine, four-square, with great clarity of detail. They are clearly labelled, offer a regimented perspective, and come with detailed measurements of size and proportions. The pictures are buttressed by the diagrams and facts of the techniques of surveying; physical science and the camera combining to proclaim the authoritative and accurate representation of the real. The maps have a higher level of technique and accuracy than any previously produced, with carefully delineated contours, outlined and labelled buildings, and are the basis of all subsequent maps of the region. Yet it is also fascinating to note that these new Ordnance Survey maps of Jerusalem still offer two scales by which to read them. There is at the bottom of the page to the left a 'modern scale' – offering English, French and Russian measures of distance – and, on the right, an 'ancient scale', offering Greek, Roman and Hebrew / Babylonian / Persian measurements. The map is designed to be read both with modern European eyes, and through ancient texts and their calculations, as if any vision of Jerusalem will be calibrated both through contemporary technological controls and through the layerings of ancient measurements, in the biblical gaze of the modern viewer – or as if the ancient measurements will be brought under the aegis of a modern technological usage (but not done away with). In contrast with the aesthetic views of Roberts – a vision of the Holy Land – and Frith's photographic profusions and chaotic narrative form, the Ordnance Survey publication structures, directs and demands a scientific evaluation of Jerusalem. The new ordering of knowledge and new technology are linked in a new vision of the holy city.

Each of these large-scale volumes offers a specific perspective, aesthetic and technology of representation to organize its collection of images. These albums – as opposed to the illustration or the individually circulated picture – organize a profusion of images into a structured whole, linked not by a thread of family life, as in a personal album, nor by the serendipity of a individual's journey, as in the collection of souvenirs of a trip, but as a paradigmatic and normatively constructed experience. Each enters the dynamics of display as such – linked into the normative values of the household or institution which made public use of the volumes. Daston and Galison's marvellous study, *Objectivity*, has described the development across the nineteenth century of the atlas of science as a 'systematic compilation of working objects' which 'trains the eye' of the scientific community, by virtue of the production of 'an idealized, perfected, or at least characteristic exemplar of a species or a natural kind', which as a model itself was later challenged by different forms of representation that recognized the messier assymetries of reality.[64] The passage from David Roberts to the Ordnance Survey takes place while the scientific atlas as a form is developing, and the album as a form, with its increasing appeals to the unmediated photographic representations of reality and its systematic compilations of images, draws on or mimics the authority of such models. They too train the eye, but do so for a differently constructed community and to a different agenda. The professionally produced album of photographs engages with the discourse of objectivity – but allows a place for the very values being actively excluded by the scientific publications: pleasure, history, personal experience, religious feelings.

These three productions are in different ways exemplary of the potential of the form of the professionally produced album; and all three are expensive, difficult to use and to circulate, and objects of status and displayed value. By the last decades of the century, however, such professional albums had become smaller, cheaper, more freely available, circulated to far wider audiences, and – therefore – were appropriated by specific groups with particular agendas.

The Franciscan order ('Latins') had a long presence in Jerusalem, centred by the nineteenth century on the Church of the Holy Sepulchre and the Latin Patriarchate, and spreading out through local mission schools and attached workshops.[65] The contest between European powers and their religious orders for control in the Middle East was enacted at a symbolic and practical level in conflict over the role of *custodia Terrae Sanctae* ('Custody of the Holy Land'). In practical terms, *custodia* indicated religious, political and social protection for pilgrims to Palestine. In symbolic terms, the privilege and authority of *custodia* implied first a history of the region – which group over the centuries had most successfully enacted the protection of Christian holy sites and Christian pilgrims – and, second, *custodia* demonstrated which group in the present had the most power and status in the imperial struggle over the current possession, protection and management of holy sites as a key to the political dominance of the region. The largest group of annual pilgrims were poor Russians, who turned to the Orthodox Church for protection.[66] The Greek Church owned more property in and around Jerusalem than any other group, and dominated the Church of the Holy Sepulchre – with the result that the Franciscans, backed by the papacy, inevitably came into direct conflict with the Orthodox Church. The historic legacy from the Crusades, the iconic model for the violence between East and West in this part of the world, grounded the Franciscan self-image, which clashed with the realpolitik of contemporary Orthodox control. Meanwhile, the British established their own protectorate through a consulate, backed soon by a church building programme, and the much contested Jerusalem Bishopric;[67] and other European imperial powers insisted on their presence in Palestine. Petty squabbles over individual cases of *custodia* repeatedly threatened to escalate into full-scale matters of international diplomacy.

In 1883, the Franciscans put together an album of 108 images, mostly photographic, though some particularly dark interiors were represented in drawings, which set out to demonstrate the scope of their mission – it was entitled *Album Missionis Terrae Sanctae* and was announced as a production of the *custodia Sanctae Terrae* (and dedicated to the Pope). It has no text attached to the photographs bar titles, and begins in Jerusalem with the Church of the Holy Sepulchre, the centre of Franciscan custodial presence, before moving around the whole Middle East, recording, mostly in photographic prints, the schools and workshops of the Franciscan order. Figure 3.5 comes from this collection, and the presence of the Franciscan monks in the picture can now take on its full ideological weight: it is a visual sign of their educational mission. Unlike the repertoire of bloody images of martyrdom or the more garish images of, say, the heart of Jesus, this expression of the Franciscan ideal of humble simplicity seems to draw on the photograph's apparently unmediated representational mode: an unadorned and simple snapshot of an unadorned simplicity.

Figure 3.6, in similar vein, is another picture from this album, this time of the school at Laodicea, a town well known for its role in early Christianity and for its mention in the book of Revelation (a central text for Victorian Christian knowledge), where it is called on to repent of being 'neither hot nor cold' (Rev. 3.16). A Victorian Christian, seeing the monk teaching the young, might well recall the promise there that 'those whom I love I rebuke and discipline' (3.19). The boys, presided over by the bearded monk, all

67. Schola Elementaris Laodiceae

3.6 Schola Elementaris Laodiceae, Franciscan *Album Missionis Terrae Sanctae*. The smudged faces of the children are the result of the long exposure time and the inability of the children to sit still.

wear their fezzes and robes, uncomfortable Ottoman youths being overseen by their Franciscan mentor. Bringing Christian education to the region – the Franciscan mission – is powerfully embodied in the image. Education was a bitterly contested arena in the Ottoman empire, conceived not just as a national and religious battle for hearts and minds but also as the 'secret to success in the modern world':[68] Ottoman educational policy was formed in part as a 'direct response to the challenges brought by foreign missionaries',[69] even to the point of sponsoring travelling preachers during the 1890s to inveigh against missionary schools throughout Ramadan.[70] The Sultan himself recognized the dangers of missionary activity. On 26 May 1892 he dictated to his private secretary a long note worrying about their influence and his response: 'By increasing the number of their followers this religious influence is then transformed into political leverage.'[71] This Franciscan image of missionary education has a full and precisely located ideological weight. The geographically organized volume thus maps out a

Franciscan world. The album offers a cartography of certain holy sites and certain towns and certain projects – a Franciscan *Weltanschauung*, for which no other groups, no other sites, seem to enter the panorama.

This 1883 album is now extremely rare indeed. But in 1893, these pictures form the basis of a two-volume album, which now has commentary on each image in Italian, French, rather dodgy English, and German, along with a rather defensive introduction in Latin, with translations, on the Custody of the Holy Land ('some reserved remarks on past vicissitudes'). This more lavish edition is far easier to find nowadays. The first volume with 146 pictures is on Judaea and Galilee; the second with 116 images on Syria, Cyprus and Egypt. For this edition, maps are also included – fully instantiating the limited Franciscan topography – but the pictures are now entirely lithographs, hand-tinted. In 1895, a further volume of 156 photographs of the Sanctuaries of the Holy Land was produced in at least two different formats. As with the earlier volumes, the photographs create a systematically blinkered map of Franciscan piety.

The reasons behind the choice of lithographs rather than photographs for the more widely circulated two-volume edition of the *Album Missionis* are likely to be primarily financial – along with the technological capabilities of publishing in this decade at Jerusalem. But what is most telling here is the self-consciously apologetic use of albums of images to propagate a vision of the world, a vision to place the religious and political self, to construct the real. 'The Western photographic gaze' is not only formulated through religious models, but also reveals competition between different Western religious groups, attempting through a visual regime to enforce their particular perspective on what is to be seen in the Holy Land. The form of the album might seem to imitate the blithe objectivity of a travelogue or even the arbitrary archive of snapshots; but these albums present a morselized, collected view which reveals the particularity and partiality of a vision of the world.

Albums are thus *sites of creative agency* – making a topography or itinerary of the real.

In 1896, three American Methodists, Bishop John Vincent, James Lee and Robert Bain, published a photographic album of their long trip to the East, with a bare commentary, entitled *Earthly Footsteps of the Man of Galilee*. The photographs were all taken by Bain; he had travelled with Lee; Vincent provided the celebrity introduction and intellectual weight for the volume. Their announced aim, 'Five hundred original photographic views and descriptions of the places connected with the early life of Our Lord and His Apostles', gave them scope for a full Grand Tour, as the Apostles fortunately were said to have travelled to Rome and Damascus and many other cities on their route. Lee and Blair organized their album according to the life of Jesus ('Part I: from the Annunciation to Zachary to the Baptism of Jesus'), and their commentary reveals the biblical gaze in its most imaginative guise. A picture of shepherds and sheep is glossed, 'Flocks near the cave where Joseph was thrown by his brethren.' The fact that not even credulous medieval pilgrims had identified any such cave did not stop the earnest Americans: 'The flocks are still feeding on the Hills of Dothan, and the shepherds watching them are dressed probably in the same costume worn by the sons of Jacob.' Only the coy 'probably' distracts at all from the extraordinary collapse of historical distance ('still').[72] When they see flowers they emote 'These nurslings of the sky were the companions of Our Saviour on earth.' Their vision of the Holy Land is inclusive (flowers, groves, Rome, Damascus, Cairo . . .), but all formulated by a biblical understanding that finds a Christian message in every vista. The Franciscans limited their perspective to Franciscan sites; *Early Footsteps of the Man of Galilee* is more promiscuous in its selection, but recuperates all to its religious lesson.[73]

Bishop Vincent is best known as one of the founders of the Chautauqua Institution, an educational movement for Sunday school teachers and other religious figures, which in 1874 established the Chautauqua camp and Palestine Park in New York state, with a celebrated large-scale relief map of the Holy Land.[74] Vincent (who had zealously studied a 'singing geography' programme as a student at Milton College)[75] set out to bring home (in all senses) the real of the Holy Land to his students, to fulfil the 'desire to see the topography which gave to [biblical] history such vividness and power'.[76] This is part of an apologetics, asserting the truth of scripture, as Prothero, the biographer of Dean Stanley, spells out: 'Geographical details not only add point to the images and vividness to the pictures of the sacred writings: they also give a solid basis of fact, which being embedded in the narratives, show that the histories they relate do not merely represent a "past which was never present".'[77] To this purpose, the 'true representation' of Vincent's modelling 'shall render a visit to it second only to the land itself'.[78] Indeed, Vincent even claimed that his 'study of the lay of the land which makes the physical Chautauqua is an allegory' of spiritual growth.[79] Visitors even dressed in Eastern costume to complete the experience of being there.[80] Twenty-two years after the founding of Chautauqua, the new technology of cheap photography (and travel) allowed Vincent to circulate his album to a wide audience of his students, as the culmination and advertisement of his commitment to the real as the royal route to religious education. Again, the album comes out of – and embodies – a specific ideological, religious agenda, in which the simpler image of Capharnaum (Figure 3.2), taken from this album, finds its place.

Jesse Lyman Hurlbut was a Methodist Episcopalian minister, also associated with the Chautauqua movement, whose history he wrote, and secretary of the Epworth League, a Methodist group for young adults, which at its height boasted nearly a million members across the United States. He published *Travelling in the Holy Land through the Stereoscope* in 1900, advertised as a tour personally conducted by the author. There were 200 stereoscope images in sequence, from arrival in the port at Joppa/Jaffa through the standard religious sites.[81] The images are what can now be recognized as a largely conventional selection of sites of particular interest to a Protestant religious traveller, but what makes them especially interesting is the commentary that Hurlbut provides. Many, though not all of the slides have paragraphs of text on the reverse, which not only identify the sites, but direct the viewers' gaze to particularly significant aspects of the photograph, offer a strong model of how to view the images, and even construct important cross-references, instructing the viewer what to think and how to construct a sequence of images: the creative agency of the album. Each is extracted from a separately published book. This commentary demonstrates the biblical gaze at full throttle, and repeatedly demands the recognition of a biblical past in the apparent exoticism of the present.

So an image of the house of a tanner in Jaffa is introduced first in the style of the personal tour: 'We are in the tanners' quarter of Jaffa (Joppa), by the seaside.' This site is immediately justified according to its biblical precedents: 'There are good reasons for believing that this house is on or near the site of the house where the Apostle Peter is said to have spent many days in Joppa.' The continuity of history is emphasized: '[I]n the changeless East, they now build houses just as they did twenty centuries ago.' This motivates a modern sense of deep contact with the past: 'Up such steps as these, outside the house, Simon Peter must have often walked' – as he received his own vision, duly cited from Acts 10, with full biblical authority. (This style of argument can be played both ways: so Arthur Stanley, reflecting on the biblical story of Abraham's trip to Egypt, comments, 'some of the main features of the country appear [in the Bible], as we see them today':[82] the real of the Bible and the real of the present are mutually confirming.) There is also a reminder that the lives of such poor modern Easterners are dependent on missionary activity: 'These women, while industrious and kindly, are quite uneducated; unless some mission school has taught them, they do not know how to read or write.' Finally, and more surprisingly, it is noted that the house is also sacred for Mohammedans. Looking at these stereoscope images is turned into an experience closer to a lantern slide lecture by the personal voice of Hurlbut. His collusive first-person plural cajoles, advises and directs us towards a religious appreciation of all we are shown to see. If Prothero worried about a 'past that was never present', the stereoscope of Hurlbut not only collapses the past and present, but brings us there, in the present: 'We are in . . .'.

The stereoscope was an invention of the 1840s which was a huge hit in the 1850s and despite a dip in sales in the 1860s continued to be popular into the twentieth century, especially in the USA.[83] As a German visitor to the United States in 1883 observed: 'I think there is not a parlour in America where there is not a stereoscope.'[84] The most famous company, which also published Hurlbut's tour, was the American firm of Underwood and Underwood, which at its height produced 300,000 stereoscopes annually and offered the public ten million stereoscopic views for sale.[85] The stereoscope was sold because of its extraordinary ability to conjure reality. As James Breasted, the distinguished Egyptologist wrote, looking through the stereoscope, 'we are gradually to realize that we are actually in the land of the Pharoahs'.[86] Breasted's breathless 'actually' is matched by O. E. Brown, A.M., B.D., D.D., Professor of Biblical and Ecclesiastical History: 'They do actually produce the realization of having seen the actual locality and not merely a picture of it.'[87] But as we have already seen with Bishop Vincent, what is at stake here is not just a technological marvel, but a Christian education: a Sunday school pupil 'scarcely regards Palestine as a real country. Bible stories were simply enacted sometime, somewhere; he almost conceives of it as a world apart, and hence never conceives Christ and Christianity as realities.'[88] Without the real experience of the reality of Palestine – the Fifth Gospel, as the tour guides termed it – or without the equivalent real experience through the heightened realism of the stereoscope, it is hard to grasp the reality of religious truth. It is this that grounds A. E. Osborne's extraordinary subtitle to his book on the stereoscope, its images and travel system: 'What they mean for individual development. What they promise for the spread of civilization.' The stereoscope, for Osborne and his co-workers, is an instrument in the spread of Protestant religion.[89]

The simplest form of album collected and republished a set of commercial images according to a simple itinerary. So Paul Bridel in 1892 published *Palestine Illustrated: A Collection of Views Obtained in the Holy Land by Messrs F. Thévoz and Co., Geneva*. The pictures start as the traveller did with the port of Jaffa and move up the hill road to Jerusalem, and conclude with the city's Christian religious monuments. This may seem no more than a tourist guidebook. But its selectivity is marked. There are sixteen images of the trip from Jaffa to Jerusalem, and thirty-four of the city itself. These include the Jaffa Gate, Mount of Olives and the other highlights of a tour, including some lepers by the gate. William Thomson tells us how a gate should be viewed. Thomson was an American Protestant missionary who first went to Syria in 1834. His widely read, topographically organized guide, *The Land and the Book*, is a textbook for the new archaeologically informed sense of how the landscape informs a reading of the Bible:

> Stop a moment. A city gate is a novelty to me, and I must examine in detail a structure so often mentioned in the Bible.
>
> What is there in a mere city gate to attract attention?
>
> Very little, perhaps, to one who has passed in and out daily for so many years; but many Biblical incidents connect themselves with gates.[90]

Thomson depicts himself as a traveller in conversation (Ruskin's *Mornings in Florence* will become the most obvious and far more elevated paradigm of this strategy), and demands we stop with him and pay attention to the biblical stories and ideas embodied in the everyday physical surroundings of this other world of the East – the classic gesture of the biblical gaze. Bridel's album appears to collect a series of images for precisely such general reflection for a Christian traveller. But it is equally striking for what it does not show. This is a city without Jewish and Muslim monuments. The album circumscribes a world. It is not by chance that it was published in London by the Society for the Promotion of Christian Knowledge.

It is within this framework that we can now more fully appreciate one of the most fascinating and commercially successful art works of the nineteenth century. James Tissot, just like Ernest Renan, was born in Brittany, went to the college of Saint-Sulpice for his education, but chose not to become a priest and remained in a tense and dynamic relation with his Catholicism throughout his life. When he was already a celebrated society portraitist, and his mistress had died, he turned back to the Church. As Degas seethed, 'He's got religion.'[91] He travelled to Palestine twice, in 1886 and 1889, to 'capture a Holy Land he imagined unchanged since the birth of Christ'.[92] The results of this trip were gradually produced and exhibited, and eventually became the extraordinary *Life of Our Saviour Jesus Christ*, 365 small watercolour pictures, none bigger than eleven inches by seven, illustrating the Gospels. The travelling exhibition of the paintings was a considerable event, especially in America and France, where scenes of devotion by the viewing public were reported, as if the paintings were icons. The pictures as a collection were bought by the Brooklyn Institute of Arts and Sciences in 1900 for the huge sum of $60,000, collected, impressively, by public subscription. The book, *The Life of Our Saviour Jesus Christ*, was published in French in 1896, and then in 1898 in English, in four volumes: each page has a selected text of one of the Gospels in the vulgate Latin with a facing vernacular translation (the English volumes used the King James Bible), framing an illustration of the text; many of the pictures also have a lengthy commentary attached by Tissot, including scholarly comments on archaeology, theology and his own travel reminiscences. Tissot made a great deal of money from this venture; and the size of the pictures suggests that he always intended a commercial project. As a set of images, they not only provided the backdrop to generations of Sunday School books, but also have been hugely influential on the image repertoire of modern cinema into the twenty-first century.[93]

Tissot's sequence of images is a visual counterblast to Renan's celebrated, provocative and humanizing *Life of Jesus*, a key popularizing text for the new critical history. It offers a forcefully Catholic, orthodox account of the divine Jesus, with portrayals of miracles, angels, spirits and a fully realized Ascension, organized in five chronological sections tracing the life of Jesus, according to the Gospels. In contrast to critical history's challenge to biblical narrative, it pointedly represents in stunningly vivid form medieval stories whose authenticity had been undermined in academic circles – such as the woman who wiped Jesus' face and thus found her cloth impressed with an image of the face of Jesus. In contrast to Protestant conventions, it lavishes attention on the tortured and scourged body of Jesus. The 365 images are like a Catholic, visual equivalent of Keble's *Christian Year*, a daily encouragement to devotional reverence and worship.

The claim that Tissot makes for his work in its introduction, however, emphasizes that he aspires to capture the real. It is time, he declares, 'to restore to reality . . . the rights that have been filched from it'. His work will be different, he states, from the long history of art, in its 'topographical accuracy' and his resistance to 'lead[ing] astray public opinion': 'I determined to go to Palestine on a pilgrimage of exploration, hoping to restore to those scenes as far as possible the actual aspect assumed by them when they occurred.'[94] Like Renan's *Life of Jesus*, Tissot's book is also a type of travelogue based on his own experiences in the Holy Land, a search for the real. So, it is fascinating, first of all, that Tissot's reality unabashedly includes angels, Satan, spirits, in forms that have seemed to many modern viewers – and to some of his contemporaries – to be baroque extravagances to the point of tastelessness. A massive pair of ghostly hands, for example, hovers above the bubbling water of the thronged pool of Bethesda, to represent with striking literalism the phrase from John 5, 'an angel troubled the water'. As I have discussed, the biblical gaze allows the biblical past to be seen in the contemporary landscape: here Tissot goes to the landscape to represent this biblical past as a historical and literal reality. The success of Tissot's images, despite some critical demurral in England, shows once again the conflict between academic critical doubts and the continuation not just of forms of faith but also of the popularity of representations that avoid such doubts. It is indeed striking that after a century of critical doubts in academic and theological circles about the status of the biblical narratives, in 1900 a huge public subscription could be raised for paintings that treated the Bible as literally true and simply real.[95]

But Tissot goes further. For in his cycle he also includes images of parables: the Good Samaritan, the Hidden Treasure, the Wise Virgins, and, more excitedly, the Foolish Virgins. It is as if the stories told by Jesus have the same status, the same visualization, the same reality, as the Gospels themselves. So even a metaphor of the threat of destruction for the non-repentant, The Axe in the Tree (Matthew 3.10), is also pictured, as, simply enough, an axe stuck in a tree, in a strange literalization of the power of words to bring an idea vividly before the listener. The boundary between different levels of (fictional) reality slip and slide, as the Gospels' parables and Jesus' images are represented physically, visually, at the same level of reality as the Gospels. It is as if the whole Gospels have one shared and visualizable level of the real: captured by an eye of faith.

Tissot's *Life of Our Saviour Jesus Christ* draws on the nineteenth-century tradition of travelogues to the Holy Land; on the claims that only seeing the reality of Palestine can ground the reality of the Bible; and on the privilege of an appeal to topographical and representational accuracy. This is all to construct a book in resistance to Renan's *Life of Jesus* that mirrors, for example, the photographic travelogue of Bishop Vincent's *The Earthly Footsteps of the Man of Galilee*. Tissot's *Life* too is structured around the chronology of Jesus' life and the author's pilgrimage to Palestine, and its 365 pictures have the coherence and the directed, selected viewing of an album. But Tissot's artistic medium, unlike photography, allows him to construct a biblical gaze of a quite different sort, where Jesus himself is seen in the real landscape of Palestine, accompanied by angels, performing miracles, and where his every word can become embodied as a portrayed reality. Within the polemical context of contemporary challenges to the status and author-ity of the biblical narrative, Tissot's painting here, I would suggest, is appropriating the reality claims of photography and archaeology, and the formal qualities of an album, to offer a quite extraordinary version of how art captures the real of the Holy Land. It is as if the religious assertion that every word of the Bible is literally true and thus visualizable as reality, is combined with the claim that the reality of the landscape of the Holy Land grounds the authentic truth of the Holy Scriptures – to create an indivisible Catholic vision. Tissot's sequence of images enacts the biblical gaze stretched to its conceptual limits. Art here seems to be in competition with photography, creating its own vision of the post-photographic real.

Perhaps the most surprising and interesting change in the last quarter of the nineteenth century, however, is the active participation of Ottoman, and especially Armenian photographers, in the production and circulation of photographic representations of Istanbul, Palestine, Jerusalem and the inhabitants of the region. Abdullah Frères published an album of images of Istanbul, as did Les Frères Gülmez (1885 and 1895); Sébah and Joailler (1895) and Kargopoulu (1884) – though here too, as Bohrer has analysed, self-consciously articulated cultural differences between East and West formed a far-reaching agenda for the normative work of self-representation.[96] Pascal Sébah's photographs formed *Côtumes Populaires de la Turquie en 1873*, an album displayed at the Ottoman Exhibition in Vienna in 1873, which brought Sébah's work to European attention.[97] The photos staged the variety and beauty of the profusion of the human world of the Ottoman Empire, as part of the ongoing politics of dress that mark the cultural politics of the final decades of Ottoman rule. National dress is fully part of the representational strategies of nationalism, and beneath the obvious exoticism and aestheticism of the images – for both Western and Eastern viewers – lies a political, visual display of the scope of the Ottoman Empire, which mirrors, for example, the list of the provinces of the Persian Empire in Herodotus' *History*, the foundational text of orientalism. This is a complex production, where the exoticism of the Ottoman Empire is put on display by the Ottoman authorities, and can be seen both as marking a difference between the subjects of Empire and the urban elite of the Ottoman court, and as indicating the sheer range of the Empire – with the added layer of the anticipated and actual responses from its Viennese audiences.

A production like this is especially difficult to fit into the simple models of the Orientalist gaze. Rather, it demonstrates on the one hand what Makdisi has called 'Ottoman Orientalism', a product of the self-conscious modernization at the centre of the Ottoman Empire that increasingly treats the provinces as backward colonies.[98] On the other, it is a perfect example of how 'official nationalism . . . was a project of modernization which strove to homogenize different cultures, different regions, and, above all, different stages of progress within a coherent culture of Ottoman modernity and civilization'.[99] Hamdi Bey's text which accompanied the pictures constructed an articulate map of Empire, and 'explicitly outlined where and how tradition fits within a modernized world'.[100] This book is a product of Ottoman Imperialism's self-portrait to the West and to itself.

Berggren, by contrast, published an album to illustrate the development of the port of Istanbul (1894) as part of the self-promotion of the city as a modern political, military and commercial enterprise.[101] The album focuses its gaze on industry, new technology, and the might of the navy as signs of the modernity of Istanbul. Even 'L'Album des chemins de fer d'Anatolie' is best seen not as a train-spotters' curiosity, so much as a contribution to the deep-seated political concerns about the German involvement in the build-ing of the railways of the Ottoman Empire, a geo-political interest taken very differently in England, France and the Ottoman Empire.[102] The rail-ways as the icon of modernity in this region always also indicate the power of foreign influence. 'Dès le début des années 1880' comment Gigord and Beaugé, 'la prise de vue devient systématique' – a systematic perspective, informed by the military, political and cultural interests of the state and embodied in the systematics of the album as form.

Although there are some very negative remarks about image making in Haddith, which result in some religiously motivated attacks on photography as a form of idolatry or, at very least, as a form of figural representation, which should not be allowed, the Sultan Abdul-Hamid II himself, as the spiritual head of the Caliphate, not only gave permission for photography, but also both sponsored photographers and was a keen photographer himself; he had his own darkroom in the harem section of his palace. Abdul-Hamid was keenly aware of the negative image of the 'awful Turk' in the West, and how photographs supported the language of political Orientalism that underpinned the political hostility, which was gathering strength as the First World War approached.[103] As one of his advisors, Ahmed Cedvet Pasha, sardonically noted, before the Crimean War, 'the Europeans refused to consider the Sublime State as European. After the Crimean War, the Sublime State was included in the European State system'.[104] But this could only make it the 'sick man of Europe' – a failed and collapsing state on European lines. Abdul-Hamid set out to re-address this negativity, with a strategy of image management.

This is a truly extraordinary story. The Sultan had prepared two sets of fifty-one albums of photographs of the modern Ottoman Empire as he wished it to be seen, and had one album sent in 1893 to the Library of

Congress in Washington, and one sent to the British Museum in London in 1894. These are wonderful collections, each with over 1,800 photographs, all taken under Muslim authority and many by Muslim photographers. There are many more pictures in the collection in Istanbul.[105] This is the East striking back in a self-conscious conflict over how it looks. It is quite remarkable that this side of the image war is so little discussed or even recognized by modern Western scholarship, intent as it is on proving its past imperialism, although historians in Istanbul have noted these collections repeatedly.[106] It must be supposed that, despite the critique of Said's work on the texts of Orientalism, this important body of material is ignored because it does not fit into the simple, politically charged model of the imperial West using images of the East to promote its cause.

In a conversation between the American Ambassador and the Sultan, the organization, display and exchange of collections of photographs is explicitly described as one of the modernizing regimes of knowledge, such as the census; and the American Ambassador, who had brought the Sultan an exemplary album of photographs of firearms of America, encouraged Abdul-Hamid to undertake a census of his own for the Ottoman Empire.[107] In the albums which the Sultan subsequently produced, we have the unique opportunity to see how photographs are selected from an archive in order to create a specific, politicized, systematic portrait of the Ottoman Empire from its political centre, rather than from Western travellers' eyes. 'Every picture is an idea', said the Sultan, 'a picture can inspire political and emotional meanings which cannot be conveyed by an article of a hundred pages; therefore I benefit greatly from photography.'

The categories are broad, though significantly linked to the modernization projects of Abdul-Hamid's regime, and the examples often assembled at numbing length (modern interest in cadet uniforms or army horses is sadly diminished, I fear). There are sections on scientific and educational institutions – schools, including girls' schools to counteract the image of the harem, and hospitals (as there were in the Franciscan albums); military installations; religious buildings; portraits. It is, however, a riveting document for cultural history both because of what it puts in and because of what it omits. It is constructed as a 'conscious antidote'[108] to the exotic and orientalizing imagery which is no more than a 'mockery that ... damage[s] national honour and propriety' – as the Sublime Porte thundered in trying to stop an English showman from collecting boats and exotic Turkish subjects to create a live panorama back in London.[109]

Figure 3.7, for example, is a modern station with trains and sidings (presumably the railway built using German expertise and capital). The

3.7 Railway Station, Abdul-Hamid's Album. Both the rolling stock and the buildings indicate a European design.

railways are the archetypal image of modernity in action. It could be a European picture. So the harbour scenes show an up-to-date navy, and the troops on parade are orderly and well-armed: 'the imperial soldiers constituted the vanguard of Ottoman modernity, rationality and national-ism'.[110] In Figure 3.8, we see the exotic mosque of the Sultan, as men cross a bridge towards it, and one turns back, nattily dressed in a familiar European suit, and carrying an umbrella; another has jaunty white slacks. Only the fezzes which some of the men wear are distinctive.[111] This is very different from the market scenes and traditional workers in the field that we saw from Bonfils: it is contemporary with it, however. So Figure 3.9, we get a modern fire brigade on an exercise. Or Figure 3.10, a major piece of artillery from

3.8 Istanbul, street scene, Abdul-Hamid's Album. Two men, turned back towards the camera, appear to notice the photographer, adding a self-consciousness of representation to the image.

inside a ship, new military technology. The techniques for making the images are the same as those of the West. The subject matter is carefully and self-consciously selected to show the world how the Ottoman Empire looks. The institutions of the State are displayed as modern and replete with Victorian principles of cleanliness, order and propriety.

3.9 Fire Brigade exercise, Abdul-Hamid's Album: civic order as a sign of modernity.

By the same token, there are no odalisques, no harem scenes, nor indeed any sexuality, exotic or otherwise.[112] There are no scenes of backward labour or biblical landscapes. With more political bite, we might also notice that there are no Armenians – this is in the middle of the Armenian massacres – despite the fact that some of the photographers were Armenians (and Christian rather than Muslim). There are no Jews and, perhaps most surprisingly, no images of Jerusalem, for all that it is the third most holy city of Islam,

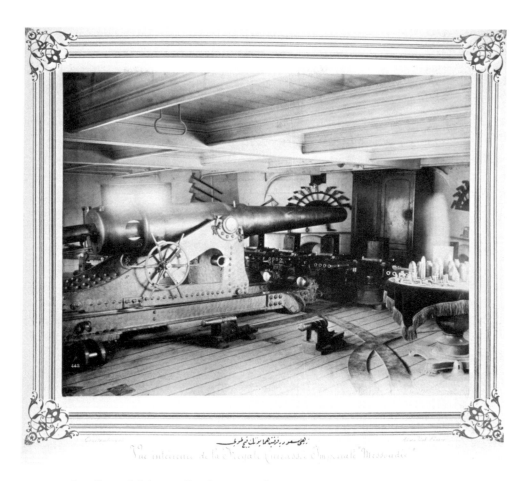

3.10 Naval artillery, Abdul-Hamid's Album – a soft power image of the hard power of Empire.

though there were many fine images of the city in the Sultan's collection, and the Sultan was persuaded to have an Ottoman exhibition including a full-scale model of the Dome of the Rock at the World's Fair in St Louis in 1904, as indeed he had made a display of Ottoman art and industry at the Chicago world's fair in 1893, including the American version of the albums.[113] Perhaps the evident backwardness of Jerusalem, combined with its profound religious associations, made it unsuitable for the Sultan's agenda.[114] Nor are there but a tiny number of adult women (though there are schoolgirls, to counteract the image of the harem),[115] which may be part of a Muslim propriety, but also may be part of a familiar patriarchal fantasy. Modernization has its own idealized imaging too.[116]

The exhibition of these albums at the World's Fair at Chicago in 1893, like the reconstruction of Jerusalem at St Louis in 1904 (with a big dipper incongruously looming behind the Dome of the Rock[117] and a cast of exotically dressed extras), shows how this image war took on an international shape and was fully acted out. For modern Jews in St Louis it was alienating and perplexing to come face to face with their own exhibition as biblical antiquities or Eastern exotics.[118] The fairground promoters of the biblical parts of the show, to the amusement of local cartoonists, found it financially expedient to advertise their exhibitions as promising the Eastern harem rather than scriptural insight.[119] The Reverend E. Morris Ferguson, general secretary of the New Jersey Sunday School Association, however, excitedly promoted the prospect of the Jerusalem exhibit, and tellingly captures how the biblical gaze was not easily to be shifted by the Sultan's projects of image management: 'It is a remarkable fact', he declares, 'that Palestine has changed little since the days of Christ, and in some respects but little, if any, since the days of Abraham. This will be vividly impressed upon the visitor to the Jerusalem exhibit.'[120] And this for the model of a Muslim shrine erected 650 years after the death of Jesus ... Palestine's modernity cannot escape, it seems, its deep religious past.

The irony is that by entering an image war with the West, in many ways Abdul-Hamid also rehearses the very categories of representation by which the East was denigrated: progress, development of civilization according to technological advance, cleanliness, order and so forth. Can the voice of the other speak back and be heard at all, without adopting the tones by which it is constructed as the other in the first place?

The final irony? This wonderful 51-volume album was sent to the British Museum in order to change the West's view of the Ottoman Empire in 1894. The packages, wrapped up in brown paper and string, were not opened and recognized and catalogued until 1983, almost a century later.[121] There is a rather shamefaced letter from the curator of the museum in 1983, admitting some blame for the nine decades during which they just sat there. It is indeed hard for the voice of the other to get a hearing. This institutional ignoring makes the subsequent undervaluing of the material, once made publicly available, all the more poignant.

IV Conclusion

The Victorian gaze at Jerusalem and the Holy Land, then, was first and foremost religiously filled and religiously fulfilled. The claim of the real was in service to a Christian teleology, and self-consciously constructed as such from the beginnings. The Holy Land, unlike the colonies of Africa and India, was not part of a Western empire, and it was the source and fountain-head of the most cherished western moral and religious values. Consequently, the landscape is never simply orientalized, despite the easy orientalism of native faces, backwards labour, and Eastern exoticism, which fills these images. Rather the landscape is formulated as religiously expres-sive, through rich symbolism and evocative tableaux: a biblical gaze. The pastoral, the backward, the simple, the humble, the poor, are not simply subject to the superior gaze of the civilized Western traveller, but are invested with the historical significance of the Christian message, as types, echoes and memories of the foundational moments of religious truth. Seeing the unseen – and worrying about the gap between such vision and the insistently disappointing physical realities of the Holy Land – structure the traveller's experience.

This biblical gaze was prepared, formed and regulated by hundreds of travel books, novels, Sunday School lessons, exhibitions, the circulation of images – and both gently mocked and then questioned as the clichés of disappointment became more intricate and pervasive. As photography became cheaper, however, a profusion of images circulated more and more freely, and became not just part of the commercial exchanges of the region but also an increasing factor in the construction of the Victorian imagination of the Holy Land. Professional albums took advantage of these cheap photographic and printing techniques to circulate more widely collections of images, collections which represent and embody systematic, ideological perspectives that seek to order and regulate the profusion of images according to the religious and political agenda of particular groups. Early photographers already collected their work into albums which imitated earlier artists' display volumes in form and use, but as the century progressed the conflict over the representation of the region by such albums became more marked.

In particular and most strikingly, normative Western imagery prompted a response from the Sublime Porte and from the Sultan who was passionate about photography as a medium and as a medium for political ideology. There was a direct engagement, a battle of the image world, where Christian Armenians and Muslims produced a new portfolio of the modern Ottoman Empire, an equally ideologically laden image repertoire. This was institu-tionalized in a multi-volume album sent to America and to England, the centres of Western photographic power. But this was first ignored for whatever reasons by the libraries; and then, even more dodgily, it has been repeatedly undervalued by contemporary Western scholarship, which has only just begun to acknowledge the role of Muslim-sponsored and Muslim-produced photography – no doubt for its own ideological purposes.

The engagement of the Western tourist with the Holy Land, then, was mapped through biblical, imperial, aesthetic agendas, and contested in zones of conflict over the image repertoire, often according to competing religious perspectives; these perspectives were in turn challenged from within the Ottoman world, which had also its own modernizing, orientalizing agenda. Photography's claim on the real is part of the rhetoric of the imagination. As identity takes shape between self-presentation and how others see you, in Jerusalem and the Holy Land, you are never just looking … The biblical gaze and the creative agency of the album formed an integral and fundamental aspect of this process of imagining the space of Empire, of seeing history in the materiality of things.

4 | Building history

A mandate coda

When the Archbishop of York announced to the Palestine Exploration Fund in 1865 that 'Palestine is ours', rather than making any simple assertion of presumed sovereignty, he was performing a gesture of affiliation and genealogy that explained the interest of his Christian colleagues in exploring Palestine as the homeland of Christianity. The Palestine Exploration Fund was one of the prime movers in the archaeological discovery of biblical sites that aimed to prove the truth of the Bible through scientific, material discovery. Yet, when Britain had such imperial interests in the Middle East, and, indeed, when the supply routes to and from India became in the First World War a strategic requirement, the imperial potential of a claim such as the archbishop's soon became fully realized.

The imperial eye had already been closely focused on the region and on British interests, as the long-anticipated break-up of the Ottoman Empire took place. Captain Charles Warren was employed by the Palestine Exploration Fund to explore the tunnels around the Temple Mount and to produce an Ordnance Survey map of the city. Warren was something of a Boy's Own hero who thought that a boy needed no other books than Baden-Powell's *Scouting for Boys* and the Bible. His archaeological and military exploits were parts of the same heroic persona that made him a celebrity in the Victorian world, and he rose to become chief of the Metropolitan Police during the Jack the Ripper affair (and General Sir Charles Warren). Warren epitomized an imperial, orientalist view of the Ottoman world in his disdainful dealings with the officials and community of Jerusalem; and his blasé daring in exploring the tunnels made archaeology seem an intrepid adventure as well as a religious mission. He set off, according to the telling words of his grandson and biographer, 'somewhat in the *rôle* of a Crusader . . . for he was stirred by the longing to reveal to the Christian world those Sacred Places which were hidden by the *débris* of many a siege and jealously guarded by the Turkish Mussulmans'. The archaeologist is a crusader, whose mission is to reveal the Christian truth embodied in the buried materiality of Jerusalem and 'jealously guarded' by Islamic opponents. His account of his archaeological discoveries – the story of whether 'the perseverance of an Englishman would not at last overpower

opposition' – became a best-seller, and its final sentences show with troubling vividness the connection between imperialism, archaeology and religion, a connection that makes the Archbishop of York's proclamation seem
disingenuous at best:

> Will not those who love Palestine, love freedom, justice, the Bible, learn to look upon
> the country as one which may shortly be in the market? Will they not look about and
> make preparations and discuss the question?[1]

The idea of a country being 'in the market' is a strikingly direct expression
of the economic roots of the British imperial project. The ideological
buttresses of the project are no less directly expressed: the Bible, justice
and freedom. When the First World War made Palestine strategically
crucial, because of its control of the supply routes to India, political prag-
matism drew on both the shifting image of the Middle East, and on the
deeply felt religious and ideological commitment to Palestine as the homeland of Christianity to found and support its realpolitik. It is from within
this milieu that the political movement of Restorationism, the desire to
return the Jews to Palestine, arose in the 1840s in particular, and by the end
of the nineteenth century had become prominent in Zionist ambition
among Christians and, latterly, Jews in Britain.[2]

From the end of the Crimean War, when restrictions on foreigners
owning land in Jerusalem began to relax, following the Ottoman government's recognition of European help in the fight against the Russians, the
major European powers each began building in Jerusalem as a nationalist
expression.[3] Church architecture in the West had, of course, long imitated
the models of the Holy Land, often in idealized and abstracted form – not
least through the structuring principle of the stations of the cross. (We will
see this at work, for example, with Templar influence on the Round Church
in Cambridge in the final chapter.) Yet this nineteenth-century importation
of Western models into the Middle East is formed through a powerful and
particular sense of nationalism and the ability of architecture to embody the
spirit of a nation. The collapse of the Anglo-Prussian Jerusalem bishopric
led to the foundation of St George's Cathedral by the British in the style of a
home counties' church with an Oxford college attached – while Kaiser
Wilhelm inaugurated the austere Lutheran Church of the Redeemer,
along with the Dormition Abbey and Augusta Victoria, built with expen-
sively imported German materials to a German design. The Italians built
their hospital as a replica of the Palazzo Vecchio in Florence; the French
built their neo-classical Notre Dame pilgrim hospice with a huge statue of
the Virgin Mary on its roof copied from Our Lady of Salvation in Paris. The

Austrian hospice, a building that would not be out of place in the Tyrol, served strudel and coffee in the Old City. The Russian compound with its Slavonic crosses, onion-domed cathedral and pilgrim hostels was almost a walled town of its own, opposite the New Gate.

The exotic, Eastern city of alleys and dirt, described in those thousands of travel reports, was being redesigned, as the European powers each constructed a major building project in their own image as a centre for their own presence in the city – and nervously, competitively, watched each other for signs of overstepping the balance of imperial interest in what all determined was a city soon to be fully 'in the Market'. The construction of national architecture was an attempt to form a national landscape and national perspective for the Holy Land, a chance to frame the material world within national lines: a claim on how the real should appear.

The representation of Middle Eastern architecture in general and the buildings of the Sacred Places in particular had been a central genre of the new technology of photography from the beginning. Long exposures made buildings attractive subjects, of course, but there was more at stake. John Ruskin's *Stones of Venice* (1851–3), perhaps even more than his essay *Seven Lamps of Architecture* (1849), was instrumental in reformulating the architectural interests of the nineteenth-century public.[4] Ruskin's work proved to have considerable reach. His writing first of all produced an intense moral concern with the material landscape of the city and its great buildings. Ruskin approached what he called the 'distinctly political art of Architecture' with the aim of demonstrating how 'every form of noble architecture is in some form the embodiment of the Polity, Life, History and Religious Faith of nations'.[5] The aesthetic judgment of the nobility of form is inextricably also an evaluation of a moral, political, and historical truth, linked to the life of a nation, with all the implications of such nationalist normativity in mid-century Europe. To look upon the buildings of a city was to be fully engaged as a historical subject, to take up a position. 'To see clearly', as Ruskin himself defined his belief in the transformative power of the visual, 'is poetry, prophecy and religion – all in one.'[6]

The *Stones of Venice*, with its wonderfully precise and evocative drawings, also encouraged a particular form of attention, which was never merely an aestheticized concentration, but always also a politics of history and faith and labour. The happy labour of the stonemason, matched by the attentive labour of the artist's drawing and the viewer's focused visual engagement, was the work of a religious faith for Ruskin, whose language never lost its evangelical cadences, even when his own faith faltered and collapsed in later years.[7] 'When we read Gothic architecture through Ruskin's eyes – at least in 1849 – we are reading exemplifications of hierarchy, of the law of supremacy, an order defined by God.'[8] Charles Eastlake, looking at the rise of the Gothic revival in architecture in Britain, saw Ruskin's moral force in precisely such terms: 'He wrote as a moral philosopher rather than as a churchman, and though his theological views found here and there decided expression, they could hardly be identified with any particular sect. His book, therefore found favour with a large class of readers ... '[9] It was Ruskin's moral fervour and sense of the religious charge in the physical world that changed the experience of observing art and architecture for a very large number of British travellers, in England, abroad, or from the armchair. As Charlotte Brontë attested with paradigmatic recognition: 'This book seems to give me eyes.'[10]

Ruskin also used photographs. He was initially extremely excited by the new invention and claimed to be the first person to take a daguerreotype of a Swiss alpine mountain – the object of sublime awe, and icon of God's majesty as expressed in the natural world.[11] Ruskin began by recognizing – as other theorists also did – the value of photography in service of the accurate preservation of images of architecture, currently threatened at the hands of the restorer and the revolutionary, as he put it, significantly enough, in 1849, the year after Europe was convulsed by the violent political turmoil of 1848.[12] He collected photographs of architectural details and complete buildings, and used them in the preparation of his books and even as illustrations for them. But as his writing on art progressed, he began to take against photography's inabilities to capture shadows, light and the visionary gleam he hoped to inculcate – and he ended writing dismissively of the technology and its products. Ruskin's complex and developing sense of how the viewer's practice should be educated, and through what visual technologies it should be formed, is integral to the history of nineteenth-century visual culture.

Ruskin had a profound influence on William Morris, of course, and many other intellectual figures who focused on the relation between the Church and the polity, especially as such thought fed into the projects of architectural restoration and the opposition to it – the subject of the final chapter of this book. But he also was the figure who inspired so many nineteenth-century travellers to visit churches as a gesture of contemplative cultural activity, and to reflect through architecture on the passage of time within the urban and social fabric of Britain and Europe (though he supported neither Holman Hunt specifically in his desire to go to the Holy Land, nor the project of biblical archaeology in general).[13]

As ever, parody makes for a particularly clear sign of this new visual attentiveness to art and architecture as a moral and religious statement of cultural value, and its association with the figure of Ruskin and the tourist gaze. E. M. Forster in *A Room with a View* (1908) delightfully describes Lucy's visit to Santa Croce in Florence with no Baedeker: 'She walked about disdainfully, unwilling to be enthusiastic over monuments of uncertain authorship or date. There was no one even to tell her which, of all the sepulchral slabs that paved the nave and transepts, was the one that was really beautiful, the one that had been most praised by Mr. Ruskin.'[14] The narrator tells us wryly that a small Catholic child 'stumbled over one of the sepulchral slabs so much admired by Mr Ruskin' – but Lucy never manages to identify the tomb she has come looking for. When she hears a clergyman lecturing a party in clichéd Ruskinian terms on how the church was 'built by faith in the full fervour of medievalism', Mr Emerson, her unwanted materialist commentator, insists, 'Built by faith indeed! That simply means the workmen weren't paid properly.' For Forster, Ruskin's influence is on a par with Baedeker's, producing an anxious tourist experience, desperate to live up to the expectations of taste and appreciation, prepared by rote from the guidebook.

The photography of architectural details of Jerusalem, however, fits well into this refashioning of the import of architecture. And the Holy Land raised specific problems and excitements for the contemplation of the 'History and Religious Faith of nations'. Thanks to Ruskin, looking at architecture had taken on a new and powerful valence for a subject's sense of history, temporality, and its embodiment in material form.

When Britain took over the rule of Jerusalem in 1917, a government formalized afterwards by the League of Nations into the British Mandate for Palestine, it was faced by a city that had been ravaged by war, famine and a brutal winter. The long history of imaging and imagining Jerusalem, in writing, art and photography, as now mediated by new British, Christian imperial concern for the Holy Land, coupled with twenty-five years of nationalist, competitive building in Jerusalem itself, provides the broad frame for the Mandate's policies on preserving the fabric of the city of Jerusalem. The authorities, with characteristic zeal, established their committees, set up administrative systems, and developed a policy for this task of the city's restoration.

But the specific line this policy took, turns out to depend to a surprising degree on one particular man, C. R. Ashbee. Charles Ashbee was the son of Henry Ashbee, the famous bibliographer of pornography, associate of Burton, Swinburne and others, who published under the pseudonym of

Pisanus Fraxi, and may, according to Stephen Marcus, be 'Walter', the author of the pornographic classic *My Secret Life*.[15] Charles Ashbee (always known in his intimate circle as CRA, or Charlie) is best known for his role in the Arts and Crafts movement in England. In 1888 he had founded the Guild of Handicrafts with £50 and four associates. Inspired by John Ruskin and William Morris, this little workshop in the East End of London grew through the 1890s to take up a central place in the Arts and Crafts movement.[16] By 1902 it had so outgrown its premises and its earlier ambitions that Ashbee could move the whole operation down to the Cotswolds, to the village of Chipping Camden, where his picnics, naked bathing, amateur dramatics and cycling trips around the countryside became a mildly shocking feature of the Cotswolds scene, and a fashionable site to visit.[17] It was in the 1890s too that Ashbee started going to America to lecture and to spread the word of his particular brand of Romantic Socialism, Garden City architectural principles, and Arts and Crafts commitment to designed objects and local materials.[18] He became a particular friend of Frank Lloyd Wright, and developed a special love for the Chicago waterfront. After his lecture in Chicago on the awfulness of the modern city had horrified his audience, who felt their city had been grievously insulted – it prompted a storm in the local press – he went on to describe Chicago's integration of architecture and nature in glowing terms, with praise for its 'creativeness ... buoyancy [and] exhilaration' and said that nothing had moved him as much, except – a typical local touch, this – standing on the back bridge of King's College, Cambridge.[19]

The juxtaposition of King's College and Chicago captures something of Ashbee's particular blend of modernism and deep-rootedness in an English tradition. This also helps explain his passion for the preservation of old buildings – as a modernist concern – or, to be more accurate, his love of eighteenth-century buildings and medieval structures. As he himself summed up his view on the value of the past, it was precisely seeing the significance of history within the materiality of objects and buildings that prompted his political activism: 'It was war with commercial vandalism that made men turn to the past as a citadel that had to be defended: the Historic conscience came with the aesthetic rebellion against commercialism.'[20] Hence: 'much of my own professional work has been the preservation and protection of beauty'.[21] But Ashbee was also conscious of how carefully a veneration of the past needs to be policed: 'This preservation of the past had its evil side, Veneration begat idolatry ... The movement ended in an orgy of bric-a-brac in which the prices were kept up by American buyers and manipulated by gangs of Jews.'[22] And this touch of racial thinking is followed through elsewhere in his writing: buildings such as Shakespeare's house at Stratford-on-Avon 'have in them a quality of their own that will not die, unless through negligence, the blindness, the death of the race itself. Beauty, in that it is an attribute of Divinity, has in it a race consciousness.'[23] Ashbee was also a friend of Lord Redesdale, father of the Mitford girls, and translator of Chamberlain's *Foundations of the 19th Century*, a fundamental text of German racism and anti-Semitism.[24] Since we will end with Ashbee in Jerusalem, it is worth noting thus that he was, surprisingly and without public acknowledgment, technically Jewish: his mother was a German Jew from Hamburg. In his reminiscences, however, he always distances himself from the Jews as other to himself, and, indeed, he is scathing both about the chances of Zionism succeeding as a political movement, and about the Jews he encountered in Jerusalem.[25]

Ashbee's campaigns and writings led not just to a new public gaze at what would come to be called architectural heritage, but also to the establishment of the Survey of London, the publication which still thrives as the official history of London, and is still used for the listing of buildings in London – probably Ashbee's greatest contribution to the cityscape of the capital.[26] His campaign to preserve Trinity Hospital in the East End of London is still recognized with a plaque on the wall of the building.[27] He was also a strong and active supporter of the Garden City movement. He designed a whole town for King's College, Cambridge to build in Ruislip – the full-scale design is still in the library, kept rather ignominiously behind a filing cabinet; the town was never built[28] – but he published increasingly polemical but still interesting treatises on how the material conditions of the city could be improved, in which, with great prescience, he called the automobile 'the enemy of architecture'.[29] In the 1890s, Ashbee became a public figure – a quirky icon for the possibility of standing out against the unthinking march of industrial progress in the name of craftsmanship, city planning and a turn back towards the traditional values of medieval artistic production.[30] He ascribed his inspiration 'to the founder of Christianity, to the Athenian citizen, to the medieval state builders, to the modern exponent of socialist economics' – a classic 1890s combination of the Bible, classical antiquity, the medievalism of the Pre-Raphaelites and modern social science – and aimed to reconstruct citizenship and production 'in conformity with the ways and methods of the medieval Guild'.[31] His art, his campaigning and his lifestyle, set him at the centre of the self-conscious sense of modern progress through a love of the past that is so typical of the 1890s. 'Aesthetics and History' could save us from 'the sordid materialism' of modern life.[32] It is as such a figure that he has entered the histories of the Arts and Crafts Movement.[33]

He also married in 1898 (though his father, from whom CRA was completely estranged, did not attend).[34] Ashbee was gay. He was great friends, as a student at King's, with Edward Carpenter, the art critic, and with the essayist, Sinologist and fellow of King's, Goldsworthy Lowes Dickinson, both of whom led him to recognize his own sexuality. (Lowes Dickinson remained Ashbee's closest and most trusted friend over many years.) In 1897, the 35-year-old artist met the 17-year-old Janet Forbes, and proposed soon afterwards. He wrote to her with a surprising candour about comradeship, the term through which same-sex desire so often expressed itself in these years. 'Comradeship to me so far – an intensely close and all absorbing personal attachment, "love" if you prefer the word – for my men and boy friends, has been the one guiding principle in life.' 'There may be many comrade friends but only one comrade wife.' 'These things', he concluded, 'are hard to write about.'[35] He hoped that the seventeen-year-old girl would understand. It is not clear she understood at all.

But they did get married ... On the wedding night, he kissed her fondly and went off to write a letter to his mother about how he would always love *her* more than any other person alive.[36] After three years of unconsummated marriage, Janet fell in love with another man, Gerald Bishop, who was also married, and who reciprocated her feelings. But duty and morality prevailed, and this relationship was also unconsummated. After six years of enforced celibacy, Janet not unsurprisingly had a mental breakdown, to which Charles responded with heartening and physical sympathy, and they had four daughters in rapid succession. The letters and diaries of this marriage give a fascinating insight into the daily workings of a relationship caught between the strictures of a public morality and the gradual development of a personal honesty deeply at odds with that public morality. He describes to her picking up a guardsman on the Strand and taking him off on a walking holiday in France; she replies that she cannot deny shedding a tear over his letter, but adds that since he had been so good to her over her difficulties previously, she gave his holiday romance her blessing. This is not exactly a traditional Victorian marriage.[37]

By 1916, however, things had taken a turn for the worse in Ashbee's career. Many of the Guild workers were killed in the Great War; fashion and austerity greatly reduced demand for the work anyway. Ashbee, now in his fifties, was too old to fight. He applied for a rather dispiriting job as a lecturer in the Egyptian Ministry of Public Instruction in Cairo and duly set off for Egypt.[38] (It is not clear there were any other applicants.) It was from Egypt in 1919 that he was summoned to Palestine by Ronald Storrs. This too is an extraordinary story. Ronald Storrs was the first military commander of

Jerusalem under the Mandate. Storrs had heard Ashbee give a talk at his school, Charterhouse, when Storrs had been a boy – and remembered it as the only interesting 'entertainment' talk he had heard at school. So he summarily invited Ashbee to become the first Civic Adviser – town planner – of Jerusalem: this is really the old school tie at work.[39] So in 1919, in late middle age, Ashbee took over in Jerusalem.

He was faced by an Ottoman town, where a significant majority of the population were poor Jews, dependent on foreign charity, and where the starvation and economic deprivation of the war had been particularly intense: it had experienced the fully biblical suffering of a plague of locusts in 1915, an epidemic of typhoid and cholera in 1916, and famine in 1917; the banks had been closed; the newspapers closed or censored; the post limited to the Ottoman service. Although the town had now begun to spread beyond its sixteenth-century walls, it still had no reliable water supply, barely a single paved road (but no cars either). Its regular tourist trade had collapsed with the War and with the Russian Revolution; it had little industry, and no natural resources. Many buildings, including those of most religious significance, combined intense politicized feeling with years of neglect.[40] Ashbee worked closely with Storrs, and they had the authority to pass the legislation they needed, and to enact it successfully. As Ashbee wrote in his first report to the War Office: 'Jerusalem is unique, a "city of the mind", and in it anything is possible.'[41] The results of his ambition are remarkable.

Ashbee's first report, prepared for Storrs and the War Office, was a review of 'Arts and Crafts in Jerusalem'. This might not seem an obvious starting point for town planning in war-torn Jerusalem – but it reveals Ashbee's particular intellectual formation all too clearly. Ashbee travelled the city, cataloguing and exploring its workshops, and collecting postcards and photographs of 'native craftsmen at work', a genre, as we have seen, popular in the nineteenth century. This led him to suggest some quite bizarre remedies for the city, such as revitalizing the industry in indigo dyeing, although there were only two elderly indigo dyers still in the city. But it also led to some far-reaching projects, as we will see, including the repair of the *Suk*.

It is fascinating – and, within the frame of contemporary dissension over the architectural fabric of Jerusalem, extraordinary – that there appears to have been minimal local resistance to his plans. The reasons for this lack of voiced 'subaltern resistance' are multiform and complex. First of all, Jerusalem had suffered very badly indeed during the last years of the War from famine, disease and the freezing weather as much as from violence, and restoration was desperately needed[42] – and only the British had the resources and organizational control to make this happen. This encouraged compliance. Second, there was already considerable antagonism between the various parties in the Holy City. There was no need to introduce a policy of divide and rule. Greeks, Armenians, Latins volubly argued and fought, while the two largest groups, the poor Jews and poor Arabs lacked the financial or political clout to realize a significant influence, and the leading Palestinian families were deeply competitive with each other and happy to express their competition by fighting over their intimate connection with the powers that be. Any localized resistance to British plans quickly became incorporated into long-standing internal divisions. The long-standing hatred of Ottoman official policy in the region and its tax collectors also eased initial acceptance of British authority. Nonetheless, although Ashbee was involved in the argument over the Western Wall (the significance of which he rather airily dismisses[43]), his own policies appear cannily to have largely avoided specific religious and political problems, and, as we will see, it was carefully arranged that leading representatives of the major religious groups were all invited to be representatives on the committee that guided the restoration programme (while the Mandate authorities maintained a majority).

It was only a honeymoon, however. The Deputy Mayor, a Syrian Greek, had already said to him, 'You English are doing so much here, planning such a wonderful city, showing us the way to so many new and strange things, that I suppose in twenty years' time we shall want to be turning you out.'[44] The Deputy Mayor's anticipated timing was only a little awry, and Ashbee may have missed any bite or irony behind his comments: indeed, Ashbee responded: 'that's the right spirit. It isn't "nationalism", or the "empire" that counts, but the idea, the fact of devotion and beauty' – as if politics or commitments (in either direction) could and should be simply subordinated to Arts and Crafts principles.[45] But Ashbee's stay in Jerusalem was also a remarkable window of opportunity, between the difficulties of the First World War and the imminent Arab nationalist riots and, later, more violent Arab/Jewish conflict – a moment when the combination of the firmness of British rule, a genuine and recognized need for the reconstruction of the civic infrastructure, and the lack of resistance in such cultural matters, made his work possible.[46] What is more, he had broad support in Britain in high places – he describes his meetings with Curzon at the Foreign Office, with the American Ambassador, with 'Zionist friends', with the Archbishop of Lambeth, and with Lord Milner, who told him to go to the Prime Minister because 'he will help you, he believes in Jerusalem'.[47] He also

Plate 1 Chasuble, made by G. F. Bodley (1882) for Watts and Co., back.

Plate 2 Chasuble, made by G. F. Bodley (1882) for Watts and Co., front.

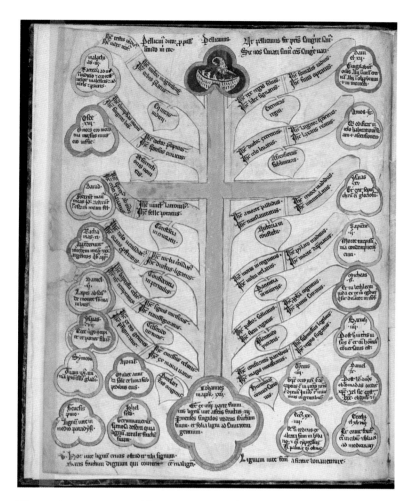

Plate 3 An image inspired by St Bonaventure's *Lignum Vitae* (1260) from Beinecke, ms 416, produced at the Cistercian Abbey of Kamp.

Plate 4 The Restoration Ball: Queen Victoria and Albert are on the right, in their resplendent costumes.

Plate 5 *The Procession to the Lists. Eglinton Tournament*, John Henry Nixon 1843.

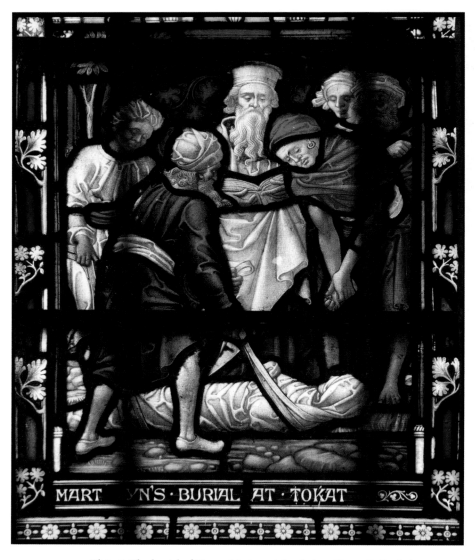

Plate 6 The burial of Henry Martyn, stained glass, Truro Cathedral.

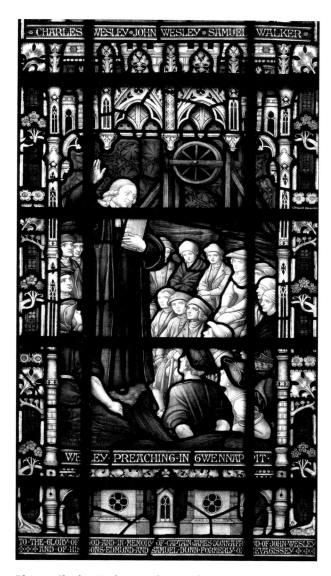

Plate 7 Charles Wesley preaching to the miners at Gwennap, stained glass, Truro Cathedral.

Plate 8 Miners at Dolcoath, stained glass, Truro Cathedral.

published a report of his work in *The Times* of 5 February 1919: *The Times* staff added its heading to his report, 'The Napoleonic Vision' which captures something of what Ashbee calls the 'effervescent optimism' of this period (though perhaps an inadequately self-aware sense of the history of Napoleon's activities in the Middle East and Egypt in particular).[48] Although he continued to intone that 'our politicians thwart our administrators',[49] in Jerusalem, the feisty administrator for once could temporarily transcend such political barriers. It was an opportunity Ashbee made the most of.

Ashbee and Storrs put in place four particularly important strategic policies in response to their initial survey of the city. First, a law was passed that forbade all building material except Jerusalem stone – and they explicitly banned corrugated iron ('We do not need Wolverhampton in Jerusalem', as Ashbee put it.) It is still the law that all buildings in Jerusalem must be at least faced with Jerusalem stone – although most people today seem to believe it is an Israeli regulation. The motivations behind this law are typical of the Arts and Crafts movement, and typical of Ashbee's own writing on the built environment: the requirement to use local materials, traditional materials, and a resistance to modern mass-produced industrial products. As we will see, this desire to recover traditional materials also led to some more paradoxical decisions. The result of this first piece of legislation, however, is a remarkable uniformity of texture and colour in the stone of the city, especially around the Old City, as an expression of historical continuity in architectural materiality.

Second, with equal imaginative scope, and ability to enact a policy, Ashbee changed the whole vista of the city. He declared that the walls, built by Suleiman the Magnificent in the sixteenth century, were the best example of a complete medieval enceinte in Europe, or at least would be when restored.[50] For Ashbee, as for the Pre-Raphaelites, the word 'medieval' was the lure of lures. And, it is worth noting, the sixteenth century could count here as the medieval. The Town Planning Report that Ashbee prepared for the War Office stated as Principle Number One for work in Jerusalem: 'To ensure proper restoration and preservation ... so that its medieval aspect may be maintained.'[51] It is rare that one can see so directly the artistic and historical principle behind a town-planning scheme. In Jerusalem, there is a constant, often violent battle over what needs to be preserved, what excavated. In order to excavate, the upper levels are inevitably destroyed. Restoring or preserving a lower level means not preserving or restoring fully an upper level. One of the great battles of contemporary archaeology thus is between the biblical archaeologists who wish always to reach the older levels, usually with the agenda of proving the biblical accounts authentic, and the Christian archaeologists who have an interest in the Roman Empire material, and the Islamists for whom the medieval Muslim palaces are central: the agendas are transparent.[52] But for Ashbee, it was his Pre-Raphaelite training that led him to privilege the medieval – with huge consequence.

Ashbee proceeded, first of all, to make the walls the centre of his development plans. Figure 4.1 is the before and after of Ashbee's imagination. Above is the photograph of the city walls, in a state of some disrepair. Below is his idealized drawing of a medieval town, with its towers rising above a verdant landscape, cleared of all unsightly impediments.

The Jaffa Gate reconstruction as at present, looking towards the city.   No. 44.

The same, as suggested when the unsightly obstructions that hide the wall line are cleared away.   No. 45.

4.1 The Walls of Jerusalem from *Jerusalem 1920–22*, edited by C. R. Ashbee. The 'unsightly obstructions' – domestic buildings – are replaced by what appear to be English oaks.

'Rebuilding the walls of Jerusalem' was a catchphrase of the British Restorationists who had worked to bring the Jews back to Palestine since the 1840s, as well as part of the rhetoric of longing in the Bible. Ashbee harnessed this imagery to the Arts and Crafts agenda. The trees that frame this picture look mostly like English oaks (they do not at any rate look like the trees of the arid environment of Jerusalem). And it is a striking contrast to the innumerable photographs and even paintings of the Holy Land that the two youths in the foreground are running playfully across the sward, rather than standing or squatting in still observation, the standard pose of the shepherd or Bedouin in Western imagery.[53] They look, that is, more like stereotypes of British boys romping.

   To keep the walls' medieval aspect, he planned to remove the large, ornate clock tower from the Jaffa Gate. Figure 4.2 is a famous picture of Allenby marching into Jerusalem to claim the Holy City for the British. The clock tower, a nineteenth-century Ottoman addition, in rather undistinguished, generic Eastern style, rises above him, registering 7.30. Clock towers were the 'first' and 'ubiquitous sign of Ottoman modernity',[54] explicitly intro-duced by Sultan Abdul Hamid II, to tell 'Western time' as a gesture of modernization and as a celebration of twenty-five years of his rule.[55] Ashbee, shocked at the aesthetic disaster of this construction (as he saw it), suggested that the tower was taken down immediately (it was placed at ground level, near the post office, as a sop to the residents who complained at the removal, on the grounds that they needed it to tell the time).[56] Buildings and other structures had been built right up against the walls or into them at various points in the circuit. Figure 4.3 shows the celebrated Fast Hotel, the most popular residence of European travellers, hard by the Jaffa Gate. There are also stalls and sheds either side of the postern. The hotel, and other such buildings abutting the walls, were also demolished to clear the view of the walls. Jaffa Gate was, and is, the most frequented point of entry for the city, and particularly concerned Ashbee. Figure 4.4 shows to the left the Jaffa Gate in its most ruinous state. The picture is actually from 1898, nearly twenty years before the British arrived – the selection of image is clearly designed to maximize the rhetorical force of the juxtaposition of the two images, and the British loved to compare the ruinously arrogant and destructive entrance of Kaiser Wilhelm with the modest, restorative arrival of Allenby. To the right is Ashbee's design for its new development (com-plete now with fully Oriental extras). Notice he reconstructs a moat (which every decent medieval fortress should have), with bridging arches, which he calls a 'fosse' to give the right touch of the Olden Days. A roadway across this territory was not in fact built for many more years, but Ashbee did

4.2 Allenby marching into Jerusalem, 1917, a staged event.

manage to restore the Citadel, the so-called David's Tower, precisely with
such civic gardens.

   In restoring the walls, he also reconstructed the walkway round the ram-
parts, the 'spinal cord of the Jerusalem Park system',[57] a task which required
some particularly awkward reconstruction and destruction, where buildings
had been incorporated into the upper level of the walls. This rampart walkway

4.3 The Fast Hotel, Jerusalem, with carriages awaiting customers. Jaffa Gate is to the right of the image.

was designed in order for Western tourists to be able to process round the city at a higher level to look out across the new town, playing the role of a medieval or biblical soldier, to appreciate the medieval enceinte. That is, there is also a constructed level of display here, of spectacle. Jerusalem also has to be viewed as well as lived in, treated as an art object. This is a turning point in Jerusalem becoming a museum or memorial of itself – something which has become the dominant aesthetic of the Old City with its constant work of new reconstructions of an imagined ancient life. Ashbee and Storrs founded the Pro-Jerusalem Council to oversee all the work of restoration.[58] They published accounts of their work in beautifully produced volumes. On the cover (Figure 4.5) – summing up the work on the walls nicely – is a calligraphic inscription which reads 'Walk about Sion and Go Round About the Towers Thereof', and below the central tondo, which combines the Star of David and the Cross in an abstract design, 'Mark Well Her Bulwarks; Set Up Her Houses; That Ye May Tell Them That Come After'. The book is a memorial of the memorializing task of reconstruction, its rebuilding of the past for posterity. The elegant lettering, so typical of the work of Morris, and the suitably biblical quotations, display and embody the aesthetics which underlie the messy business of civic planning.

The Jaffa Gate as it was when the " Kaiser's breach" was being made, and before the building of the Turkish Clock Tower.   No. 40.

Suggested reconstruction of the fosse at the Jaffa Gate.   No. 41.

4.4 Jaffa Gate, Jerusalem, the site of what is still the main entrance to the Old City of Jerusalem. Ashbee's proposed fosse is populated by stereotypical figures of Middle Eastern iconography.

The removal of buildings next to the walls stretched not only to a ban on any new building near the newly cleared walls, but also to a full town-planning policy based on Ashbee's passionately held Garden City principles. Figure 4.6 is one such plan, with a neat grid pattern, with hubs of public space, constructed memorials, and diagonal cross streets. There are linked gardens, a green belt ('clear belt . . . in natural state'), and an image of public life based on Letchworth or Hampstead Garden Suburb – despite the fact that the walled city and the style of architecture throughout the region was based on low-lying houses crammed together around small alleys and courtyards, with agricultural fields and hills beyond. This plan was never enacted. It is entitled a plan for 'Restoration and Preservation of the Ancient City' – which perhaps obscures any tension between the two aims, as well as any precise temporal reference for the antiquity to be maintained. The different concentric areas are calibrated with clearly marked boundaries. In the Old City, its 'medieval aspect' is 'to be preserved', which means 'no new buildings': the Old City is not to be developed in any way to

4.5 The cover, *Jerusalem 1920–22*, edited by C. R. Ashbee, an image whose design captures the Arts and Crafts paradigm.

compromise its perceived medieval form (but embalmed). The next circle will become the 'clear belt'; then there is a further area where buildings will only be given permission under 'special conditions' determined by their 'harmony with the general scheme'; finally there is an outer circle for redevelopment: that is where modernity may be placed. Here live 'Public

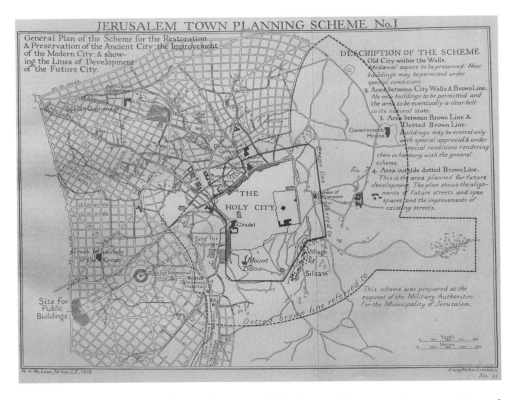

4.6 City plan for Jerusalem: an unfulfilled proposal for restoration, preservation and modernization.

Buildings'. Figure 4.7 shows a more extended, proposed green belt marked off in the shaded section, with some new trunk roads schematically indicated, and the University added. If the construction of a new city was beyond the power of Storrs and Ashbee to fulfil, the ability to stop new building in the 'clear belt' was rigidly enforced, and despite some encroachments, is still mainly in operation today. Figure 4.8 is taken from Ashbee's 1917 manifesto, *Where the Great City Stands*, and is his pen and ink drawing of the plan of Letchworth Garden City, halfway between Cambridge and London. It is not simply that similar principles motivate both plans: it is also remarkable – and hilarious for anyone who knows both places – just how similar the footprint of Jerusalem and Letchworth are made to appear, with their framing of green spaces around urban development around a central cross street. The two plans show with striking clarity how the ground-plan of Ashbee's vision was carried from the English Garden City into the Middle East.

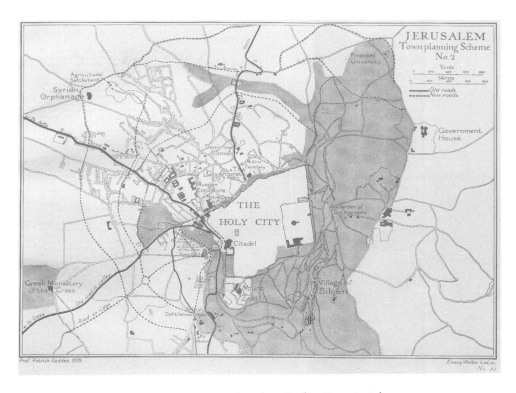

4.7 City plan for Jerusalem, a zoning system, based on Garden City principles.

The walls of the Old City are one of the most familiar images of Jerusalem. That we can see them the way we can, with such an unimpeded view of their cleared stonework, is the result of bringing the Arts and Crafts aesthetic and the policy of the Garden City movement to Jerusalem in 1919.

Thanks to papers that have only very recently come to light, we can see Ashbee's imaginative thought in process. He travelled the region, collected photographs, his own and those of others, and *in situ* or back at his house, painted rather beautiful watercolour images of proposed developments, which he put together in juxtaposition in his personal albums. Figures 4.9a and b make up one example of a scheme for a Thomas Cook Hotel on what is now the major thoroughfare, Derech Hevron. The black and white photograph (Figure 4.9a) is re-portrayed in the pastel colours of the future (Figure 4.9b). The real of the photographic image becomes the imaginative leap of the artist's hand. Yet Ashbee was also in a position to enact at least elements of his vision. In these lovely sketches, we can see in physical form how Ashbee's artistic vision is the grounding of his work as civic advisor.

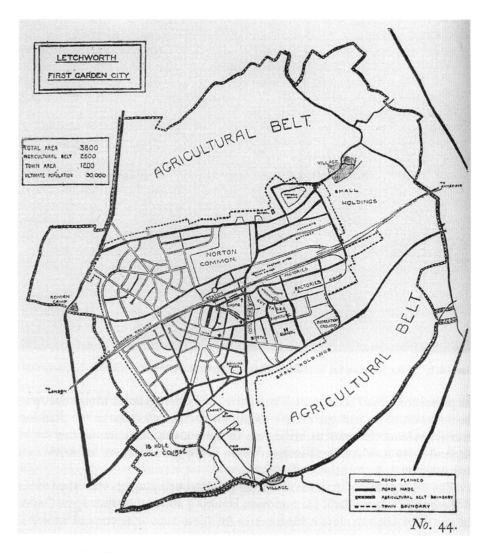

4.8 City Plan for Letchworth Garden City, from C. R. Ashbee, *Where the Great City Stands* – the Hertfordshire model for the Middle East.

The third plank of Ashbee's reforms involved bringing his cherished ideas of the guild to Jerusalem. He had been thinking about this already in Cairo: 'In our view none the less it were better for these lads – the sons of weavers, potters, glass-blowers, cabinet makers – to be practising the crafts they love and studying their much needed service to Western Industrialism than shouting catchword politics in the streets and class rooms', he wrote in a letter to a friend (a remark which reminds us how easily Arts and Crafts

4.9a *Derech Hevron*, photograph by C. R. Ashbee, taken by him on one of his investigative tours of Jerusalem and its environs.

4.9b Watercolour of envisioned *Derech Hevron*, by C. R. Ashbee, painted after his walking trip around the city.

became integrated with an imperial policy).[59] His idealism of the male group working together was also tied up with his own sexual attitudes, inevitably, and he wrote sweetly that he often chose young men to join the guild because of what Art could do for them rather than what they could do

4.10 Indenture Ceremony for apprentices, Jerusalem, in the *suk* in the Old City.

for Art. His interest in guilds and the first report on 'Arts and Crafts' in Jerusalem led directly to the restoration of the *Suk*, the covered market of the Old City, which was falling down both from years of disrepair and from the particularly severe blizzard of 1920, which had an especially deleterious effect on the fabric of the buildings. Ashbee prepared photographs for the Pro-Jerusalem Council, and published a carefully organized before-and-after report in the volumes of the Council. He not only set about repairing the fabric of the *Suk*, but also established new guilds for Palestinian weavers in particular, institutionalizing his principles of work, once again, now from the position of imperial authority. Figure 4.10 is a wonderful portrait of the ceremony of indenture for new apprentices. The arches of the newly constructed *Suk* rise cleanly above the ceremony. On the right sit the British matrons in their hats. On the left sit and stand the Arab families. In the middle standing at the official desk is Ashbee in military uniform. The ceremony performs the Imperial Mandate at all levels: re-educating the natives into their own traditions, now socially restructured with an admixture of the medieval guild; demonstrating and enacting the divide between rulers and ruled in clothes, deportment and language; developing an economic system which will maintain the wealth of the centre; and doing it all with pomp and circumstance. The *Suk* is the centre now of Arab Old

Jerusalem, visited for its exoticism, its old-style Arab market life, and local colour by thousands of tourists. It is a piquant irony that its material form comes again from the link of an 1890s aesthetic policy with a British imperial power structure. What is regarded by so many modern tourists as the most authentic and ancient sign of eastern exoticism in the Old City is a restoration reliant on the predilections of one British Mandate official.

For the Old City, the Pro-Jerusalem Council also established a system of small grants for repairs. This too, however, was tied to a policy of maintaining the traditional fabric of the buildings. They required, for example, that wood windows were replaced or repaired with wood, despite the fact that wood was expensive, and difficult to obtain in the environs of the city. The overhanging alley windows also had to be kept in their traditional design. Figure 4.11 from the publication of the Council shows the paraded fruits of the policy. Metal windows may have been cheaper, longer lasting and desired by the residents, but the Council, led by Ashbee, took control of the details as much as the broad policy of civic development. Again, this policy has to be seen within the context of the Arts and Crafts movement's passion not just for local materials and continuity of traditional crafts but also for the 'through design' of the fittings of any building.

The fourth strategy I wish to stress is the inverse of the preservation of medieval Jerusalem and the restoration of traditional crafts as the substructure to the medieval city – and it shows in the starkest manner how policies of preservation come hand in hand with instituted attitudes of wilful disregard. This fourth policy, it should be clear, was repeatedly enacted in a series of surprising, indeed swingeing decisions, but, unlike the first three policies we have been discussing, it was never explicitly encoded. It is, rather, the flipside of the love of the medieval, prompted as ever by the distaste for modernity as no more than a progress towards unthinking materialism and commercial vulgarity; and it consists in a stance of sniffy dismissal towards recent, contemporary building, where it did not conform to the aesthetic principles of the viewing critics. The test case, which displays the policy most strikingly, concerns the Russian Compound.

Throughout the nineteenth century thousands of Russian pilgrims came to Jerusalem for Easter week.[60] Many were very poor, and took weeks of arduous travel to reach the city. They came with the aim of receiving sparks of the Holy Fire from the Church of the Holy Sepulchre at the climax of the Easter celebrations. They would catch the sparks in their hats, and would aim to return to Russia and to be buried with their hats in their graves with them. This influx of pilgrims was part not just of the calendar of the year but

No. 11.

Old wooden window.

No. 12.

On the roof of Sûq el Attarîn.

4.11 Windows, from *Jerusalem 1920–22*, edited by C. R. Ashbee.

also of the economic expectations of the residents of the city. In the 1870s, a huge compound was built outside the walls for the pilgrims: a domed cathedral, a hospital, two dormitories for ordinary pilgrims, a fine hostel for noble pilgrims, a council house.[61] This project was completed despite the fact that Russia and Turkey had been at war in the Crimea only a few years before. Indeed, the parade ground on which the Russian Compound began was a gift to the Russian Tsar from the Sublime Porte. Both the fact that

Jerusalem's military presence lost its parade ground and the fact that this was a gift from the Sultan to his recent enemy in war are testimony to the intricate and sometimes baffling turns of diplomacy and national interest in this era. The Compound was walled, and made its own little Russian town. As new Jerusalem spread, the Compound was gradually built all around (and now what was once a free-standing and distinctive monument to a foreign national presence in the Holy City, is wholly absorbed into the city's landscape). The Russian Compound was one of the most distinctive and largest developments outside the city walls in nineteenth-century Jerusalem.

These fine buildings are all from the decade of Ashbee's youth, and some of the best examples of nineteenth-century Russian national architecture outside Russia – and therefore of little interest to Ashbee. 'Bastard Moscow' he called it with a sniff. The Compound was turned over for civic use. One hostel became a prison, its classical pediments topped now with barbed wire, its courtyard turned over to armoured vehicles and checkpoints, (Figure 4.12); the other, with oppressively neat symmetry, became the law-court. They have remained dedicated to these functions. The hospital is now the administration offices for parking offences.

The central vistas, a ceremonial approach across a rather grand square to the elaborate façade and multiple domes of the cathedral, are now ruined by traffic (Figure 4.13). What could have been a superb Victorian plaza, with elegant buildings around courtyards, has become a sour, overcrowded, mishmash of the cheapest redevelopment – which, with an inevitable irony, now also houses the Israeli Authority for the Preservation of Historic Buildings. Ashbee cared to preserve the medieval and what he could call the traditional: he had no eye for 'the Victorian' – near contemporary work – especially when foreign. Decisions about preservation are always also decisions about destruction. Here too the whole shape of the city and how its administration relates to its architecture has been constructed according to a very precise aesthetic agenda, forged in the 1890s and focused on the Arts and Crafts in the Cotswolds.

Ashbee did not stay long in Jerusalem. He worked there for only four and a half years, before retiring to the house where his wife had been born near Sevenoaks in Kent. He died as late as 1942, largely a forgotten figure. His last surviving daughter, Felicity, who had travelled with him to Jerusalem, died in 2008. Although he has been justly reclaimed as a leading light of the Arts and Crafts movement, and of the historic buildings movement, and even, to a lesser extent, of the Garden City movement, his influence in Jerusalem has been far less appreciated, not least because Ronald Storrs is very chary about any reference to him in his memoirs, even when they starred together in a

4.12 Russian hostel, now a prison, Jerusalem.

performance of *The Merchant of Venice* (of all plays!) during that first Christmas in the Holy City. Storrs was 'quite furiously angry' at the publication of Ashbee's warts-and-all *mémoires* of his Jerusalem stay, and this rage may explain his *damnatio memoriae*.[62] But most importantly, what has been systematically ignored is the influence of Ashbee's intellectual development in the Arts and Crafts and Garden City movements on his activities in Jerusalem. He was responsible for the fabric of the buildings, the design of restorations, and overall policy of development and preservation for the first years of the Mandate, and much of what he put in place is still determinative of the visual culture of the Holy City. Ashbee brought the Cotswolds to Jerusalem.

It would be hard to imagine a more important symbolic cityscape than Jerusalem, or a place where preservation is more intimately connected with politics, religion and empire. But here in Jerusalem we have an extraordinary case of the principles of Morris and Ruskin, as taken up and developed by Ashbee, affecting the policies of preservation and planning. The shape, the design and the use of one of the most important cities in the imagination of the world was fundamentally altered, through 1919 to 1923 (and beyond), according to aesthetic principles laid down in the 1890s. The life of an aesthetic theory is not limited to its immediate years of production or immediate influence but can spread with unpredictable time-lags

4.13 Russian Cathedral, Jerusalem, its vista marred by modern traffic.

following unpredictable personal narratives of the artists in question. Ashbee and his theories had their greatest impact when they were no longer fashionable, or even much recognized: but this is when they were most fully enacted. In part, this is because of Ashbee's involvement with the imperial system. The Mandate set out to improve Jerusalem: it brought in a water supply, reliable electricity, trains, tax, justice and so forth. It saw itself as bringing much-needed civilization to the Holy City, and, with the classic cognitive dissonance of empire, the Mandate officials were always baffled and upset by the ungratefulness of the inhabitants who continued to fight for self-determination. Ashbee's cleansing of the city – and the metaphors and realities of cleansing were also central – is an integral part of this imperial project. The aesthetics of the Arts and Crafts movement here becomes fully implicated and intertwined with the structures of imperial authority and power. The surprise of Ashbee's story finally is simply the surprise of seeing how the material life of a Middle Eastern city in the 1920s could be so affected by the emergence of an 1890s British Arts and Crafts aesthetic – and all because Ashbee had gone to give a schools talk at Charterhouse . . .

For Ashbee, the Great War was also a turning point in his ideas of how a city should be preserved. 'The disaster of the Great war has forced upon all men and women the necessity of preserving all that is possible of the beauty and the purpose, in actual form, of the civilizations that have passed before.'[63] He saw the previous thirty years of work 'shot to pieces by the war'.[64] 'The War has shattered the system', he reflected, but he saw in the idealism and plans of the young as much chaos and despair as hope.[65] Preservation was now not just 'aesthetics and history' aiming for the 'protection of beauty', but the struggle to save civilization itself and create a new civics from the horrifying destruction that mechanization, materialism and political violence had brought about.

Yet it was the very contingency of war that gave Ashbee the opportunity to enact his theories. In a way that was impossible in London or in England, he could enact a full programme of civic and architectural reform in Jerusalem. 'One isn't allowed to do "reconstruction" at home . . . one does it here', he reflected, with a sadly triumphant note that he had achieved more in his short stay in Jerusalem than in his previous eighteen years of work in England.[66] 'We have really got great things underway', he wrote, 'I have started two new industries; restored some old streets; am laying out parks and gardens; saving the walls of al-Quds; have rebuilt Nabi Samuil; started an apprenticeship system among the weavers; am planning new roads, parks, and markets, and making designs for half a dozen important buildings.' There was, as he declared, 'a great idea in it'.[67] The Empire was also a place where preservation, reconstruction, a 'new civics' could be tested and embodied without the compromises, negotiations and vested interests of politics that dominated policy in Britain. The power relations of imperial rule established the civic advisor in an unprecedented position to fulfil the idealist artistic aims by which he had been nourished over so many years – and gave an unexpected and practical sense to the old promise of building a New Jerusalem.

This, then, has turned out to be a story about distance. Jerusalem was once an archetypal city of distance, a city from which Jews and Europeans were exiled and to which Mamaluk political renegades were exiled. The difficulties of travel and the exigencies of politics made it a city much longed for, and much idealized. Jerusalem became a way of expressing the distance between the ideals of a heavenly city and the mundane corruptions of contemporary society. The Victorian age changed the practicalities of this as in so many areas. Baedeker in hand, travelling with Thomas Cook by steam-ship, sending a wire home with news, suddenly the Holy Land of Bible study was a holiday destination, and the disappointments of the smelly, poor, unpaved, unimpressive eastern city, needed some . . . distance: a renegotiation of the image, of the viewer's historic subjectivity, located between the past and the present. Archaeology re-discovered the truth of the biblical past, and re-authorized the city as a *lieu de mémoire*; exploration re-mapped the city and the countryside as the Holy Land; religious seriousness produced an experience of the past: here was where Jesus had stood: the past's distance collapsed by historical imagination into the experience of the present. When the Mandate took over, with its passion for order and practical solutions, Jerusalem offered unique and pressing historical and religious injunctions. If, as the Archbishop of York said, 'Palestine is ours', what, then, is the gap between us and them, and how should it be handled? Whose past is this urban landscape? These questions are, of course, still being worked through, but the answer of the first civic advisor who set British policy in the city came from his intellectual formation. He brought his own past with him: his 1890s aesthetics which privileged the medieval on the one hand and the new Garden City movement on the other: a specific blend of topographical distancing – the Garden City movement is all about creating green distance between urban experiences – and a vision of histor-ical distance, the search for a lost integrated past of labour and architecture in the medieval world. But when I see Ashbee standing between the Arab parents and the British rulers in the *Suk*, where Ashbee hoped to create an integrated community, what one sees most vividly, as so often in the Empire and in Jerusalem above all, is the distance still inscribed between the figures captured in this historical moment.[68]

With Ashbee in Jerusalem we can see how the buried life of things – finding historical significance in the material world, and articulating a historical consciousness through physical objects – has its own history, its own afterlife. We can also appreciate how the aesthetics of historical materiality in the 1890s led to an active attempt to reconstruct a historical landscape to match an already formulated internal, imagined vision in the 1920s. 'All is possible', contemplated Ashbee, as he worked to make the landscape in which to find the historical vision he wanted to see.

5 | Restoration

> For nature brings back not the mastodon,
> Nor we those times; and why should any man
> Remodel models?
>
> Tennyson

> Oh, flog me at the old cart's tail!
> I surely should enjoy
> That fine old English punishment . . .
> I should not feel the pain
> If *one* old English custom
> Could be brought back again!
>
> Monckton Milnes

I Rebuilding Jerusalem, here

In 1807, a devastating fire wrecked the Church of the Holy Sepulchre in Jerusalem. This iconic building, the very centre of Christian religious topography, had been destroyed and rebuilt more than once before, and there was no question of not repairing it. What grew from the ruins, however, did not simply reproduce what had been there before. Rather, the Greek architect Kommenos followed current style and constructed an Ottoman baroque dome in place of the flat-topped, open conical roof, familiar from eighteenth-century engravings, especially this frequently reproduced image of Cornelis de Bruijn (Figure 5.1) – to be the first dome over the Rotunda since the ninth century. In 1867–8, this whole roof, leaking severely since the 1840s and in dire condition (Figure 5.2), was taken off again, and rebuilt with new, Victorian technology based on a prefabricated cast-iron framework, a dome to compete at last in size and splendour with the Muslim Dome of the Rock (Figure 5.3 – the camel on the roof is particularly redolent of a clash of technologies here). Restored, it stood out as distinctively modern and shiny in its metal casing against the dusty jumble of its surroundings (Figure 5.4).[1]

CHIESA *del* SANTISSIMO SEPOLCRO

5.1 Church of the Holy Sepulchre, engraved by Cornelis de Bruijn in the seventeenth century.

How was this dome to be viewed? The Church of the Holy Sepulchre, as it changed in appearance, was also changing in the imagination of Western nineteenth-century culture: it was caught between its status as the military and spiritual destination of the Crusades, on the one hand, as the Crusaders themselves became integral to contemporary European self-representations,[2] and, on the other, Protestant distaste for the 'pious fraud' of Catholic and Orthodox 'worship of fetishes', 'orgies', and 'blind fanaticism';[3] it was perceived now within the new archaeologically inflected critical history of early Christianity, which challenged the historical status of the site; and implicated with imperial Christianity, Protestant and Catholic, strongly cathected as ever on Jerusalem and the Holy Land and all its monuments, validated by history's patina.[4]

What is more, in the last decades of the century, as we saw in chapters 3 and 4, the imperial European powers also stamped their national visual

5.2 Church of the Holy Sepulchre, dilapidated, in the nineteenth century.

repertoires on the landscape of the city, as the British constructed St George's, an Anglican cathedral in the style of a Cotswold church crossed with an Oxford college, and the Italians reconstructed the tower of the Palazzo Vecchio of Florence by the walls of the Old City, and the Germans raised the austere Lutheran tower of the Church of the Redeemer in the city itself, modern buildings reconstructing an image of an absent homeland, and reframing the stately dome within a European imaginative panorama. The question is not just what was to be seen on the skyline of the Holy City, or from within the church itself above the tomb of Jesus, but rather what was to be experienced in such a viewing? What is at stake here, of all sites, is authenticity, an authenticity of feeling, of history, of aesthetics, of true religion – and it is an experience of authenticity tied up integrally with political, religious, national and artistic self-positioning – and competing claims of authority. Reconstruction inevitably provokes an anxiety of authenticity. Yet, strikingly, for so much of Victorian thinking about its own age and relation to the past, it was only through restoration that

5.3 Church of the Holy Sepulchre under reconstruction in the nineteenth century. This picture was taken by Conrad Schick, the German architect, who also designed Mea She'arim, the best-known ultra-Orthodox Jewish settlement in Jerusalem.

authenticity could be found. Paradigmatically, Disraeli's Tancred, named for the Crusader hero, sums up his decision to visit Jerusalem with 'It is time to restore and renovate our communication with the most High.'[5] To get (back) to a full and real spiritual experience, it will take restoration.

The Church of the Holy Sepulchre in Cambridge, now usually known as the Round Church, was itself reconstructed in 1841. This church was first built in the twelfth century, inspired by the Rotunda of the Church of the Holy Sepulchre in Jerusalem. In the fifteenth century it was extended and a polygonal bell-tower added. By 1841, the building needed major repairs. The Cambridge Camden Society offered to take on the project and hired

5.4 Church of the Holy Sepulchre, finished, in the nineteenth century, its dome set against the jumbled and rundown cityscape.

Anthony Salvin as architect. The Camden Society, as we saw in chapter 2, had been founded by two Cambridge undergraduates only in 1839 for the study of Gothic architecture and ecclesiastical antiques.[6] It was on its way to becoming one of the key institutions in the restoration movement that changed the landscape of England. In the nineteenth century fully 7,000 of the country's 10,000 parish churches along with many cathedrals were restored, and the Cambridge Camden Society stimulated and epitomized the ideological driving force behind this remarkable reconstruction programme ('the villains were the Camden Society', as a later Heritage wallah accuses).[7] The restoration of the Round Church is a harbinger of what would happen to many churches. The bell tower was removed and replaced with a pitched roof. The Gothic windows were taken out and replaced with narrow Norman arches. The north aisle was completely rebuilt and extended to make it now the same length as the chancel. A south aisle was added to create symmetry. The gallery inside and the staircase to reach it were removed. The result of the restoration was not just the systematic removal of the signs of the fifteenth century and other later periods, but also the fulfilment of a design that no period had

5.5 Round Church, Cambridge, 1809, from the standard guide-book, *Description of Cambridge*, published by Richard Bankes Harraden.

ever seen – a Victorian idealized imagination of a supposed Norman blueprint (Figure 5.5 and Figure 5.6), now advertised for tourists as the second oldest church in Cambridge. With a sanguine sense of consensus, which would turn out to be wholly misplaced, the young Edward Augustus Freeman comfortably asserted that 'no one probably objects to the destruction of the superincumbent storey, and the restoration of the nave to its original state.'[8] Restoration takes us back to the desired, fantasized 'original state.'

5.6 Round Church, Cambridge, after restoration. This picture is from the early 1970s.

Restoration – and its close relative reconstruction – goes beyond its dominant political and physical expression in the architectural, where this chapter suitably enough begins, to become a central discursive marker of Victorian culture, linking, as we will see in this chapter, architecture to religion, to philology, to social reformation, to national identity, to epic poetry, to moral regeneration. Restoration encapsulates a longing for whole-ness and integrity to be projected from an idealized past into a sought-for future, that veins the self-aware Victorian conceptualization of progress. Chapter 1 of this book began with the restoration of Bulwer's house; chapter 2 took the Round Church's restoration as one of its central exam-ples; chapter 3 touched on the restoration of the Jews as part of Christian responses to the Holy Land; chapter 4 focused on the restoration of Jerusalem. It is time in this concluding chapter to look in detail at restora-tion as a central, organizing expression of nineteenth-century conceptual-izations of how history and the material world interact. Yet it is also integral to understanding the importance of this discourse of restoration, that, as with the cases I have been discussing so far in this book, although we start with material restoration, we will see how the language of restoration is repeatedly used to instantiate the invisible, the ideological, the conceptual – national identity, religious truth, personal fulfilment. The discourse of restoration cannot be limited to physical acts of rebuilding, as it becomes the culturally dominant language for articulating how the physical, material world and the idea of the past are dynamically interactive in the politics of progress that mark the Victorian present.

The projects of these two Churches of the Holy Sepulchre open a vista onto the 'great building campaign of the Victorian churches [which] had a profound impact, not just on the lives and habits of churchgoers, but also on the economic, cultural and physical composition of the larger society'.[9] Disrepair is one obvious motive for such work, and the images of Jerusalem above are a vivid demonstration of the combination of new technology and violent boldness of concept that typifies and makes possible the nineteenth-century response to this need. Technological innovation goes hand in hand with major cultural shifts, as we have seen throughout this book.

But the arguments for restoration as a thoroughgoing reconstruction to a new model were vociferously promoted at an ideological level, and gradu-ally opposed (and defended again) with even more strident voices in the name of preservation: 'restoration' is always cited in rhetorically sneering inverted commas by its opponents as they attempted to reclassify it as destruction. When the opposition started – first most notably from Ruskin and then from Morris and the newly formed Society for the Protection of Ancient Buildings – it published heated statements of princi-ple, which had little power to slow the programme of projects.[10] The *Builder* regularly lists ongoing and completed restorations, and the number of projects, as well as the *Builder*'s sensible appraisal of them, continues unabated. But the sheer volume of discussion – the *Builder* published twelve articles in a single year on the debate 'restoration versus preservation' – does begin to have an effect. Even a major figure of the restoration movement such as Gilbert Scott, president of the Royal Institute of British Architects and restorer of hundreds of churches and public buildings, starts to talk in his opponents' terms of conservatism, preserving what is great of the past, 'tender, loving handling' of the ancient fabric,[11] and so forth, in a way which is in stark and confused contrast with his own practice and many of his other more forceful statements. But this opposition became and has remained the orthodoxy of the now dominant heritage ideal, with the result that much of the history dedicated to this area has proved unrepentantly teleological in its disdain for the Victorian practice of restoration as a violent misdirection on the road to contemporary expectations and regulations of conservation.[12] In an absolutely emblematic Victorian gesture, however, the claims of restoration were seen both as a sign of the time and as a demonstration of the period's unique sense of historical (self-)awareness: 'The idea of restoration is a product of recent civilization, due to our modern historical self-consciousness.'[13] 'Church restoration is a business peculiar to this age.'[14] Indeed, Eugène-Emmanuel Viollet-le-Duc, the great maven of restoration, makes its modernity the first line of its very definition: 'Both the word and the thing are modern.'[15] Restoration starts out as a proclamation of a pressing modernity.

What, then, were the motivations of the Cambridge Camden Society and its heirs who published in the *Ecclesiologist* and who trained and promoted the architects who worked so assiduously on restoration projects? In the space here, the detailed ins and outs of the often vitriolic and petty debates will need to be sacrificed to the lapidary statement of some more general principles.[16] There are four main ideological frameworks in which the demand for restoration is articulated. The first, inevitably, is religious. It is not by chance that the great period of restoration begins with Wyatt (whom Pugin called 'the master of architectural depravity')[17] at around the same time as the evangelical movement of the early years of the century, and grows in intensity through the Oxford Movement and the pursuit of earnestness: 'The exact parallel growth of the Oxford Tracts and clerico-architectural Treatises, affords at least a very plausible reason for concluding that the seed from which they have both sprung is of like quality.'[18] For some, the threat of the Oxford Movement and the Cambridge Camden Society was the same fear of Catholicism: 'Romanism is taught *Analytically* at Oxford, it is taught *Artistically* at Cambridge.'[19] Yet for the majority of its practitioners, the return to a pre-Reformation, Gothic architecture was part of a broad religious movement to revitalize the Anglican Church, and which consequently saw architectural restoration as the reconstruction of the necessary and symbolically charged topography for a proper religious life. Restoration, as we began to discuss in chapter 2, was thus fully embroiled in the fierce debates about ritualism, which swirled around the Oxford Movement. The connections between liturgy and architectural structure were made frequently and intently: 'The question of restoration has been associated with, if, indeed, it has not arisen from a great religious and social change. Revivals of form and ceremonies have much to do with architectural restoration of churches.'[20] Ritualism, in short, 'caused the Gothic revival'. As Scott calmly observed: 'The revival has, for the most part, assumed an ecclesiastical character' and, with bland complicity, 'It is obvious that in refitting churches we must have our own ritual and our own necessities in view.'[21] So church design is evaluated according to the criterion of 'ecclesiological propriety';[22] restoration was 'holy work. It was a crusaded square, and trowel, and broadcloth';[23] and each architectural feature was religiously evaluated: the grand raised pulpit could be dismissively removed from its place because 'how symbolic is this position of an age which put preaching before praying, the word of man before the addresses of GOD!'[24] The structure and order of the church was to express a religious idealism. The restoration of communication with the divine that Disraeli's *Tancred* sought in the Holy Land found ritual expressiveness in a new purity and earnestness, and sought to recreate the physical world of the church to accommodate such a revival.

The second major framework is aesthetic. This is put with disarming straightforwardness by Freeman: 'The building is to be simply brought back to what we know or reasonably suppose from analogy to have been its original state.'[25] Like so many claims of simplicity, this statement is layered with complex ideological appeals and assumptions. Restorationists aim at 'the original state' – by which is not necessarily meant the first construction of the building, it turns out, but the idealized form of its structure as it existed in the mind of the medieval designers, even and especially when they did not have the technology or the wherewithal to construct that ideal. This is where restoration is to be distinguished from reconstruction: where reconstruction aims to create a new whole from fragments or ruins – and as a term is particularly prevalent after the devastation of the American Civil War and the First World War in England – restoration is to turn back the increments of time to rediscover an authentic originality. Restoration is 'to seize the opportunity to render the building as nearly as possible what it must have been in the mind's eye of its original designer'.[26] Hence the weasel slide in Freeman's credo between 'what we know' and what we 'reasonably suppose from analogy'. This allows space for the claim, in the case of the Church of the Holy Sepulchre in Cambridge, for example, that symmetry *would have been* the aim of the designer (by analogy), although the church had not previously ever been built like that (we know). So, Viollet-le-Duc's definition again: 'To restore an edifice means neither to maintain it, nor to repair it, nor to rebuild it; it means to re-establish it in a completed state, which may in fact never have actually existed at any given time.'[27] 'Brought back' is a nicely passive veil for this reworking, which also conceals the destructive effort required.

It is hard to trace any explicit intellectual link between this religiously informed architectural theorizing with its search to restore an unrealized ideal and the pervasive German idealism already flowing through English philosophical thinking of the time, but there are certainly fascinating echoes to be found of similar styles of argumentation in popular religious writing and other cultural modes. So, Ernest Renan, whose *Life of Jesus* was a huge and scandalous success from the moment it was published in France in 1863, with 60,000 copies sold in the first four months – it was translated four times into English, first as soon as 1864 – describes the Gospels themselves in extraordinary and evocative language: 'These details are not true to the letter, but they are true with a superior truth, they are more true than the naked truth, in the sense that they are truth rendered expressive and articulate – truth idealized.'[28] This bizarre category of 'truth idealized' captures the heart of the restorationist idealizing doctrine.

Most churches had accretions of years of development: restoration removed centuries of fabric as disfiguring interpolations, as if they were wrongly added lines in a text which could be cut out by an editor. So, George Cavendish Bentinck, a bluff Conservative politician and grandfather of Mark Sykes, also found the aesthetic question quite simple: 'It is perfectly justifiable to sweep away what is utterly bad and devoid of artistic merit . . . we ought to preserve what is original and good.'[29] There is, of course, for Bentinck no question about how the utterly bad and the good in artistic terms are to be distinguished. To privilege the medieval is a familiar and heavily freighted slant of Victorian historicism, but in architecture, as in archaeology, such privileging has dire consequences for the survival of any later era's achievements. Restorationists argue about which period of Gothic architecture is the really pure and perfect model, which the already degenerate, but they are consistent in their aesthetic principles of consistency of style, the value of the original, and an interventionist aesthetic practice to achieve their artistic ideals: the choice, Edmund Beckett argues with exemplary crudeness, is between letting churches fall down or making 'them as useful and as beautiful as we can get them'.[30] Beckett, known for his arrogance and bile, put his money where his mouth was: he was the architect who, as Baron Grimthorpe, was responsible for the substantial restoration of St Alban's Cathedral, at his own expense, after there had been a public outcry at his proposed changes. The extent and aggressive innovation of the restoration prompted a storm of protest, which Beckett high-handedly ignored, and for a short while afterwards 'to grimthorpe' was used to mean to 'ruin a building by reconstructing it'.

The third framework further extends the values from religion and art towards what we could call the politics of history. At one level, the appeal to history takes a turn through the common nationalist rhetoric of the nineteenth century. The masterpieces of Gothic architecture need the care of proper restoration because they are 'strictly *English*, and form a special and most delightful illustration of *English* history. How precious, then, are they to us as *Englishmen*!'[31] The link of Church and state makes the condition of the Church and the condition of the nation easily intertwined, and the initial, massive funding, which started the church building programme, was provided by the government.[32] As we will see, this appeal to history also becomes a centrepiece of preservationist opposition to restoration. At another level, however, there is an attack on the political values of the past, which are to be swept away by restoration. The removal of closed pews, for example, as we saw in chapter 2, was repeatedly defended as a gesture to reduce an unchristian politics of class snobbery and elitism within the church. The work of restoration is a radical desire for renewal of the religious values of the community as they are embodied in the fabric, liturgy and architecture of the church.

Fourth, there is the argument from need. That buildings are falling down, and need for repair is the simplest case offered (again and again). But it is fascinating to see how this need finds expression, especially as the arguments over restoration intensified. Scott is characteristically eloquent and muddling: churches have been 'allowed to fall, step by step, into a state of sordid and contemptuous neglect, decay and dilapidation, while they became encumbered with galleries, pews and all manner of incongruous interpolations'.[33] The language of decay stretches from physical collapse into moral and finally the ecclesiological, as the galleries and pews become signs of aesthetic and religious error – so that any apparent contradiction between lack of work ('neglect') and new work ('encumbered with galleries, pews . . .') is veiled in a general disdain. Indeed, in this perspective any church which has *not* been restored is likely to be the victim of degradation:

'sordid neglect, barbarous mutilation and ruinous dilapidation are the most frequent characteristics of an unrestored church'.[34] For Beckett, the decay is viewed as dirt and disease in need of modern medically informed sanitation: so, those who oppose restoration 'are only fit to rank with anti-vaccinators and objectors to interference with other filth' – the enemies of modernity and the enemies of social progress towards a more pure world – as if galleries in a church were like polio or typhus in society.[35] The desire for restoration feeds on an ideologically laden construction of the corruption of the present.

The arguments of the opponents of restoration respond directly to these four ideological frameworks, though in some rather surprising ways, and with a telling change of emphasis. The change of emphasis is to avoid the argument from religion. There was plenty of vocal Broad Church and Low Church resistance to ritualism, of course, but generally the preservationists concentrated their fire elsewhere, and failed to recognize as primary the question of 'how far architects were bound to go in their attempt to combine their work with a religious object and intention'.[36] For Morris, at least, such a stance was part of his heated anti-clericalism, easier to express persuasively later in the century. Paradigmatically, the church architect J. J. Stevenson offers three reasons why one might be emotionally attached to a church – because it is 'old', 'picturesque' or 'contained history of great art'.[37] The absence of religion here is a screaming silence. Rather, aesthetics and the politics of history ('old', 'picturesque', 'art') together form the base from which 'reconstruction' is repeatedly and viciously attacked as 'nothing less than the complete destruction of those monuments which they pretend to restore'[38], a destruction that is a 'national loss'.[39]

Ruskin put this point with characteristic rhetorical verve when he described restoration as 'the most total destruction a building can suffer; a destruction out of which no remnants can be gathered; a destruction accompanied with false description of the thing destroyed'.[40] Restoration thus 'is cutting away all that was associated in our minds with the history, legends, and traditions of the past'.[41] Indeed, the buildings are the historical records of the nation: 'I look on the architecture of all great public edifices as historical, and the edifices themselves as the most authentic record.'[42] So to destroy the fabric of a building in the name of restoration is 'to tear a page out of the record of English history', 'obliterating the history of the country', 'historical records . . . destroyed'.[43] Age is also intertwined with the aesthetic valuing of the very incongruities and developments of time which the restorationists rejected in the name of aesthetic consistency and purity. The Cathedral of St Alban's thus, before it was restored by Beckett, 'was full of incongruity and picturesqueness; there was a venerable bloom on the bricks; the oak was black with age. It had upon it, more plainly than any building I ever saw, the attestation of its vast antiquity.'[44] This is a question of 'true harmony not of form but of spirit'.[45] Thomas Hardy, a novelist particularly darkened by the imperatives of genealogy and an acute sense of place, worked as a church restorer and in 1906 reflected back on the 'tragic and deplorable' 'loss this country has sustained' from 'the damage done to this sentiment of association by replacement, by the rupture of continuity': an emotional destruction.[46] So even Scott, looking at what he self-servingly determines as the excesses of bad restoration, can declare that 'A restored church appears to lose all its truthfulness and to become as little authentic, as an example of ancient art, as if it had been rebuilt on a new design.'[47] Such buildings are no more than a 'provider of fancy dresses in brick and stone' – inauthentic, sham, deceptive.[48] In the eyes of the preservationists, restoration did not merely destroy the fabric of buildings but English history, human memory, the value of age, the very relation between people and the past: '"Restoration" denies the psychic importance of human memory, which invests brute matter with sentiment, deep resonances and a seemingly independent existence.'[49] The authentic and the truthful have to be grounded in history, and our historical self-consciousness cannot be experienced fully and properly when restoration has ruined our relation to the past.

Perhaps the most surprising and moving sense of this valuing of the past is expressed in a wonderful paragraph of James Anthony Froude's *Nemesis of Faith* (a book sufficiently provocative to be publicly burnt in Oxford). Froude's narrator, unlike the committedly religious figures I have been quoting so far, is on his way to losing his faith and living in an adulterous and self-destructive relationship with a foreign woman, which grounds his nostalgia in an intellectual and emotional crisis:

When I go to church, the old church of my old child days, when I hear the old familiar bells, with their warm sweet heart music, and the young and old troop by along the road in their best Sunday dresses, old well-known faces, and young unknown ones, which by and by will grow to be so like them, when I hear the lessons, the old lessons, being read in the old way, and all the old associations come floating back upon me, telling me what I too once was, before I ever doubted things were what I had been taught they were: oh, they sound so sad, so bitterly sad.[50]

The word 'old' intones like a bell through the description (with 'oh' a fading echo of the tolling). Froude's sense of the past is acute and produces an intense emotional reaction of loss, sadness and change. But the layers of the word 'old' are what drive the complexity of his nostalgia. The 'old' church is both an antique building and a former source of comfort. His 'old' child days are temporally distant. The 'old, familiar bells' invest 'old' also with a sense of longing and care, as in an 'old friend'. The 'old troop' is aged – and the 'old well-known faces' are both familiar and aged. The 'old lessons', however, are tied not so much to the Old Testament as to the sense of religious change which challenges the primacy of the old through critical history – the nemesis of faith of the title. They are read in the 'old way' – that is, they do not partake of the new religious forms set in motion by the Oxford Movement or the Cambridge Camden Society, its ecclesiological mirror: the newness and oldness of liturgy is a topic painfully relevant to Froude and his friends.[51] But these different senses of a past and a lost time produce reflection ('old associations') and awareness of psychological change 'what I too once was' – a sense of alienation ('I too once …' marks the current separation from the scene and the community, something Froude experienced all too directly after the book was published). He is moving away from the teachings of the past – in all senses – and it produces in him bitter sadness: the final, affective state of historical self-consciousness, tinged by loss, progress, and, above all, traumatized self-awareness, is exemplary of a changing nineteenth-century experience of historical, religious and psychological time.

The alternative to restoration's destructiveness is not, however, simply the careful cherishing and protection of ancient monuments. The most shockingly bold policy, starting from Ruskin but continued into architectural circles and the more general press, demanded that buildings should be allowed slowly to decay according to the normal wearing down of time. '*We have no right whatever to touch them*. They are not ours.'[52] What to do with buildings in need of repair? 'I would answer, Let them alone.'[53] So Samuel Huggins, the architect who stridently opposed Scott's restoration of Chester Cathedral. If a cathedral is needed for worship, then build another, new building next to the old, preserving both modern usefulness and antique beauty. It is unclear to what degree such a policy was no more than a rhetorical or theoretical posture; Stevenson, for one, against the tide of abuse, denied that it was to be taken seriously as a principle.[54] But it prompted a great deal of response from practical architects and property owners, who took the proposal very earnestly indeed. It should not be forgotten that the debate over restoration takes place during 'the largest redistribution of landownership since the dissolution of the monasteries',[55] a major shift in the principles and practices of church patronage, and intense concern over the relation between land, status and income:

stewardship of property and especially church property is a major theme of Victorian novels as well as Victorian politics.[56]

So, restorationists sharply attacked preservationists as supporters of slow decay. 'Let us have some inevitable mutilation rather than countenance such destruction as would follow from mere conservation, seeing that many old buildings would inevitably be swept away.'[57] It is 'a kind of abject fetichism [*sic*], a bowing down in an unquestioning humiliation before every brick put in place by one of their ancestors'.[58] Scott, with a characteristic self-interested feint, distinguished between ruins, which could be let alone, and churches, where restoration remained essential (in at least its proper form as observed by Scott himself). To be a slave to the past is 'to load us with fetters'.[59] Why should the moderns not be allowed to work on churches as all previous generations had? For the restorationists, preservationists were dismissed as impractical, ideologically led, even trivial: 'are churches to be left for archaeologists to amuse themselves with as long as they will stand?' sniffed Beckett.[60] Alexander Beresford-Hope, who became both president of RIBA and MP for Cambridge, put it most strongly. Preservationist policy was, he declared 'a gospel of despair and death'; 'all is to be petrified. All rottenness, all death . . .'[61]

The arguments over the policy and principles of church restoration set the rhetoric of progress against the rhetoric of loss, with competing accusations of wilful destruction and petrified ruination. Progress finds itself in restoration, and privileges an aesthetic of consistency to an ideal model, of proper religious use, of social process, of active engagement to make the ideal physical world; the rhetoric of loss turns to preservation, and extols a beauty of age, the serendipity of incongruous development, the continuity and contiguity of history, and the slow gaze of the single observer to find the beauty in the world around. Both sets of rhetorical self-positioning – and many commentators and practitioners tried to mediate between these extreme stances – are tied up with claims about the state of the nation; with professional status and authority – who has the right to speak for the buildings around us? – and with a shift in the economy of patronage and landownership. (One of the most scandalous claims, because partially true and partially misleading, is Morris' assertion that the system of payment for architects was responsible for the continuing activity of restoration.)[62] What is most deeply contested in this clash of rhetorics, however, is, first of all, authenticity. It is the aim and criterion of judgment for all participants in the debate, but quite differently comprehended: is authenticity to be found in the ideal image of the original designer, or in the layers of historical growth? Can authenticity be made or can it only be found? Consequently,

the questions that also underlie this battle of aesthetic and religious politics
are the central questions of this book: how is the past to be experienced, how
do humans relate to time, how is historical self-consciousness instantiated?
Above all, how should the physical, material world embody or reveal history
and man's relation to it?

II Philology and national culture

Gilbert Scott's use of the word 'interpolation' for a church's added pews and
galleries is a marked term. Its usual sense from the Renaissance onwards is
textual – the insertion of a misplaced line or word in a text; and the
reconstruction of the author's original wording is the aim of textual criticism,
which is a master science of the tradition of classical philology, the subject at
the heart of Victorian elite learning from school through university.
Interpolation supposes an excision to come (hence Scott's metaphor, which
works to justify his removal of the offending architectural details). The search
for the original state of the manuscript, by reconstructing the tradition of
transmission, grounds classical scholarship. Reconstruction runs through
nineteenth-century linguistics, and, as with church restoration, 'the original
state' is a defining goal. But if the grail of the eighteenth-century linguist was
the Adamic language, the original human language, the pursuit of nineteenth-
century linguistics was national identity.[63] (Marking its self-aware modernity,
the first professional organization of linguistics, the Société de Linguistique de
Paris, actually banned communications on the origin of language!) The roots
of nationalist linguistics were formed in the eighteenth century, however, and
two philologists can stand as exemplary and seminal figures for a complex tale
of scholarship, politics and fantasy, which takes us from the restoration of
buildings via the restoration of the materials of language to the restoration of a
national identity.

The first is Johann Gottfried Herder who made his name in 1770 with a
prize-winning essay on the origin of language, the archetypal eighteenth-
century passion. But his interests in language fed into his life-time project of
exploring *das Volk*, the people, the nation. Herder argued that the original
unity of mankind, located in central Asia, had become disseminated into a
series of different *Völker*. There were three main elements that determined
difference. First, climate and landscape: the physical conditions in which a
nation lived over many centuries constructed its *ethos*. There is, thus,
an integral and determinative link between a nation and its *Vaterland*.
The wanderers – Jews, Gypsies – are deracinated from such an essential

self-definition. Second, *Nationalbildung*, the culture, civilization and education of a people: a true nation has a distinctive culture, which defines its identity and the identity of its members. The mixing of cultures is not 'hybrid strength' but dangerous and corrupting weakening through diminution of distinctiveness. Third, language forms identity: each nation's specific linguistic template structured their thought and culture. The German language is formative of the German people, *das deutsche Volk*. Herder's influence is pervasive in nineteenth-century German writing on nationhood, race, culture and identity, and, more indirectly, throughout Europe, with a long and unpleasant historical legacy. Linguistics became increasingly part of a nationalist project. The brothers Grimm, for example, not only collected so-called folk-tales as indications of an original and formative *Nationalbildung* but also pursued linguistic researches into early German language. So in dictionaries and other normative systems, Cöln and Coblenz were now to be spelled Köln and Koblenz as 'the effeminate Latinity of the C was replaced by the rough-hewn Teutonic masculinity of the K'.[64] As Tacitus' *Germania* apparently gave classically authorized access to the earliest history of the pure and noble tribes of the German people, so linguistics aimed to discover and police a continuity of the German people through the German language. Similar work took place across northern Europe.[65] Reconstructing the linguistic past to rediscover the authentic history of the nation became a multiform scholarly enterprise in the nineteenth century.

This project was enabled by Sir William Jones, my second seminal eighteenth-century linguist. Jones delivered his famous 'Third Anniversary Discourse' on 2 February 1786 to members of the Asiatic Society, where he laid down the grounding for Indo-European Studies. He noted the evident similarities in morphology, phonology and lexicography between Greek, Latin and Sanskrit, and added the similar though 'less forcible' parallels between these languages and Gothic and Celtic, along with Old Persian. He proposed a single 'common source' (though he prudently hesitated here to suggest where it might be located). The labour of developing this suggestion was undertaken by a string of nineteenth-century scholars headed by Jacob Grimm, Franz Bopp, Antoine Meillet (and continued into the twentieth century by Emile Benveniste and others). The idea of reconstructing this Indo-European Ur-language, and an Indo-European Ur-society was particularly well received by German linguists, who had been primed by Herder's thinking on the single, Asian origin of mankind and the distinctive development of *Völker*, and it not only allowed a culturally charged link between German and the privileged classical antiquity of Greek (the tyranny of Greece over the nineteenth-century German imagination stretched from Romantic Philhellenism to Wilhelmine educational policies), but also provided a foundation for the construction of the idea of an Aryan race.[66] The reconstruction of Indo-European took place under the increasingly professional technology of linguistic science, but it continued to play a significant role in the invention of race and nationhood as nineteenth-century concepts.

Richard Wagner, for example, studied German philology with his customary obsessiveness, which led him back to the Norse tales of the *Nibelungenlied*, which provided him with the mythic material for the *Ring*, the opera, dedicated to the spirit of the German people, which was the summation of his *Zukunftsmusik*, the music of the future, itself an artistic summation of the *Sonderweg*, the unique path linking the sublimity of Greek culture to the promise of German transcendence. Wagner's great opera cycle, performed in the festival at Bayreuth, was a defining cultural moment for nineteenth-century Europe, and it is a moment which can only be understood within this appropriation of linguistics, myth and a commitment to a nationalist aesthetics in order to reconstruct a deep past of the nation – within an appeal, once again, for restoration. For Wagner, as we saw with the proponents of church restoration, this return to the past to found a new future was conceived as a revolutionary cultural politics: 'We do not try to revert to Greekness', he writes in *Art and Revolution*, 'only *revolution* not slavish restoration can give us back the highest art work'.[67] So, claims Wagner, in a strained attempt to capture this paradox, the artwork of the future will be 'conservative afresh'.[68] It is only by a return to the ideal past that art can find form at all: 'In any serious investigation of the essence of our art today we cannot take a step forward without being brought face to face with its intimate connection with the art of ancient Greece.'[69] But social and artistic revolution requires not imitation of the past but a thoroughgoing reconstruction of its essence. Cultural revolution requires a restoration that is not slavish, but active, German, modern. Wagner's aesthetics turns on this sense of revolutionary restoration.

The *Nibelungenlied* was not widely read before Wagner appropriated it; his choice of material caught the wave of public imagination. Across northern Europe in particular, national epic was being rediscovered as part of the reconstruction of national literary culture. *Beowulf*, the *Chanson de Roland* and *Reinhardt Fuchs* follow the same pattern of rediscovery as the *Nibelungenlied* (a pattern also evidenced in large-scale academic projects for the publication of the sources of national history such as the *Monumenta Historica Germaniae* or the *Rolls Series* in England) – a pattern formulated according to an intellectual template which Leerssen has termed *philo-logical*. 'National literatures are philological constructs.'[70] The *Kalevala* of Finland is a telling paradigm here. A series of disparate folk poems were disinterred from the archive and collected into an integral epic form and published as a continuous poem in 1835 by the philologist and Finnish nationalist, Elias Lönnrot. The new collection constituted now a literary heritage – a reconstructed cultural past, which was assumed to be determinative of the cultural and national future of the Finnish people – and duly became so. It entered Finnish culture in numerous ways of which Sibelius' music based on the saga is the most celebrated. In a similar spirit, William Morris, arch preservationist of church architecture, translated *Beowulf* into a ballad-based form, to reclaim the literary past for a socialist sense of the collective: the poems 'rightfully belonged to peoples whose commonality antedated, and in good revolutionary time should supersede, the high-cultural restriction of access to which nationalism and the mystique of Romantic authorship had conspired to habituate nineteenth-century audiences'.[71] Morris's idealism took a very particular shape, but the structure of the argument that led to his translation follows the same template as Lönnrot's with the *Kalevala*. The epic past is reconstructed with laborious philological effort, in order to demand restoration of a national culture based on it.

Macaulay's *Lays of Ancient Rome* is a particularly fascinating example of this drive towards reconstruction, and emerges from the same philological model. In the *Lays of Ancient Rome*, Macaulay, whose *History of England* was profoundly instrumental in the formation of a national history for the nineteenth century, imagines he is writing a ballad 'made about a hundred and twenty years after the war it celebrates'.[72] He is consciously echoing Niebuhr's argument about the important role of minstrel's songs in the preservation of early history here, and, as we will see, also finds support for this project in Walter Scott 'who, united to the fire of a great poet the minute curiosity and patient diligence of a great antiquary, was but just in time to save the precious relics of the Minstrelsy of the Border'. There must have been early 'ballad-poetry' in Rome. '"Where", Cicero mournfully asks, "are those old verses now?"' – Macaulay re-discovers them, as it were, in his own imagination.[73] His aim, he states directly, is 'to reverse that process, to transform some portions of early Roman history back into the poetry out of which they were made'.[74] The historian, that is, re-creates the old fictions that earlier historians had mistaken for history, as modern critical historians had revealed. This act of reconstruction turned out to be wildly popular, and his ballads of Horatius and other Roman heroes were staples of schoolboy reading for generations, as English boys found their epic past in models of ancient Roman heroism.

In this philological reconstruction of a national past, Walter Scott, as in so much, is a founding father for the nineteenth century's cultural imagination. His poetry, as Macaulay indicates, was based on a philological reconstruction of ancient ballad form, its language and narrative. It was the best-selling poetry in Britain before Byron, and helped create an image of the Scottish landscape and its past, and to define the form in which such an image could express its own sense of antiquity. But it is the *Waverley* novels that show the full range of the language and narrative of restoration. The *Waverley* novels revel in the apparatus of philological antiquarianism, with a reconstructed Scottish brogue that requires a glossary at the end of each volume, and, in *The Antiquary*, a gently tongue-in-cheek satire of the very process of antiquarian reconstructions. In Scott's narratives, however – *Waverley* itself is a good example – this philological apparatus is also framed by a narrative that links personal and political revenge with a desire to re-assert a fractured genealogy and with it to reconnect a family and its property, and, at the broadest level, to reassert a national identity. *Getting's One's Own Back* is a repeated structure: children returned to their proper family place, men reclaiming their property and their rights against usurping authority, homes rebuilt and rededicated to ancestral practice and ownership. Since the *Odyssey* at least, revenge, return and the continuity of the house have been the concerns of Western culture's privileged normative narratives. But Scott's sense of the house restored (in all senses), linked as it is with nationalism, philology and a defining historical self-consciousness, has a specifically nineteenth-century articulation.

It is, then, not by chance that Scott constructed his own house at Abbotsford as if it were a baronial castle of the Borders, designed indeed to look as if it had grown through the serendipities of time and as if it embodied a family history. As we saw in chapter 1, its rooms were filled with antiquarian relics of lost houses, churches and battle sites as well as of famous figures of Scottish history. The fragments are reconstructed to make up a historical fiction. The author's narratives of the house restored and his design for the building of his own house share in the project of imaginative historical reconstruction.

Disraeli, with his customary leery eye on all matters genealogical – he had his reasons – was fully aware that contemporary reconstructions of national history were riven with fantasies, ideological projections and silences: 'If the history of England be ever written by one who has the knowledge and the courage, and both qualities are equally requisite for the undertaking,

the world would be more astonished than when reading the Roman annals
by Niebuhr. Generally speaking, all the great events have been distorted,
most of the important causes concealed, some of the principal characters
never appear, and all who figure are so misunderstood and misrepresented,
that the result is a complete mystification . . .'[75] Yet *Sybil*, the novel in which
this historiographical sniping occurs, is obsessed precisely with the restoration of family fortunes, the genealogical imperative, the authorization of
class by history, the restoration, indeed, of Sybil to her true identity. It is a
state-of-the-nation novel; and its promotion of the idea of Young England,
which had considerable purchase in the political rhetoric of the day, is fully
imbued with the sense of restoration I have been discussing. 'They had
steeped their minds in the resonances of chivalry. They had bowed a willing
knee before the lofty seat whereon Sir Walter Scott sat enthroned.'[76] As John
Manners, Young England incarnate, confessed to his diary, 'We have now
virtually pledged ourselves to restore what? I hardly know – but still, it is a
glorious attempt.' Others were clearer, and clear in their echo of the arguments for church restoration with which I started: 'If Young England was
strongly anchored to the past, secure, so to say, in the moorings of feudalism
and chivalry, its members were as firmly attached to a belief in the Church
and its influence.'[77] Or, as *Sybil* concludes, the task of Young England – 'The
youth of the nation are the trustees of posterity' – is to struggle 'once more to
possess a free Monarchy, and a privileged and prosperous People'.[78] That is,
it is only by restoring what we imagine we once had that true progress can be
made. This is the revolution of the conservative afresh.

III   Reconstruction from the ground up

Historical fiction, a self-consciously nineteenth-century genre (and, thanks
to Scott, a supremely popular one), found intellectual roots, then, in the new
science of philology and a shared nationalist imagination.[79] The restoration
of a house such as Knebworth from its actual Elizabethan form to a more
chivalric representation of an Elizabethan form goes hand in hand with –
and finds its authority in – this philology of nationalism. Yet historical
fiction as a genre was also deeply complicit with the new science of archaeology. This is nowhere more strikingly evidenced than in the founding novel
of 'toga fiction', Edward Bulwer Lytton's *Last Days of Pompeii*, which I
discussed in the first chapter of this book. The buried town of Pompeii was
rediscovered in the eighteenth century, and its excavation and publication,
particularly by William Gell through the first quarter of the nineteenth

century, had a huge imaginative impact in fiction, art and music, as well as in the understanding of the classical past. Bulwer Lytton's novel was a best-seller, and, in the usual way of publishing, much imitated, especially in the classicizing aesthetic era of the last quarter of the century. Its narrative strategies, as chapter 1 showed, reveal the extraordinary literary fertility of the idea of reconstruction.

Chapter 3 of *Last Days* I have saved for now, however, as it is an extended reconstruction in words of Pompeian architecture, as it had been disinterred and reconstructed by archaeology on the ground. It begins with a general picture of Pompeian housing ('The reader will now have a tolerable notion of Pompeian houses . . .'),[80] as a frame and foil for the house of Glaucus, the hero of the novel: 'But the house of Glaucus was at once one of the smallest, and yet one of the most adorned and finished of all the private mansions of Pompeii' – and, with the easy and stylish snobbery that typified Bulwer Lytton – 'it would be the model at this day of "a single man in Mayfair" – the envy and despair of the coelibian purchasers of buhl and marquetry'.[81] The house is described in the style of a tour guide: 'You enter by a long and narrow vestibule, on the floor of which is the image of a dog in mosaic, with the well-known "Cave canem" – or "Beware the Dog".'[82] Bulwer here is referring to one of the best-known excavated artefacts of Pompeii ('*the* image'), a charmingly domestic mosaic in the so-called 'House of the Tragic Poet'. Indeed, Bulwer's description is not only a close picturing of this particular building, excavated in 1824, but is formulated through the current museum holdings ('You may see them now transplanted to the Neapolitan Museum') and through the critical works discussing the house: 'This room is usually termed by the antiquaries of Naples "The Chamber of Leda"; and in the beautiful work of Sir William Gell, the reader will find an engraving from that most delicate and graceful painting of Leda . . . from which the room derives its name.'[83] Sir William Gell, it will be recalled, had been Bulwer's guide to the site of Pompeii (which they visited with the dying Sir Walter Scott), and Bulwer's prose derives from Gell's detailed archaeological account of the house. This is a very emphatic and extended version of what Barthes calls 'the reality effect'. The archaeology provides not just a stage set for the story but a guarantee of its authenticity. So at the end of the story, as we saw in chapter 1, Bulwer returns to the archaeological site ('nearly seventeen centuries had rolled away when the City of Pompeii was disinterred from its silent tomb'),[84] and finds in the ruins the remains of his own characters. Bulwer has, he claims, merely reanimated – restored to life – what can be seen in reality on the ground of Pompeii.

Perhaps the most extraordinary act of reconstruction at Pompeii, however, was the casting of bodies from the impressions in the ground. The flesh of bodies imprisoned in a case of ash had decayed leaving only the skeleton, but the shape of the body was preserved by the moulding of the ash covering. The Italian excavator Fiorelli developed a technique of pouring plaster into the hollow space, thus producing casts of the body. These 'bodies' became one of the most evocative sights for tourists – the captured flesh, as it were, of antiquity, caught in the final moment of life. We can now appreciate more precisely Bulwer's delight in this empty echo of a body: 'The sand consolidated by damps, had taken the forms of the skeletons as in a cast; and the traveller may yet see the impression of a female neck and bosom of young and round proportions – the trace of the fated Julia!'[85] In the ground you can still see the tangible shape of the breast of the – fictional – Julia. The wilful manipulation of levels of fiction and material reality set in play by *The Last Days of Pompeii* shows just how vertiginously complex the staging of reconstruction can become.

Glaucus' house, that is, the House of the Tragic Poet, was reconstructed in the Crystal Palace at Sydenham in London in 1854. Bizarrely, it was first intended to act as a tea-room for visitors, though 'plans changed, and the only visitor ever officially to sit down to tea there was Queen Victoria'.[86] Crystal Palace, part museum, part gallery, part industrial exhibition, was a self-consciously modern display, from the building itself to the courts and categories of exhibition, individually and collectively.[87] Ruskin, predictably, hated it. Not only were the materials of construction resolutely and aggressively not local materials, worked and time-honoured by the knowledge and concentration of medieval artisan skill, but also the exhibition itself celebrated the very industrial machinery of mass reproduction; and the courts, the Roman, the Egyptian, the Assyrian and so forth, proclaimed the theatrical seductions of reconstruction.

Thomas Hardy gives a particularly vivid sense of the disruption that the Great Exhibition caused for a nineteenth-century sense of time and history. Looking back from 1893 to 1851, he offers a fictional account of the shock produced by that remarkable event:

For South Wessex, the year [1851] formed in many ways an extraordinary chronological frontier or transit-line, at which there occurred what one might call a precipice in Time. As in a geological 'fault,' we had presented to us a sudden bringing of ancient and modern into absolute contact, such as probably in no other single year since the Conquest was ever witnessed in this part of the country.[88]

For the rural world of South Wessex, a nostalgic, imaginative landscape created by Hardy, the exhibition is as disruptive a national event as the Norman Conquest. It appears as a dividing line in history and in the self-consciousness of change – a true 'precipice in Time', as Hardy memorably terms it. This break is expressed as a 'geological "Fault"'. On the one hand, the inverted commas around the word "fault" mark it as a new technological term – it is indeed a nineteenth-century innovation as a standard geological term – performing the rupture of old and new with a word typographically marked out as new-fangled. On the other, to make geology the field through which to image the change in a sense of time, is pointed. Geology, as is now well appreciated, was the discipline which revolutionized Victorian understanding of deep time, and produced a model of the long history of the material world which challenged in particular the possibility of Christian chronology – and in its invention of stratigraphy offered a way of conceptualizing, representing and articulating the past, which, in combination with evolutionary science, made cyclical or non-dynamic natural history harder to maintain.

The shock of the exhibition is expressed, however, as a violent juxtaposition, 'the sudden bringing together of ancient and modern'. This is an 'absolute contact'. There are, again, at least two ways to understand this bold expression. On the one hand, it recalls the physical effect on the visitors of the extraordinary modernity of the glass and iron building, conjoined with the shock of the old that the discoveries of Layard, for example, provided. The building itself, and the later Crystal Palace, was taken – for praise by many and for disgust by Ruskin – to embody the potential of contemporary industrial innovation: a marvellous and awe-inspiring sign of the times. So the modern exhibits were paraded in precisely such self-congratulatory terms, coupled with nationalist competition. But the ancient exhibitions themselves were equally startling. For many, despite the British Museum's permanent collections, this was the first time that the new finds of biblical and classical archaeology were on display. This was not just an aesthetic experience, but intimately connected with the status and authority of the past as it had been challenged by critical history.

Ruskin's voice was marginal in the debates over the Crystal Palace and the authenticity of its displays, however visionary he may now appear, and however powerful his general views on art and viewing churches continued to prove. But there was a careful rhetoric about the status of the courts' reconstructions in the official guidebooks too. The Assyrian court was designed by James Fergusson, one of the most distinguished architectural historians in London, especially on the architecture of the east (although he also passionately expressed the totally bizarre claim that the true site of the Church of the Holy Sepulchre was the Dome of the Rock).[89] We have already seen Fergusson's support of biblical archaeology as a proof of the Bible and his proclamation of archaeology's 'promise to supply us with exactly what we wanted to understand and realise what we there [in scripture] find written'. On sale was not only the official general guidebook by Samuel Phillips, but also – and the visitor was directed to it by the general guidebook – an extended account of the court by Austen Layard, the archaeologist who had famously excavated the site of Nineveh on which the display was based.[90] The official guide noted briefly that the exhibition was 'an architectural illustration which, without pretending to be a literal copy of any one building, most certainly represents generally the architecture of the extinct but once mighty kingdom'.[91] We may hear an echo of the church restorationists' appeal to the general and ideal model as the template for reconstruction. Layard's book, however, is far more extensive on what 'restoration' might entail.

The introduction lays out 'the grounds for restoration'[92] with a history of the Assyrian kingdom and of Layard's discovery and excavation of Nineveh. The exhibition was the first opportunity, he underlined with pride in the triumphs of the modern age, to see this lost architecture, buried without apparent trace or echo for so many hundreds of years. Layard too was clear that 'the Court is not a complete restoration of any particular Assyrian building'. Rather, 'It has been the endeavour to convey to the spectator as exact an idea as possible of Assyrian architecture.'[93] He freely recognizes Fergusson's use of analogy, as Freeman termed it: 'as a similar mode of admitting light and air is still found in parts of the East, Mr Fergusson has not hesitated to adopt it in his restoration'.[94] Indeed, Layard scrupulously underlines the uncertain procedures of restoration: 'The ceiling has been restored by Mr Fergusson, who has carefully selected from the various ornaments found in the ruins of Nineveh . . . The arrangement is of course arbitrary, as no ancient ceiling has been preserved.'[95] Philologists often described their work as an organic process, 'reconstructing the body of the manuscript from its mutilated members';[96] Layard is bracingly clear that the reconstruction here is arbitrary. But he also extols the values of accuracy, carefulness and the authenticity of each of the parts. At stake in part here is the professional authority of archaeology and of Layard himself as one of archaeology's leading scientific figures. So the guidebook insists on a proper historical background for the objects, and a full account of the excavation. The Assyrian court is to be viewed through the guiding light of history and archaeology, twin critical sciences of the modern age.

What is also at stake, however, is, once more, the word of God. Archaeology's promise was precisely of a material reconstruction to set against higher criticism's articulate doubts: 'The period of skepticism is over, the period of reconstruction has begun', proclaimed A. H. Sayce, Professor of Assyriology at Oxford, as he challengingly reviewed the history of archaeology for the Tract Committee of the Society for the promotion of Christian Knowledge.[97] Nineveh is a biblical city, where the prophet Jonah preached. Amid the materials found by Layard were both wall inscriptions and cylinders which explicitly mentioned Sennacherib, the Assyrian king, whose invasion of Israel is recounted in the books of Kings and Chronicles. According to the second book of Kings, Sennacherib returned home after accepting tribute, for which Hezekiah ransacked the Temple; according to the second book of Chronicles he fled after the angel of the Lord brought plague on his forces (it was actually a plague of mice, who ate their bow strings and shield straps, according to an Egyptian story told by the Greek historian Herodotus). Layard's newly discovered sources suggested two invasions, a convenient way to reconcile the biblical sources. One inscription mentioned the same figure as the Bible of thirty talents of gold in tribute; different figures in the new Assyrian sources and the Hebrew texts for the amount of silver were as easily persuaded away as the coincidence of thirty talents was celebrated as proof of the Bible's veracity. The texts of the Bible had been subject to fierce analysis by the techniques of critical history, and with this threat to the exactness of the text came a threat to the exacting normativity of its precepts as well as to its narrative of the early history of man. Archaeology appeared to offer solid, material evidence for the veracity of the holy book. *The Times* heralded Layard's work precisely for 'its remarkable verification of our early biblical history'.[98] The Assyrian Court reconstructed in Crystal Palace not only displayed the stunning architectural resources of a lost and previously unseen palace culture from antiquity, but also exhibited the proof of scriptural writing. Layard's guide is criss-crossed with references to the Hebrew Bible, comparisons of Assyrian and Jewish culture, and an easy familiarity with the morality of the prophets' denunciations of 'the danger of being corrupted by the superstitions and idolatrous worship of their neighbours'.[99] To view the Assyrian Court was to place oneself before the nineteenth-century anxieties about the status of biblical history. Every statement of the accuracy, care and authenticity of the archaeological reconstruction is a pointed contribution to this debate. When Layard was presented with the freedom of the City of London in 1853, it had been precisely for demonstrating 'the accuracy of Sacred History'.

Layard was a radical and complex person who used his celebrity as an archaeologist to enter a political and later a diplomatic career – though he ended his life with a somewhat tattered reputation, after his feisty forthrightness, as well as his political opinions, led him to make bitter enemies of Gladstone and even Queen Victoria. His particular trajectory enables us to see two further ways, however, in which archaeological reconstruction is connected to what I have been outlining as the broader politics of restoration. First, Layard worked closely with the architectural community. He was a close associate of the architect James Fergusson, the designer of the Assyrian Court, and was appointed by the Gladstone administration as Commissioner of Works. In this capacity, he campaigned actively for a broad, state-funded aesthetic education, and drew up plans for the beautification of London with a Thames-side complex of museums and public buildings (plans which were scuppered, to his chagrin, by government budgetary restrictions). Layard's involvement with the discovery and public exhibition of the great art of the Assyrian kingdom in London is part of a far more general debate, in which he is playing a leading administrative role elsewhere, a national, public debate about the degree to which the material condition of the city is an aesthetic as well as an economic and religious concern. It is a debate conducted across Europe, and especially heatedly in Germany, with the post-Humboldtian politics of *Bildung*.[100] Archaeological exhibition finds a link with the arguments over church restoration in their shared concern for bringing the artistic and material culture of the past to the people, restoring a connection to history through aesthetic experience.

Second, Layard was intimately connected to the British Museum. Thanks to the sponsorship of Stratford Canning, the powerful ambassador to the Sublime Porte, Layard's dig at Nineveh was funded by the British Museum. Layard later became a trustee of the museum; he bequeathed his Assyrian treasures to the museum, and they still form the basis of its collection. There is a deep complicity between the museum and the archaeologist, which inevitably draws this chapter's interest in reconstruction close also to the chapters on excavation and destruction – and underlines the connection between nineteenth-century English archaeology and the power structures and foreign policy of the British Empire.

Take the case of Charles Cockerell and the Temple of Apollo at Bassae. Cockerell trained and practised as an architect – he was appointed Professor of Architecture at the Royal Academy in 1839, President of RIBA in 1860, and he designed the Ashmolean Museum at Oxford as well as the interiors of the Fitzwilliam Museum in Cambridge – and the obituary written for the Royal Academy of Arts stressed that 'at the heart of Cockerell's emotional

experience of the power of the antique to fire the imagination lay an extraordinary visual sensitivity to the mass and volume of the components of
architecture'. When he came to Bassae as a young man on his Grand Tour in
1811, he had already helped excavate the fragments of the pedimental
sculptures of the Temple of Aphaea in Aegina, which had been purchased
and sent back to Munich for the philhellenic Ludwig I, where they were
restored by the neo-classical sculptor Bertel Thorvaldsen (in a manner 'soon
to appear over-confident and old-fashioned')[101] and, thanks to their display
in the Glyptothek, had a major influence on the developing neo-classical
architecture and culture of Munich. The Temple of Apollo at Bassae, mainly
because of its isolated location, was in remarkably well-preserved condition. It
had been designed by Iktinos, the architect of the Parthenon in Athens, and
praised for its exceptional beauty by Pausanias – and thus came with all the
prestige of classical authority. Over two years, Cockerell obtained permission
to excavate with his international team of aristocratic friends, and found
twenty-three slabs of the frieze of the temple – almost the complete frieze –
with images of a Centauromachy and an Amazonomachy. It was bought at
auction for £19,000 by the British for the British Museum. It was seen
immediately as a project of national aesthetic politics: 'This liberal application
of public money can have but one object in view, the eventual perfection of
Sculpture in England, by affording free access to rising artists, and a leisure for
pursuing their studies in the national repository.'[102] As Cockerell himself
noted of the national competition of the sale of the Aegina sculptures, all the
excavators of the international team were 'anxious to strain every nerve for
their respective countries'.[103]

     After the excavation, the Temple itself could certainly be seen more clearly
and its beauty appreciated, but in view of the export and re-display of the
frieze, Cockerell seems only to highlight the paradox of archaeology's work
when he writes proudly, 'The enterprise was crowned with the happiest
results, the architecture of the Athenian Ictinus was restored in almost
every particular.'[104] The sculptures were installed in a specially made gallery
in the British Museum (where they still are) – and their reconstruction, here,
has been a source of scholarly controversy ever since. The frieze is made up of
twenty-three self-contained slabs, carved by different hands, and found dis-
jointed around the site. The sequence of the slabs – how they construct or
obscure any narrative – is quite unclear. Even the positioning of the two
battles around the inner roof is debated. There was certainly paint used on the
sculptures, though how much and in what colour scheme is again a matter of
fierce disagreement. The sculptures were designed to be viewed from some
seven metres below; now they are at face height, and the details can be

observed intimately. What once went round the outside of the building, now runs round the inside walls of an exhibition hall.[105] The restoration, we could say, goes too far and not far enough.

The multiplying ironies of this idea of restoration are instructive. The Temple was founded for Apollo Epicourios, the Helper, because he restored the people to health after plague. The imagery of the Greeks defeating Centaurs and Amazons 'amounts to the restoration of the "natural" ordering of Greek society'.[106] The shattered frieze was taken back and reconstructed in the British Museum in London, where it was to provide an exemplary form to train modern artists' reconstructions of classical ideals, in part at least in order to assert a connection between the ancient past and the modern *Nationalsbildung*. Cockerell used the frieze to reconstruct an image of the Temple, which itself is a contribution to the reconstruction of a Victorian idea of Greek religious practice; the imagery of the frieze is used by modern scholars to reconstruct a picture of the classical Greek ideology of social order, as much as its artistic or religious history. Cockerell circulated an engraving that reconstructed the work of archaeology as a romantic discovery (Figure 5.7 – note the dog, gun and open book, marking the

5.7 Cockerell's image of the Temple at Bassae, under archaeological investigation: the rifle, dog, stool, umbrella and book all mark the absent presence of the presiding scholar.

5.8 The staircase at Oakly Park (1823), incorporating the Bassae frieze.

absent presence of the gentleman archaeologist). Cockerell himself reused the frieze in his own architectural work. Although he 'reject[ed] the archaeological notion of a Greek revival' in architecture, he declared that we must 'appropriate the Greek style, engraft it in our wants and recast it for our necessities'.[107] Figure 5.8 shows how he managed to build elements of the temple into the staircase hall at Oakly Park. A cast of the full length of the frieze was duly engrafted into the monumental, neo-classical Ashmolean Museum in Oxford around the top of the Grand Staircase; the Travellers' Club, of which Cockerell was a founding member, occupies a building designed by Sir Charles Barry, and its library is also decorated with a cast of the Bassae frieze. The Fitzwilliam Museum in Cambridge, where Cockerell designed the interiors, has its copy too. Plaster casts of classical sculptures over the course of the nineteenth century became coloured by their inauthenticity as mere copies; but they remained essential tools for the teaching academies well into the twentieth century. And, as the Bassae frieze shows, were incorporated into neo-classical architecture as integral reused reconstructions.

Similar stories could be told of the German excavation of the Ishtar Gate from Nebuchadnezzar's Babylon and its reconstruction in the Pergamon Museum in Berlin: another archaeological triumph with biblical associations, at the centre of a self-consciously national expression of monumental artistic value, especially charged through the connections of Germany with both scholarly and political Orientalism.[108] (As Charles Alison, a friend of Layard's cynically observed, 'If you can by any means humbug people into the belief that you have established any points in the Bible, you are a made man.')[109] The Parthenon at Athens provides one of the most extreme cases, which links German and British endeavours in this form of destructive archaeological restoration. Otto, the son of Ludwig I who had received the restored sculptures from Aegina, was set in place as the first sovereign of the new kingdom of Greece after the Ottomans were turned out. A plan was hatched to make a palace on the Acropolis for him and a design was drawn up to assimilate the Parthenon into a new, modern royal compound – by Schinkel who had built the Altes Museum in Berlin (the links between imperialism, philhellenism and museums are enacted at every level of culture). In the end, the newly established royal party along with the scholars were satisfied by clearing away from the Acropolis all signs of buildings that dated after the fifth century BCE. The shanty town that had grown up there, the Muslim mosque, the military installations, the everyday detritus, and even the landmark of the so-called Frankish Tower (built by Venetians) were all removed, and the site reduced to bedrock. Archaeology, in the voice of the director of the excavation, claimed to have 'delivered the Acropolis back to the civilized world, cleansed of all barbaric additions, a noble monument to the Greek genius'; but restoration, once again, in its search for the ideal of the past had created a vision, a site, a material environment that had never before existed.

Church restoration gave way to a principle of preservation already by the turn of the twentieth century. So, too, preservation of secular buildings had become – and remained – a fashionable cause already by the end of the century, as, for example, with Ashbee's campaign to save Trinity Hospital in Mile End in 1896. (After the Second World War, as

Europe attempted to find some sense of salvageable history, reconstruction took on a different significance again, and many European cities were desperate to rebuild as precisely as possible what had been lost to violence.) But the archaeologists, and especially the archaeologists working abroad in the Empire or in the penumbra of Empire, followed a different timeline. Sir Arthur Evans, for example, used the technology of reinforced concrete, a nineteenth-century invention, to reconstruct the palace of Knossos on Crete well into the 1930s, working from ruined fragments to create a soaring structure.[110] Evans had been educated to a Victorian curriculum and had absorbed much of his classicism from it. Like Ashbee in Jerusalem, away from the metropolis, he could undertake a project which would have been hard to contemplate in the full glare of the contemporary capital's institutional gaze. The Parthenon itself took on its familiar, splendid profile only in the 1920s and 1930s, with a restoration whose technological flaws have required an almost constant process of re-restoration since.

From Bulwer to Layard to Cockerell, the institutional connections that frame the principle of restoration stand out in high relief. The novelist and politician finds – and plays with – his resources in the archaeology of Pompeii, manipulating the authority of the real to alter the imaginative experience of visitors to the rediscovered city: he reanimates and renames the cast, anonymous bodies and empty houses. The archaeologist who becomes a politician with an agenda of rebuilding the aesthetics of the city is funded by and stocks the British Museum as a national repository of the Empire's material culture, a place to educate the people's aesthetic experience. The architect who made an archaeological discovery, which he incorporated in reconstructed form into his buildings, reconstructs the fragments of a classical ideal, brought home from abroad and built into the British Museum, an assertion of the importance of the classical past for modern British, elite cultural identity. For German philhellenism, with its genealogy back to an Indo-European, Aryan racial origin, this cultural identity had a heightened nationalist charge. Before the disciplines are fully professionalized and demarcated, novelist, architect, archaeologist, museum curator, exhibition organizer, exhibition handbook writer, politician, traveller, diplomat, from within their different and overlapping institutional contexts, share and mutually inform a discourse that seeks to restore a historically self-conscious engagement with the past through a reconstruction of the fragments of the material culture of the past. This is the aesthetic politics of restoration at work: making the buried life of things speak a script.

IV Seeing the past

In 1851, Queen Victoria and Prince Albert held the 'Restoration Ball'. This was the third costume ball which the royal couple hosted at Buckingham Palace, and guests were invited to attend in the dress of the time of Charles II. Queen Victoria's costume was silver-grey, watered silk taffeta over a shimmering brocade petticoat, with the distinctive deep lace collar and cuffs of the Restoration period (as the current exhibition guide describes it). Albert's orange silk number was even more florid (Plate 4). Queen Victoria had a particularly close association with Scotland, and dressing as a Stuart 'allowed Queen Victoria and Albert to play out their inheritance of the Scottish throne',[111] and Albert to appear as a fully English monarch. The clothing 'performed a genealogy'. This performance, as with the performance of Greek plays later in the century, made a virtue of archaeological, historical accuracy. The costumes for the 1842 ball were devised by a theatrical designer, J. R. Planché: 'Tissues must be woven expressly – spurs, weapons, and jewelry modelled and manufactured on purpose . . . boots, shoes, gauntlets, hose, nearly every article of apparel must be made to order.'[112] The reconstruction of medieval costumes had to be thoroughgoing and authentic, and, with a full show of scholarship, manuscript sources from the British Museum are cited in the magnificent souvenir volume.[113] Albert came as Edward III, the founder of the Order of the Garter, Victoria as Queen Philippa of Hainault, in costumes inspired by their effigies in Westminster Abbey, and they enacted the historical meeting with Anne of Bretagne (played by the Duchess of Cambridge). A magnificent portrait of the couple in costume was promptly commissioned by the Queen from Landseer. Bulwer Lytton with his customary flair for fictional self-dramatization came dressed as his own ancestor. Lady Ernest Bruce came as Rebecca from *Ivanhoe* (though it is unclear whether she danced with Ivanhoe in the Waverley Quadrille). Poor Mr Wylde, one of the Prince's equerries, made the unfortunate choice of a full suit of steel armour. The ball, as one paper gushed, 'restored in vivid truthfulness the long-departed glory of the middle ages'.[114]

Dressing up was a Victorian fascination, made thrilling by the insistent investment in the proprieties of outward appearance as a criterion of social evaluation. As Lady Eastlake commented in 1847: 'Dress becomes a sort of symbolic language – a kind of personal glossary – a species of body phrenology';[115] and Carlyle in *Sartor Resartus* made dressing up integral to his extraordinary social satire: 'Man's earthly interests are hooked and

buttoned together, and held up, by clothes'.[116] But these full-scale performative reconstructions added elements of ritual theatricality and social display that made them events of a broader cultural and even political
significance. Charles X of France, who reigned from 1824 until he was
deposed in the July Revolution of 1830, was committed to restoring the
values of the pre-Revolutionary royalist era in 'an attempt to remedy the
ravages of time and undo the damages of the intervening years'. So, in an
extraordinary ceremonial display, he 'went so far as to reinstate royal rituals
of medieval vintage such as bestowing a magically healing touch on scrofula
patients'.[117] The reconstruction of medieval ritual is an attempt to bolster
the irredeemably collapsing monarchy, as if the ceremonials of the divine
right of kings could dress over the wounds of the revolution.

The turn back to the age of medieval chivalry for a costume party was as
value-laden a choice as the selection of the Restoration. The reconstruction
of medieval costumes was a gesture within a more general reconstruction of
British history that privileged the imperial splendour of Elizabethan triumphs and the harmonies of medieval society woven through the Church,
the chivalrous crusaders, and the dignity of medieval artistic production: an
idealized picture of Merrie England as a model for contemporary projections of social good.[118] The Queen's ball was expressly established to
provide work for impoverished weavers, but its politics – the ball was held
ten days after the spectacle of the Chartists' march to Parliament – was also
viewed more leerily: as Sarah Tooley later lamented, 'There were papers
which printed the costs of the Court pageants in one column, and gave the
list of those who were dying of starvation in another.'[119]

The most lavish, absurd (the description is Queen Victoria's), and publicly discussed performance of reconstruction was the Eglinton Tournament
of 1839 – a re-enactment of a medieval joust, held at Eglinton Castle in
Scotland and attended on the first day by 100,000 spectators. A painful
tension within the concept of restoration can be heard in the most laudatory
account of the tournament: 'It was not a theatrical representation, got up for
the hour, to capture and deceive the eye, but it was an actual representation
of a real event.'[120] It was 'bringing back to Eglinton Castle the reality as well
as the reminiscence of the fifteenth and sixteenth centuries'. The category of
the real, the authentic, the actual is rather desperately invoked for the
Etonians in hired armour – and many other spectators testified to a far
less embracing sense of the theatricality of the day.

The immediate inspiration was the huge popularity of Walter Scott's
novel *Ivanhoe*, and, tellingly, Lord Eglinton himself modestly reflected back
on his grandiose project, 'I have, at least, done something towards the

revival of chivalry.'[121] The preparations for the joust were lengthy. In 1838, a list of 150 prospective knights was whittled down to 40 largely aristocratic heroes (most were put off by the expense of the armour: Lord Glenlyon spent the huge sum of nearly £350 on his own costume and £1,000 on his retinue). There was daily training in London, and 19 knights attended a dress rehearsal in a garden on the road to Golders Green, watched by a carefully selected elite audience of over 2,000 spectators. The success of the sunny, well-organized, and politely fought dress rehearsal was a false omen. On the day itself, the unexpectedly huge crowds, excited by the anticipation in the press, many incongruously dressed in costumes from a range of eras, crammed all available accommodation, blocked the roads and turned the paths of the estate into muddy chaos.[122] Lord Eglinton had widely publicized his offer of free tickets, but his initial expectation of 4,000 spectators turned out to be a wild underestimation (even though he refused tickets to those suspected of not being true Tories). The parade of knights was meant to start at noon. But they had not rehearsed together; dressing took far longer than expected, no-one had anticipated that with only one path the knights would have to go and return on the same route. In the end, the parade was half a mile long, three hours late, and gridlocked from the start.

The biggest disaster, however, was the weather. At the very moment of the parade's start, a violent thunderstorm broke. The knights were soaked, the ladies returned to their carriages, the spectators took what shelter they could, with umbrellas if lucky. The grandstand roof leaked. The fields were turned to mud pools. It was hard for anyone to remain dignified exemplars of chivalry (as the newspapers gleefully reported) when trying to protect their knightly plumes from the rain. As Lycion, the lead character in Edward Fitzgerald's novel *Euphranor*, mocked, it was an 'absurd thing' when the knights 'threw down their lances and put up umbrellas'.[123] Even Aikman, whose celebratory description begins with a lengthy and glorious paean to chivalry and to the family of Lord Eglinton 'that their genealogy stretches into the remote regions of antiquity, and that their scutcheon is emblazoned with many heroic deeds', found the whole thing 'melancholy', 'ludicrous', a 'misery', a 'disappointment', a 'mortification'.[124] Even the banquet had to be cancelled. The remaining days of the tournament had better weather, and far smaller audiences. When the fighting did begin, however, the Knight Marshall had to separate the Marquis of Waterford, a famously drunken brawler and vandal, and Viscount Alford, a young Tory MP, who engaged too earnestly in the violence (they had been at Eton together).[125] There were many writers and artists who found the event laughable, but Louisa Stuart, who went on to marry the dashing reprobate Waterford, responded as the

WAITING FOR IT TO LEAVE OFF TO BEGIN.

5.9 *Burton's Gentleman's Magazine and American Monthly Review, 1840.*

organizers had hoped: 'the procession into the lists, and the tilting, the
mêlée, were such beautiful sights as one can never expect to see again'.[126] So
Aikman rejoiced, 'the dullest eye glistened with delight'.[127] The magazines
may have had a field day – Figure 5.9 makes the obvious joke – but Plate 5
shows that the romanticism of the event could still be painted.

Although the Eglinton Tournament was organized and fought largely by
the very highest levels of the aristocracy (the Queen, however, despite earlier
rumours to the contrary, did not attend), the size of the crowd and the
general interest in the event indicates a far wider engagement. There were
commemorative jugs and cups and plates manufactured on an industrial
scale; scent bottles, jigsaws and waistcoats designed to celebrate the occasion; and not only was there a huge press coverage of the preparations and

the aftermath as well as the tournament itself, but also a host of illustrations were produced. A good handful of the aristocrats had portraits painted in their armour; there were commemorative pictorial volumes of the whole event; and a large number of mass-produced images for broader circulation. (Amid those who mocked or praised the event were many who made a living from it.) Even those who sneered at the pageant saw it in terms of its chivalric aims: Fitzgerald's *Euphranor* concludes it was 'only an affair of old armour with little of the essence of chivalry about it';[128] John Richardson in *The Times* commented: 'The age of chivalry, for the present, has certainly departed.'[129] It is very much on its own terms, by the 'essence of chivalry', that the event was publicly judged. There was also a wider politics at stake, however. For Charles Mackay, a reporter for the *Morning Chronicle*, the affair was no more than upper-class, silly posturing: he reported himself 'utterly weary of the Tournament and its frivolous and scarcely picturesque unrealities'.[130] No authenticity or higher purpose here. By contrast, Disraeli, who missed the Tournament because he was on his honeymoon, saw the reconstruction as part of a broader social and religious revival. The Tournament at Mountfort, a thinly disguised Eglinton, has a prominent place in his novel *Endymion*, where one character declares:

A great revivification. Chivalry is the child of the Church; it is the distinctive feature of Christian Europe. Had it not been for the revival of Church principles, this glorious pageant would never have occurred. But it is a pageant only to the uninitiated. There is not a ceremony, a form, a phrase, a costume, which is not symbolic of a great truth or a high purpose.[131]

Disraeli's list – ceremony, form, phrase, costume – brings together the rituals, clothes, language, and social process which make 'revivification' – restoration, reconstruction – an idea which links so many apparently disparate aspects of culture into a significant 'great truth', a 'high purpose' for nineteenth-century thinkers. This high purpose was linked – for Disraeli – to a Conservative awareness of historical value vested in religion and the old ways. This is the period of reform, of challenge to the position of the aristocracy, and Lord Eglinton represents the most conservative opposition to radicalism. Eglinton's tournament was 'a symbol of Tory defiance, of aristocratic unity, a hatred of the Reform Bill, of protest against the sordid, heartless, sensuous doctrines of Utilitarianism',[132] a knowing performance of a politically charged look backwards. And it was consequently attacked in the Liberal/Whig press precisely as a mere aristocratic entertainment, frivolous and insulting at the time of the bitter conflicts of Chartism, and the social and economic crisis underlying them.

Even Robert Owen, the Scottish social reformer, wanted to get a look in. He wrote a public letter to Lord Eglinton (published in *The Northern Star and Leeds General Advertiser*, which it is hard to imagine Eglinton reading with any regularity, but Owen also prudently sent a copy to the lord himself). It listed twelve points of political principle, which he wanted Lord Eglinton to read aloud to the assembled spectators.[133] The point is not that Owen seriously imagined that Eglinton would indeed recite the manifesto to the assembled aristocratic knights, but that the readers of the paper were to be encouraged to view the event as an opportunity for thinking about political community (which is exactly how Lord Eglinton described the Tournament in his speech at the final dinner, though in terms of a feudal Conservative social order). Owen is an extreme and radical case, for sure, but he also demonstrates how the reconstruction of the battle-ground of chivalric knights becomes the battleground for the reconstruction of historical value for contemporary society. The multiform responses to the Eglinton Tournament – celebration, scorn, political projection, and a host of other misrecognitions – charge it with a particularly complex and contested political significance as a cultural event.

The Tournament at Eglinton marks a summit of the nineteenth-century visual reconstruction of the past, a performance watched by thousands of spectators, and rehearsed in hundreds of subsequent reproductions and memorials. New technologies of visual representation, however, dedi-cated in many cases to the reconstruction of other places and other times, were a distinctive feature of the Victorian city. Reconstruction shades into illustration, especially where historical imagery in books is concerned; but public exhibitions and shows, especially panoramas and dioramas, took reconstruction to a new level of sophistication and technological achievement.

The panorama was patented by Robert Barker in 1787, and with his son, Henry, a far better painter, he opened the first commercial panorama in Leicester Square in 1794. The panorama brought the spectator through a dark passage into a large rotunda, lit from above, to be surrounded by a huge canvas painting that encircled the rotunda. Henry Barker teamed up with John Burford, a pupil of his father's, and they ran the Leicester Square business successfully into the 1860s. There were many imitators (though few that had the purpose-built, fully circular building for the complete panoramic experience), and there were many variations – Cyclorama, Diorama, Europerama, Cosmorama, Neorama, Nausorama, Octorama, Physiorama, Typorama, Udorama, Uranorama, Eidophusikon – that also used a similar visual technology to Barker's panorama, though without their regular success.[134] The largest such construction in London was the Colosseum in Regent's Park designed by Thomas Hornor. It opened in 1832 after years of financial and practical difficulties, all of which, reported in the press, greatly increased public interest. Its star attraction was the view of London from the top of St Paul's (Hornor had some years before made 200 sketches from the scaffolding on the cathedral during its repairs, a feat also reported at length in the press). The first passenger elevator in London could carry ten or twelve people to a platform in the centre of the dome of the rotunda, from where 'you cast a glance into the terrific depth around. And obliged almost to reason with yourself, to be persuaded that it is not nature, instead of a work of art on which you are bestowing your admiration.' The painting showed London and its environs as they could be seen for twenty miles around (under perfect conditions). 'Everything was depicted with microscopic particularity', and the effect was absolutely 'hypnotic', 'all-engulfing'.[135] The Colosseum was a sensation.

The Colosseum never recouped the huge costs of its construction, and it declined into a shoddy showroom and pleasure dome, sold on and refitted first in 1843 (with a 300-foot reproduction on silk of Elgin's marbles of the frieze from the Parthenon), and ending up in the 1850s as a theatre. Although it was a grand building with a hefty admission charge, it did not attract the sort of contested political response that Eglinton stimulated. The *Penny Magazine*, a paper for working men, was happy to celebrate it as encapsulating ' "the best possessions of civilization" and the accumulated advantage of the British people'.[136] Yet it changed the expectations of spectatorship. For the first time, it was possible to get a bird's eye view of the city in its extraordinary extensiveness. For many of the panoramas, guidebooks were produced to direct the experience of viewing. The vast confusion of London was laid out to an ordering, sovereign gaze. Reconstructions of battle scenes gave the viewer the sort of comprehension Tolstoy in *War and Peace* denies to any participant in the battle (though Wellington was said to have enjoyed seeing reconstructions of Waterloo at the Leicester Square panorama). As *The Times* reflected, a panorama gave 'a completeness and truthfulness not always to be gained from a visit to the scene itself'.[137] Reconstructions of foreign cities or majestic topographical scenes added the awe of the exotic to the sublime experience. These reconstructions reordered the viewing experience, and, as the American visitor quoted above indicates, it was a self-aware process where recognizing the startlingly new perspective was itself part of the thrill of the experience. This shift of perspective, enabled by the new technology, is a formative element in the construction of the historically self-aware Victorian subject, seeing oneself seeing.

These panoramic reconstructions also staged the scenes of reconstruction I have been discussing in this chapter. So Vauxhall Gardens had a large-scale reconstruction of Vesuvius, the volcano that buried Pompeii, in front of which firework displays were held in the evening. Panoramas offered Canterbury Cathedral and other churches to a close view through the years of the restoration debates. But no site was more caught up in this culture of reconstruction than Jerusalem and the Holy land, where this chapter began. As Mr Poole – 'the Panoramist, the Stereoramist, the Dioramist, and all the other "ramists"' – lamented in an interview to the *Pall Mall Gazette*: 'They always ask for the Sepulchre.'[138] When the Great Exhibition opened in 1851, there were three competing views of Palestine, 'A Grand Moving Diorama of the Holy Land' in the Egyptian Hall at the Exhibition itself, a 'New and Magnificent Diorama of Jerusalem and the Holy Land' at St George's Gallery, Hyde Park Corner, and a much-used Jerusalem Panorama at Leicester Square. Such panoramas also toured the provinces (and abroad). At the same time, models of the churches or city of Jerusalem also toured with great success, often accompanied by expository and evangelical talks. Lantern-slide performers repeatedly advertised lectures on the Holy Land. Exhibitions in town halls staged oriental markets, reconstructions of famous facades, and other fragments of eastern archaeological tourism. 'Many have long desired to visit the Holy Land, but now', one show advertised, 'Palestine has come to them.' In 1892 alone, Palestine exhibitions were held in Woodbridge, Plymouth, Croydon, Norwich, Clifton, Tunbridge Wells, Cambridge, Cheltenham, Bath and Stroud (Figure 5.10 is Stroud in 1892). Although more than 60 such exhibitions had been held around the country, in 1907 the Islington show still attracted 350,000 visitors. As Eitan Bar-Yosef remarks, the English school nativity play with tea-towels on the head to mark Oriental authenticity, finds its roots in these town hall reconstructions of Eastern bazaars.[139] In Chautauqua, up-state New York, in 1874, as we saw in chapter 3, a new religious group constructed a large-scale topographical model of Palestine as the icon of its community;[140] each World's Fair had its Middle Eastern display – often with a full-scale reconstruction of major buildings as well as 'typical' scenes.[141] From children chanting the geography of Palestine in Sunday School, to the rebuilding of a model of the Dome of the Rock to be visited by millions of visitors at a World's Fair, the reconstruction of the Holy Land filled the imaginative space of nineteenth-century culture.

It is hard, here too, to keep religion, politics and Empire from the project of reconstruction. It was a 'mockery that . . . damage[s] national honour and

5.10 Palestine and Eastern Exhibition, Stroud (1892): a very British suk.

propriety', thundered the Sublime Porte, that an Englishman tried to collect boats and exotic Turkish subjects to create a live panorama back in London.[142] It was also a statement of English, imperial and national identity, based on superiority and a dismissive disregard for the Eastern other. From the display of live natives in reconstructed native villages, to the museum dioramas (in the modern sense of a three dimensional model) designed to allow an easy transition from the scenes of animals to the scenes of pygmies or bushmen, reconstructed scenes are there to be stared at in order to locate the self through the captured image of the other – whose reality (hence the value of reconstruction) validates the work of self-formation as authentic and natural.[143] Reconstructions of Jerusalem and the Holy Land allow and require the viewer to perform a religious self-positioning.

Hence, finally, we return to the religious and imperial politics of restoration in the Middle East. The English 'Palestine Exhibitions' were organized by Samuel Schor, who was born to converted parents in Jerusalem, and his shows and lectures were sponsored by the London

Society for Promoting Christianity among the Jews, which had a strong missionary presence in both London and the Holy Land.[144] From at least the 1840s, the mission to convert the Jews was directly connected with a political and religious plan to resettle the Jews in Jerusalem. In 1840, against the background of the blood-libel massacre in Damascus, *The Times* published a series of letters and articles supporting the restoration of the Jews to Palestine (with the nice demurral that it should be checked whether the Jews actually wished to return to Zion).[145] As Britain became more involved with the Holy Land through archaeology – all too often to an imperial agenda – its heroes, like Captain Warren, followed the same Restorationist principle. Warren, as we have seen, demanded that Britain should lead the race to take over Palestine – which, he underlined with shockingly insouciant economic and political realism, would soon be 'in the market' – but they should engage in such imperial policy 'with the avowed intention of gradually introducing the Jew, pure and simple, who is eventually to occupy and govern the country'.[146] Restorationism combines the biblical prophecy that the Second Coming would take place only after the Jews had returned to a rebuilt Jerusalem and converted, with the Victorian imperial willingness to realign populations and boundaries. It was a project passionately supported by many leading English politicians, including the Earl of Shaftesbury, and constitutes the historical and religious framework within which the Balfour declaration has to be seen. The Holy Land, in Herderian terms, was the land which would make the Jews a proper nation. This project was an integral part of the idealism of Victorian political, theological and intellectual culture (though not for the majority of Jews). George Eliot in her novel *Daniel Deronda* captures the projected ideal beautifully with her hero's commitment to restoration: 'The idea that I am possessed with is that of restoring a political existence to my people, making them a nation again, giving them a national centre, such as the English have, though they too are scattered over the face of the globe.'[147] As we have seen throughout this chapter, from tea towels to armour, from panoramas to the exhibitions of the Crystal Palace, from the sculptures of the British Museum to the facades of churches, the materiality of history is mobilized in the service of an idealized time to come: restoration as an idea is forged between religion, archaeology, linguistics, history, aesthetics and politics, as an ideal that promotes revolutionary modernity through a turn to the deep, but determinative past, which needs fulfilment in a projected future, as an answer to the ills of today.

V Conclusion

The concept of Restoration and its poorer sibling Reconstruction (with cousins Revival and Reanimation) are central discursive organizers of nineteenth-century culture, with an impact that lasts into contemporary social, religious, political and aesthetic divisions. We could say that we have traced the use of the idea of restoration/reconstruction through the different privileged arenas of nineteenth-century thinking – church and politics, philology and critical history, architecture and archaeology, nationalism and narrative fiction, popular culture and elite display, familial and national inheritance – a shared thread, that is, through the disciplines and across social structures. But this would be to misread the institutional and conceptual work that these concepts are performing, for all that it is true enough that restoration / reconstruction are terms with significant purchase across a huge range of thinking and practice in the nineteenth century. For the professional regulation of the disciplines (and with it the hardening of boundaries between them) is taking place over the nineteenth century, and the language of restoration / reconstruction is one way in which this process is taking shape.[148] Debates over restoration and reconstruction are not so much 'interdisciplinary' as one way in which the disciplines are being formulated as disciplines. Hence the sometimes easy and sometimes bitterly contested overlap between arguments which we would call religious, political, cultural, scientific, when restoration and reconstruction are invoked. It is through the idea of restoration, for example, that architecture discusses the degree to which religious belief is or is not part of architectural practice: the discipline is shaped by these discussions, within formal institutions, the journals, and in more marginal arenas. Hence arguments about restoration and reconstruction turn easily to questions of (professional) authority and authorization.

The reason why these ideas of restoration and reconstruction have such a broad efficacy is, then, the work of thought they enable across a range of interlinked areas. I have described the general structure of restoration as a self-consciously modern, progressive stance: an ideal that promotes revolutionary modernity through a turn to the deep, but determinative past, which needs fulfilment in a projected future, as an answer to the ills of today. Consequently, authenticity is a key criterion of evaluation and contestation. The authentic past is the guarantor of an authentic and hoped-for future. What such claims of authenticity set at stake is a person's national, individual, cultural sense of self as a historical being. Reconstruction and restoration, that is, are signs and symptoms of how a historical self-consciousness is to be enacted. They are notions integral to how the nineteenth century conceptualized, experienced and performed a relationship between the historical past and the present.

Restoration and reconstruction always enacted an idealized version of a historical past, for all the compromises and failures any particular project might have involved. Yet, the projects of restoration and reconstruction were contested and provocative precisely because of competing notions not just of what the past itself was like (the Rankean principle of 'wie es eigentlich gewesen ist'), but also of what the political, aesthetic, national, emotional significance of the past could be for the present, and, consequently, for a person's self-positioning as a historical subject. Reconstructions and restorations were repeatedly re-presented in textual discussions and visual forms, an intermedial debate about the sense of history's impact.[149] These debates crossed genres, class boundaries, confessional boundaries and professional interests. Reconstruction and restoration became for Victorian culture, therefore, a key battleground to dramatize why history mattered to the nation, and, in particular, how the materiality of historical things embodied the past and thus demanded attention, care, engagement.

Restoration aims to remove the increments of time to find an authenticity of the original; reconstruction hopes to create an authentic version of an original from the fragments or ruins of a lost past. Both practices in the nineteenth century depended on new orderings of knowledge and new technologies. The roof of the Church of the Holy Sepulchre could not be reconstructed without new steel casting and new building techniques. But it also could not have happened as it did without a new sense of the importance of church architecture for the self-definition of the modern subject, a specific commitment to an imperial vision, a willing political and aesthetic boldness actively to create an image of the past that answered to ideological, genealogical needs. The rediscovery of the *Nibelungenlied* or the *Kalevala* answered a profound longing for a nationalist mythological epic; and its reconstruction required and found authority from contemporary, post-Lachmanian philological science. The Parthenon emerged as a fresh white visual icon of Philhellenic idealism hand in hand not just with the new science of archaeology, but also with a German national engagement with Greece, and a Greek search for national independence and identity. For many years, the restoration of the Jews had been an aim of the militant Church; it is only in the nineteenth century that Restorationism first conjoined political will, imperial agency, religious fervour with the potential of the technology of transportation and communication to make such a project possible. New tools and new questions served to make a new world. Reconstruction and restoration were ways of giving form to a historical sense of the past in the present. The physical world, the world of things, became the means and the matter of history, history embodied, experienced, projected: the buried life of things.

Coda

A final dig

I began this book with a picture of a Victorian drawing-room, represented by Mrs Gaskell through the eyes of her heroine in *North and South*, as if it had been preserved by an entombment under lava, like Pompeii, and excavated a millennium later – an image of aesthetic, emotional and political estrangement from the present. I want to end with an image of digging from the land, which will open a further, final vista onto the Victorian engagement with the material culture of history.

Edward White Benson was a dominating and frightening personality, an intense Protestant of unshakeable public belief and commitment. He rose from the obscurity of an impoverished childhood and improvident parents to become Archbishop of Canterbury at the height of Victoria's power and at the height of the association of the Church of England with the institutions of government and crown.[1] He was married to Mary Sidgwick (always known as Minnie), from the celebrated Sidgwick clan of Cambridge intellectual grandees.[2] He had proposed to her when he was twenty-three and she was only twelve years old (and she was sitting on his lap at the time, and he kissed her), and they were married when she was eighteen, and he had just been appointed headmaster of the new school of Wellington College, established under the patronage of Prince Albert. She was the same age as his sixth-form pupils. They had six children, two of whom to their parents' long-lasting despair died in their youth. The remaining four all disappointed the Archbishop in varying forms of rebellion and emotional disorder – and none were married or had children. Mary Benson, who was erotically passionate about women throughout her pious life, ended her time, after the Archbishop's early death from a heart attack in church at Gladstone's Harwarden, living with and sleeping in the same bed as Lucy Tait, the daughter of Archbishop Tait, who had been so instrumental in the Public Worship Regulation Act. Edward White Benson in one sense epitomized a grand Victorian career, moving from relatively ordinary origins into a fellowship at Trinity College, Cambridge, then into school-teaching as a headmaster in the pioneering tradition of Thomas Arnold, and then into the Church, where he rose to the centre of institutional power. In another sense, he is a quite extraordinary figure, whose bouts of depression

184

scarred his family life, and whose family became, despite or because of his fierce evangelical domination, an icon of sexual, religious and intellectual transgression, or, at least, of the transition from mid-Victorian earnestness into the uncertainties of modernity.

Edward White Benson's first really major religious appointment was as Bishop of Truro. This was an especially exciting opportunity because Truro was the first cathedral to be founded in Britain since Salisbury Cathedral in 1220 and Benson was to be its first bishop. It brought for Benson an opportunity not just to found a new institution of Christianity but also to live out his evangelistic zeal with a new region to bring into his fold. He threw himself into the job with characteristic energy and ambition – a stirring image of Victorian imperial thrustingness and progress. It was, typically enough, taken as a sign of the new era of Victorian Britain that a new cathedral, a project so bold and at such a grand scale, could be established. Benson himself dismissed accusations against the project's extravagance with a telling turn to ancient Greece: 'The one man whom the ancients describe to us as ... the very author and model of domestic economy is he who built the Parthenon – Pericles, the Athenian.'[3] The see was established in 1876, the bishop consecrated in 1877, and the building, after the necessary fund-raising and design discussions, was started in 1880. The service of consecration took place in 1887, by which time Edward White Benson had become Archbishop of Canterbury.

The architect of the building was John Loughborough Pearson, already a renowned figure in the Gothic revival movement, and the design was formed resolutely in the tradition of the movement's understanding of Gothic principles. Pearson had been the architect for the restoration of Lincoln Cathedral, where Benson had been Canon Chancellor, and there are clear resemblances between Truro and Lincoln, as well as the great cathedrals of northern France. For the first time, an architect from the restoration movement could create in England a cathedral from scratch according to his idealization of the past.[4] Unlike all the great cathedrals, which were its models, Truro could be of a piece, a single, synchronous design (though it has since been extended and ... restored). Integral to this design was the stained glass. It is one of the great monuments of a genre of Victorian art that has not yet been studied with enough comprehensiveness or rigour, although it transformed the physical appearance of so many churches in the nineteenth century.[5] The glass of Truro is a truly remarkable piece of work by Clayton and Bell, the leading firm for the Gothic revival: Clayton was trained by Scott, introduced to Bell by Salvin, and their partnership worked with all the major restorationist architects.[6] It is but one small window from this masterpiece that I wish to consider finally here.

The sequence of glass, in simplest terms, as the cathedral authorities themselves declare,[7] represents the history of the church from its foundations to the establishment of Truro Cathedral itself – it ends indeed with a fine image of Benson and the contemporary foundation, in full medieval guise. A material account of history ... It was thematically designed by Benson specifically for the new church, although, after his elevation to Canterbury, a committee saw the installation through to its conclusion, with the inevitable push and shove of pious argument and alteration. But, as we have seen throughout this book, there are few subjects so charged and so open to ideological manipulation for a Victorian theologically informed audience than the history of the church. Truro is no exception.

This is seen most strikingly at either side of the west door. On the north side, there is an extraordinary trio of images of John Keble, F. D. Maurice and Henry Martyn. This is a pointedly constructed symposium. Keble may have been in the minds of hundreds of thousands of Christians through the poetry of *The Christian Year*, which from its publication in 1827 was one of the best-loved and widest selling books of poetry in the nineteenth century; but he was also the founding father of the Oxford Movement.[8] F. D. Maurice was an inspiration to many Christian intellectuals as a Christian Socialist; but he had been sacked from King's College London, because of his heterodox views on eternal punishment, and remained a rebellious figure in the view of many evangelicals in particular.[9] Henry Martyn is less well known today, but is a hero of the Christians of Truro.[10] He was born in 1781, and his father was a mine captain at Gwennap (a few miles west of Truro). He became a convinced evangelical, missionary Christian, after meeting Charles Simeon at Cambridge, and he not only went to the East to proselytize, leaving his one true love behind unfulfilled, but also translated the gospels into Urdu, Persian and Judaeo-Persian, and the Psalms and the Book of Common Prayer into Urdu. He died from a fever in Tokat in Turkey on his way home in 1812. Below the three men is a further image of Martyn debating points of translation with turbaned Persians. In the baptistery there is an extraordinary sequence of the life of Martyn, as if he were a saint, complete with a thoroughly medievalizing climactic representation of his burial (Plate 6). Martyn's epitaph was composed by Macaulay and his life and letters edited by Samuel Wilberforce: he was a paradigm of the pioneering missionary for a period besotted with the idea of the Christian mission.[11] The combination of these three figures by the west door is a fascinating snap shot: a Tractarian, a Christian Socialist and a philological missionary, each exemplary of a strand of Christian life in the nineteenth century, each a remarkable figure, but together offering a surprisingly ecumenical picture of inspirational counter-trends to main-stream Anglican religiosity.

The imagery on the south side of the door might seem equally surprising for an Anglican cathedral. It shows John Wesley, his brother Charles Wesley, and Samuel Walker. Samuel Walker (1714–61) is another local hero – curate of St Mary's, the church on whose site the cathedral was built. Walker had an archetypal Damascene conversion, and became a close friend of John Wesley. 'The transformation in the life style and preaching of Walker provoked much hatred, opposition and persecution',[12] but he seems to have been a remarkably successful preacher, and stayed within the Anglican church, despite his Methodist sympathies and the sometimes bitter resistance to him in the Church itself. Wesley was a frequent visitor to Cornwall and had particular success with the miners and other workmen: a striking image below the three men, parallel to Martyn discussing with the Persians, shows Wesley preaching to the miners at Gwennap where Martyn's father worked (Plate 7). Benson himself acknowledged the strength of Methodism in the region: 'He always recognized quite fairly that Methodism had kept religion alive in Cornwall when the Church had almost lost the sacred flame, and he treated Nonconformity as an enthusiastic friend.'[13] Martyn, however, had not been welcome in his home church because he returned from Cambridge 'tainted' with 'Methodism'. Here, too, we see represented both a strong sense of local Christian activity, and a willingness to include figures often seen as resistant to or at least in a combative relation with mainstream Anglican orthodoxy.

Now, throughout Christian history stained glass and paintings in churches have acted as a form of public memorial both of benefactors and of religious leaders, as well as providing an educative and inspirational depiction of the life of Jesus and the saints. The suitability of such imagery has been debated certainly since Paulinus of Nola, and various upheavals of iconoclasm mark in most violent form a continuing anxiety about the powerful effect of such imagery. In the Victorian era, there is a breathtaking expansion of the types of figures on show, individually and as groups. Mansfield College, Oxford, has Vinet, Brown and Schleiermacher, two staunch non-Conformists with a provocative German in a black-suited row (but Mansfield is a non-Conformist college); Wesley himself is shown as a fiery preacher at the Anglican St Botolph's, London and in Sheffield Cathedral;[14] the founders of D'Oyly Carte opera get their window; Archbishop Benson himself is next to Queen Victoria in Canterbury Cathedral. Yet even so, the combination of these particular local and international figures by the west door of Truro Cathedral constitutes a particularly self-aware positioning within Christian history, a narrative of how the nineteenth century has unfolded.

The other windows in the sequence of church history along the nave also have trios of significant figures, which, individually and as a sequence, indicate a particular take on the unfolding history of England, the Anglican Church and Cornwall's part in it. Queen Victoria, an inevitable presence, is squired by General Gordon, devout Christian, imperialist and military hero, and Alfred Lord Tennyson, poet laureate: the divine right, supported by military might and soft power. The eighteenth century is represented by Bishop Joseph Butler, a celebrated theologian, whose *Analogies* defended orthodox Anglicanism against deism; Isaac Newton, the scientist who was also a serious theological writer; and George Frederick Handel, who provided so much of the musical score for Victorian public life. The seventeenth century has a more directly Cornish colouring with Margaret Godolphin, a saintly woman from the court of Charles II, married to a Cornish statesman; Sir Beville Grenville who led the Cornish Royalists during the Civil War; and Sir Jonathan Trelawney, Bishop of Winchester and a Cornishman, who was one of the Anglican leaders of opposition to the Declaration of Indulgence by James II, which would have introduced a religious tolerance into Britain. Indeed, the trial of the seven bishops who opposed the king is a set piece of Thomas Babington Macaulay's history of Britain, a best-seller which for mid-Victorian readers created a narrative of national and imperial self-formation.[15] This window combines piety against the corruption of royal power, the defence of the divine right of kings, and opposition to a royal interference with the religious autonomy and the monopoly of the Anglican Church over public worship: an extended gloss on *noblesse oblige* in its grandest political and moral form. This is matched by the next window which shows Charles I (described in the guide today with a full-blooded rhetoric as 'saint and martyr . . . who might have saved his crown and his life had he abandoned the Church . . . His suffering and death made the causes of Monarchy and Anglicanism sacred to the English people'). He is joined by George Herbert, Anglican priest and poet (as we saw in chapter 2); and Sir John Elliot, leader of the House of Commons which had opposed the king. The imagery and its modern commentary are of a piece in its construction of a one-sided account of what was, after all, a civil war. Thomas Cranmer, John Wycliff and Thomas Coverdale are linked in their commitment to the Bible and Book of Common Prayer in English translation, the cornerstones of the Anglican liturgy; Colet and More, the only pair rather than a trio, are key figures of the English Reformation. Thomas à Kempis, Savanorola and John Huss take us back to the fifteenth century and its turmoils (the last two were burnt as heretics).

Now, each one of these chosen figures, their combination into groupings and the juxtaposition of windows in a sequence, could certainly be expanded into a more detailed exposition of their historical significance, specifically for a late nineteenth-century audience. But enough has been said to underline the two crucial points that need to be made. First, it is typical of the Victorian historical self-consciousness, and a fine example of the way in which history is told through material culture, that the construction of a sequence of images in this newly conceived and built cathedral turns to a representation of the history of the Church itself, culminating self-reflexively with the very construction in which the viewer is standing. It is a history told through great men (and two women), across the centuries, each expected to stand for a turning point in the ecclesiastical narrative. This has no parallel in earlier stained glass.[16] Benson himself, as inaugural headmaster, had also been instrumental in the design of windows for the chapel at Wellington, though these, now largely lost, seem to have been rather obscure biblical scenes, to encourage (he hoped) the boys towards reflection. There are, of course, great sequences of the life of Jesus with typological mirrors from the Hebrew Bible in the paired windows of the chapel of King's College, Cambridge, for example, which Benson and his sons loved, and this has a claim to be a history of things – but this typological narrative demonstrates a quite different sense of history, of the nature of the Church as a historical development, and of the connection between scripture and modernity from Truro. As Benson declared on his enthronement: 'It is no foolish dream, no reverie, no indulgence of fancy, when we look to the old past.'[17]

Second, the history represented is not – and could not be – a simple, orthodox, pietistic account, however naïve or pious some images may appear to a cynical modern spectator. Rather, within the conflicts over the history of the church that we have traced throughout this book, this sequence necessarily represents an engagement with contemporary arguments over the history of the Church. Edward White Benson was instrumental in the design of the sequence. He was himself, typically for the academics and theologians we have met so often in this book, obsessed with the early Church as a model for modernity. Of his own writing, the piece he regarded as his most significant and lasting was a life of Cyprian, the third-century bishop of Carthage. He held strong views on the apostolic succession. It was Archbishop Benson, it will be recalled, who delivered the judgment that paved the way for the increasing acceptance of ritualist worship – a judgment based on the extensive citing of historical sources, a recognition of the determinative history of the Church.

It is within such a historical narrative, then, that the image I wish to discuss is also to be placed (Plate 8). It consists of a small window, which is topped by a far larger picture of a guardian angel. It was completed as late as 1907; and although the towering guardian angel was specified by Benson, this final image was added to the design. It is, however, as we will see, fully and brilliantly within the logic of Benson's agenda. The glass shows four miners working, and is labelled 'Cornish Miners Working at Dolcoath'. A young, angelic boy on the right looks back over his shoulder towards an older man who is pushing a trolley on rails. The boy has an inverted pick over one shoulder, a little like a cross. The man is trudging heavily, and wears a working-man's clothes with a hat and neckerchief. Behind him, and partially concealed by a massive wooden mine prop, there are two further miners digging. The men all work intently, and their faces are characterful and beautifully articulated. The boy seems to mirror and direct our gaze at them, as they all look down at the ground that they are working. Behind them is the recognizable landscape of the hills around Dolcoath, Carn Brea. Above them, the huge guardian angel floats, with a pick over one shoulder (also helping the association with the cross, a more normal angelic orna-ment, or a sword of angelic power) and a Davey lamp in the other hand. The angel's iconography makes him the guardian of the miners.

The poor, always with us, are regularly represented in stained-glass windows, though usually as backdrop figures to the life of Jesus, and often as the sneering and faithless populace that humiliate Jesus on his way to the crucifixion. It is not common, however, to commemorate the poor, and even less common to commemorate the working poor, for all that guilds have their own celebrations and memorials, which also played an important role in the Victorian imaginative reconstruction of the medieval past.[18] It is this striking image of Cornish miners at work that I wish to try to understand.

Truro Cathedral is particularly aware of its role in the community as a building and as an institution for the new Cornish diocese, and it celebrates this local history throughout, as we have already seen with the commemo-ration of Henry Martyn and Samuel Walker in particular, as well as its choice of Cornish figures in its window representing the seventeenth cen-tury. No doubt, one primary aim of this window was to reach out to the local people through a memorial of their best-known industry. This gained added poignancy from an accident at Dolcoath in 1893, which killed seven men. There is a parallel window, also topped by a huge guardian angel, which shows Cornish fisherman – another paradigmatic industry, touched here also by associations not just with the well-known Christian imagery of fish and the fishers of men, but also with the local history of Methodist preaching to the workers at the coast. John Wesley's Methodism also found a particular audience in the working miners and the success of Wesley among the working poor is an integral story of the official biography of the Methodist movement. Wesley indeed did regularly preach to the workers of Cornwall in particular. The miners, like the fishermen, have a role in the church's own history of Cornwall, which further justifies their place in the cathedral's narratives. The pair of images places the dangerous industries of Cornwall under the protection of huge Christian angels, and recalls the mission to the workers, paradigmatic of local Christianity. Its imagery fits Cornish industry well into the teleological sequence of the windows' Christian history. But I think the historical depth of the image goes much deeper than this understandable evangelical thrust. For the choice of the mine of Dolcoath, the largest and best-known copper and tin mine in the region, also looks back to a more ancient history.

It is a frequent trope of the histories of early England that the first visitors to Britain were Phoenicians who came to Cornwall to trade for tin and copper. It is this trade route that provides one basis for the legends of Joseph of Arithamea coming to Glastonbury. Irish genealogists for their part claimed a link for themselves with ancient Palestine via the Phoenicians who made it to Ireland from Galicia following the same trade pathways. Cornish tin and its mining links England to antiquity. So, in 1890 *The Wonderful Adventures of Phra the Phoenician* was published in serial form in the *Illustrated London News* and was the only novel-writing success of Edwin Lester Arnold. It is perhaps not the greatest novel, but it reveals how a sense of historical untimeliness becomes almost a cliché of the era. Phra is a Phoenician, a race who provide a starting point not just for the alphabet, but for many constructed pasts. Phra is visiting England from Egypt in pursuit of Cornish tin, way back in the mists of time, but, when he is faced by death, he falls into suspended animation, and returns – repeatedly – to face another crisis, first as the druids resisting Caesar's Roman forces, then to a Saxon community at the time of the conquest; to join the knights of Edward III; and he ends up finally reawakened in the days of good Queen Elizabeth, the Merrie England of Shakespeare and Empire. He is on each occasion awakened and finds himself amazed at change, and out of kilter with the age, and acutely aware of his own untimeliness. This becomes for him a question of identity – a national identity: 'Was I a Roman, I wondered . . . What was I? Who was I?' Centuries later he concludes comfortingly, 'In truth I was more English than I had thought.'[19] Phra, like Lucian's Anacharsis, is the Eastern outsider, whose bafflement reveals the oddity of the normality of his hosts – but this is now troped through a temporal rather than a spatial or simply cultural matrix. Phra finds it easier to reconcile himself to the present – again and again – than many of his readers seem to have done – but his figuration through contemporary concerns about fitting into time seems clear enough. Like so many characters we have seen in this book, Edwin Lester Arnold is caught up in an anxiety about historical self-understanding. For him, however, the story starts with Cornish tin mining, because it enables him to link the outlying and obscure island of ancient England with the grand narratives of antiquity.

I am sure that Edward White Benson did not read Edward Lester Arnold. He could not even finish his own son's best-selling first novel, which he regarded as too trivial to waste his energy on. But Phra the Phoenician's adventures in Cornwall indicate the importance in the popular imagination of the antiquity of the tin mining industry and its connection with the privileged origins of cultural authority in the antiquity of the East. Here, then, we might see a further sense of the deep historical past emerging in the representation of Cornish miners here in the cathedral of Truro.

The digging miners, then, provide an apt final coda for this excavation of the buried life of things. For all that it was completed in 1907, this small stained-glass widow is a supremely Victorian moment of representation, where history is deeply encoded within the material decoration of a new church. The church itself is built to old models by a restorationist team as a conscious act of historical reconstruction, an ambitious religious and polit-ical gesture within a contest over the place of the Church in society, the role of the past for modernity, and the passions of faith and worship. The window shows working men in an era where industrialization, social con-flict and political revolution had made such an image especially charged. It was constructed in the name of an evangelical bishop renowned for his care and contact with working men, as a gesture, it seems, of building affiliations and commitments in this new community. But it is an image that is also set within the frame of a historical narrative constructed by the cathedral's unique sequence of stained-glass windows. This adds a historical depth to the window's significance. It ties the miners into the local tradition of Methodism and Wesley's celebrated evangelical work among the miners of Cornwall, also celebrated in the other windows. It also allows a long vista back into Cornwall's place in the history of England, as it was told in the nineteenth century, where trade between Phoenician merchants and Cornish tin miners constructed a genealogical link between the early history of England and the privileged origins of culture in the East. That this wonderful piece of stained glass is all too often today regarded as no more than a quaintness seems to capture something of our contemporary loss of understanding of the profound Victorian engagement with the histories of the Church and of classical antiquity and their expression of this engagement in and through the material culture of things. It is something of this loss of understanding which this book has sought to repair.

    This image, thus, epitomizes a set of nineteenth-century concerns that I have been tracing throughout this book. It also captures a range of questions that has motivated the project. First, although I have focused on things, things require people to make them talk, even and especially within the rhetoric which insists that 'things speak for themselves'. The sequence of windows was conceptualized by Edward White Benson (and made by Clayton and Bell); and Benson's conceptualization is both located within its specific cultural context – he is, of course, 'of his time' – and the product of a specific and individual engagement with that context; and the meaning of the windows over time is also produced by a set of spectators, who engage partially, in all senses, with their imagery. The cast of characters and biographies that run through this book are all testimony to how individuals have invested in the semantics of things. I emphasize this perhaps obvious point for two reasons. On the one hand, it allows us to see how important *desire* is to the buried life of things: the need for restoration, the search for historical meaning, the longing for an ideal, the melancholia of loss, the repression of blindness, make things speak as they do. The intense emotions that have surfaced in the stories of this book are testimony to the force of this desire. On the other hand, this desire is a constitutive element of a historical subjectivity – seeing and wanting to see oneself located within a historical narrative: placing oneself. In the case of the sequence of windows, this subjectivity is literalized, materialized, in the windows' narrative teleology, which ends with the church itself in which the windows are placed. It is, if you will, Benson's public, historical account of how he came to be where and who he now is. What I have been calling 'historical materiality' is motivated by a desire for historical placement, to have the past make sense of and give a sense of rootedness to the unstable present.

    Second, the miners window's modernity and its echo of a deep, historical past underline how important a particular construction of temporality has been for this book. I suppose all history is told for the present; but these test cases have revealed a more complex hankering for what has been lost and for what might be, more complex, that is, than the simple and familiar assertion that the past provides an exemplary, instructive or genealogical model for the present. Repeatedly, we have seen not just the cliché of Victorian historical self-consciousness, but rather a structuring pattern of an idealized construction of a past that needs restoration to remedy the present – a pattern that becomes a point of contest in which the nature of modernity is set at stake. The fragments of the past need reconstruction to tell history; this history becomes an idealized model to be revivified in the present; because progress depends on appreciating the ideal values of the past which have been lost or corrupted, and which can promise a new future. One insistent desire, thus, is to collapse the gap between past and present, so that the time of the Bible is still present, the architecture of the past surrounds us still, the literature of the past is our modern culture, our national identity fulfils an ancient paradigm. And at every step, this model of engagement with historical time is open to challenge by those who would have buildings slowly decay, who would resist the perspective of faith, commit to a modernist aesthetic, discover a new cosmopolitan brotherhood or sisterhood of class or gender, or insist on the irremediable abyss of geological time, where the ice age has passed for ever. The historical materiality of Victorian modernity makes temporality a battleground of self-definition.

It is within such a context that my focus on forgottenness takes its shape. It is striking how often in the preceding chapters a thing that has flared into passionate significance has been forgotten or turned to dismissed triviality within a short period. It is also integral to the book that I too in my writing have been recovering what has all too often appeared as forgotten people and forgotten worries (and thus potentially open to the charge of scorned irrelevance, nowadays). Stained glass, after all, as a genre, is so easily treated as no more than colourful ornamentation, and really looking at and thinking hard about a stained-glass window, especially a nineteenth-century one, might well mark you out as a crank or obsessive. Victorian stained glass is not, I know, modishly fashionable. The general point, however, stands: that where cultural memory has been the subject of much contemporary research, cultural forgetting has received much less attention. Yet the flip-side of the desire which makes things speak is the drive towards oblivion or obscurity. Things, things in and as history, are less solid, more fragile than the long history of the rhetoric of material permanence would have us credit.

The desire that makes things speak of the past, and the fragile temporality of the significance of such things, betoken one of the oldest questions of art history – it certainly goes back at least to the fourth century BCE[20] – namely, how an art object can make the invisible visible. Whether the miners window is taken as expressive of the history of the Church, or of the contingencies of this church; or as an evangelical appeal to the mining community; or as a sign of Cornwall's tradition of tin-mining; or as a gesture within the politics of poverty and industrialization; or, as I would insist, as a combination of all these narratives; the glass is significant precisely for the way it cues and provokes thought that goes beyond its visual materiality, its beauty, as it were. The title of this book may be 'The Buried Life of Things', but things do not have a life of their own, simply awaiting the excavator's spade, but always take shape and meaning within a cultural milieu, a cultural milieu which is reciprocally created and moulded by things. Things take on cultural authority because they can be taken to express value, ideology, history; things can lose their authority because this invisible, soft power is not integral to them.

When it comes to telling the story of the past, it is in the nature of things that things are buried, disburied and re-buried, and this book, my partial story of our relationship to the nineteenth-century material culture, contributes to that continuing process, as well as reflecting on it. To attempt to disinter the buried life of things is not just to explore the past's now obscure investments in stuff, but also to bring to light our own contemporary gestures towards Victorian material culture, gestures of engagement and forgetting, misrecognition and resistance, carelessness and obsessiveness, gestures that are never less than a self-defining self-placement before the materials of history.

Notes

Introduction: The buried life of things

1. For this shift see Berg, *Luxury and Pleasure* for the eighteenth-century start, and Cohen, *Household Gods* for the change in the 1860s.
2. Gaskell, *North and South*, 108 [chapter xv].
3. Gaskell, *Charlotte Brontë*, 4. On Gaskell's role in the Brontë myth, see Miller, *Brontë Myth*; and, less critically, the Brontë industry: Fraser, *Charlotte Brontë*; Gérin, *Charlotte Brontë*; Gordon, *Charlotte Brontë*. See also Freedgood, *Ideas in Things*, 55–80 on Gaskell's 'thing culture'.
4. See the exemplary works of Daston ed., *Things that Talk*; Fritzsche, *Stranded in the Present*; Brown, *A Sense of Things*; Brown ed., *Things*; Cohen, *Household Gods*; Freedgood, *Ideas in Things*; Gell, *Art and Agency*, with Osborne and Tanner eds., *Art's Agency*; Plotz, *Portable Property*; and, of course, Briggs, *Victorian Things*.
5. Plotz, *Portable Property* 1 (smartly reviewed by Pettitt in *Victorian Studies* 51, 2009: 766–8).
6. Brilliantly achieved by Price, *Things With Books*, following on from Lamb, *Things Things Say*.
7. See Melman, *Culture of History*; Mitchell, *Picturing the Past*.
8. See, for example, Miller, *Novels Behind Glass*; Watson, *Literature and Material Culture*; Freedgood, *Ideas in Things*; and on American sources, Brown, *A Sense of Things*. Appadurai ed., *Social Life of Things* and Fritzsche, *Stranded in the Present* are especially stimulating for such work; Douglas and Isherwood, *World of Goods* proved foundational.
9. See Higgins, *Under Another Sky* for one such journey.
10. See Boak, *Sacred Stitches*.
11. On classical education see e.g. Stray, *Classics Transformed*; on classical privilege see Richardson, *Classical Victorians*; on the tension between classics and religious commitments see Goldhill, *Victorian Culture*.
12. Freud, *Standard Edition* iii 192; see Orrells, 'Rocks, Ghosts and Footprints'.
13. Koselleck, *Futures Past*; Koselleck, *Conceptual History*; and Fritzsche, *Stranded in the Present*, have been especially important for my thinking here.

1 A writer's things

1. Background in Girouard, *Return to Camelot*, especially 86. On restoration, see chapter 5 below.

2. For the 'toga novels', see Goldhill, *Victorian Culture*, chapter 5; Turner, 'Christians and Pagans' and in general the seminal Rhodes, *Lion and the Cross*; Jenkyns, 'Late Antiquity' is characteristically second rate. On Bulwer Lytton, see Mitchell, *Bulwer Lytton*; Christensen ed., *Subverting Vision* especially the chapter of Brown; each with extensive bibliography of the earlier lives.

3. Oliphant, 'Bulwer', 223.

4. [Kingsley], 'Sir E. B. Lytton', 111.

5. Thackeray, 'Highways', 725.

6. G. Ray ed., *Letters and Private Papers* iii: 181.

7. Armstrong, *Scenes in a Library*; on thing theory, see Brown, 'Thing Theory'; Brown, *A Sense of Things*; Brown ed., *Things*; Gell, (1998) *Art and Agency* with Osborne and Tanner eds., *Art's Agency*; Daston ed., *Things that Talk*; Freedgood, *Ideas in Things*; Plotz, *Portable Property*. A set of questions, rather than a coherent theory . . .

8. See Watson, *Literary Tourist*; (Watson ed., *Literary Tourism* is, however, disappointing). Gill, *Wordsworth* is exemplary, though Bourke, *Romantic Discourse* adds a crucial political dimension. See also Hendrix, *Writers' Houses*; Ousby, *Englishman's England*; and for a later period Fuss, *Sense of an Interior*. For the broader sense of celebrity in the first half of the nineteenth century, see now Mole ed., *Celebrity Culture*.

9. For the 'home as a stage', see Cohen, *Household Gods*, 122–44.

10. See e.g. Hon. Mrs M. M. Maxwell-Scott, *Abbotsford*; Crockett, *Abbotsford*; Crockett, *Scott Country*; Pope-Hennessy, *Laird of Abbotsford*; Shelton Mackenzie, *Sir Walter Scott*.

11. Gaskell, *Charlotte Brontë*.

12. See Marchand, *Down from Olympus*; Schnapp, *Discovering the Past*; Stiebing, *Uncovering the Past*; Challis, *British Archaeologists*; Hoselitz, *Imagining Roman Britain*; Levine, *Amateur and Professional*; Gere, *Prophets of Modernism*.

13. See e.g. Meskell ed., *Archaeologies*; Boivin, *Material Culture*, which is surprisingly unreflective about its use of visual materials, however; the theoretical impact of Clark and Chalmers, 'The Extended Mind', directly and indirectly, is also becoming more influential in cultural studies.

14. Auldjo is briefly discussed by Bulloch, 'Auldjo', with background in Bulloch, 'Family of Auldjo'; by a letter in *The Times* 18 May (1886): 9; a full-length biography has recently appeared – Jamieson, *Auldjo* – but it is very disappointing, only partly because the surviving biographical material is so thin.

15. Now in the Hertfordshire Archives and Local Studies Centre in Hertford.

16. Auldjo, *Narrative of an Ascent*, reprinted in 1830 and 1856 (which is surprisingly not even mentioned by Robertson, 'Mid-Victorians'. He first appeared in

the papers in a scandalous trial, after he had lost a huge sum of money playing cards with some young rakes, who were accused of conspiring to cheat him.

17. Auldjo, *Sketches of Vesuvius*.
18. Auldjo, *Visit to Constantinople*.
19. Gell, *Gell in Italy*, 108, 157. Gell bequeathed Auldjo a pocket sextant, inscribed, as a memorial of their friendship.
20. Bulwer Lytton, *Last Days*, 170. The page numbers here and in subsequent citations are from the 1905 edition published by Funk and Wagnell, London.
21. Gell, *Gell in Italy*; Scott also wrote to Auldjo; see Bulloch, 'Auldjo', 329.
22. The story is made public in *The Times* 18 May (1886): 9.
23. Bulwer Lytton, *Last Days of Pompeii*, xii 'a casual conversation with a gentleman, well known among the English at Naples for his general knowledge of the many paths of life'.
24. The diaries and journals are in the British Library.
25. Bulloch, 'Auldjo', 327. He also took brandy, champagne and some chicken.
26. This letter – which in places is now difficult to read – was transcribed and published in Lytton, *Edward Bulwer*, 445–6.
27. This is the quotation Auldjo put in the case with the skulls when he gave it to Bulwer. Bulwer may have been thinking of Byron's description of a skull here: 'Look on its broken arch, its ruin'd wall, / Its chambers desolate, and portals foul; / Yes, this was once Ambition's airy hall. / The dome of Thought, the palace of the Soul'. *Childe Harold's Pilgrimage*, Canto 11.6.
28. See Davies, *Phrenology*; Cooter, *Cultural Meaning*; Colbert, *Measure of Perfection*; Hartley, *Physiognomy*; van Wyhe, *Phrenology*, and especially Pearl, *About Faces* for the history of physiognomics and phrenology; Tytler, *Faces and Fortunes* discusses the long influence of Lavater in the novel but surprisingly does not mention race; Eastlake, *History of the Gothic Revival* gives a useful snapshot of the *status quaestionis* from mid-century. Quigley, *Skulls and Skeletons*, 99–154 discusses the collection of skulls.
29. Combe, *System of Phrenology*; see also Combe, *Elements of Phrenology* – which also went into several editions. Combe's *Constitution of Man* sold 350,000 copies and was influential in spreading a materialist, and phrenological view of the world: see below p. 19, and, in particular Cooter, *Cultural Meaning*; van Wyhe, *Phrenology*.
30. Davies, *Phrenology*, 120–6.
31. Tuckerman, 'Allusions to Phrenology', 460–1.
32. See in particular Cooter, *Cultural Meaning*, quotation from 86.
33. See Cooter, *Cultural Meaning*; van Wyhe, *Phrenology* for Combe in context.
34. *Examiner* October (1831) cited by Cooter, *Cultural Meaning*, 86.
35. See Goldhill, *Victorian Culture*; Rhodes, *Lion and the Cross*.
36. Bernal, *Black Athena*, 51; the Victorian nature of Bernal's writing is well brought out by Orrells, Bhambra and Roynon eds., *African Athena*.

37. See Taylor, *Diegesis*, published after his spell in prison. Like the Christians in Bulwer's novel, Taylor was famous for walking the streets proclaiming his ideas.

38. Leland, *Memoirs*, 47, on his childhood reading: 'I little thought then that I should in after years be the guest of the author in his home and see the skull of Arbaces.' For the visit see 397–401.

39. Asserted without a source by Leppman, *Pompeii*, 136, for example. Bell, *Introduction*, 104 notes the skull of Arbaces is at Knebworth; Lager, 'Interview', 144 bizarrely claims the skull, kept on the desk, was the inspiration for the character of Arbaces; Mulvey-Roberts, 'Edward Bulwer Lytton', 88: 'in the study of his fantasy Gothicised home, Bulwer kept his opium pipe and Gothic relic of the actual skull of the ancient Egyptian high priest, Arbaces'.

40. See Quigley, *Skulls and Skeletons*, 99–154. Morton, *Crania Aegyptiaca* is the fullest scientific account of Egyptian skulls specifically.

41. See Zimmerman, *Anthropology and Antihumanism*, especially 86–107, 135–46; and, with good bibliography and background, Massin, 'From Virchow to Fischer'. Virchow had to keep many of his collection of 10,000 skulls and skeletons in his house.

42. For the figure of the antiquary see Brown, *Hobby-Horsical*; for the background on the professionalization of the field, see the excellent Levine, *Boundaries of Fiction*.

43. Goode, 'Dryasdust Antiquarianism', 75. In general, see Ferris, *Achievement of Literary Authority*.

44. Irving, *Miscellanies*, 43.

45. Crockett, *Scott Country*, 275; see Crockett, *Abbotsford*, 184–5. Cf. Maxwell-Scott, *Abbotsford*.

46. See Crockett, *Abbotsford*, 184–8.

47. Irving, *Miscellanies*, 57–8.

48. Freud, *Standard Edition* 11: 139. For the metaphor discussed, see Reinhard, 'Freudian Things', 57–79; Ucko, 'Material Culture'; Gamwell and Wells eds., *Freud and Art*; Forrester, 'Freud and Collecting' and Gere, *Prophets of Modernism*, 152–71.

49. Forrester, 'Freud and Collecting' is fundamental.

50. See Armstrong, *Compulsion for Antiquity*, Rudnytsky, *Freud and Oedipus*, and, especially, Leonard, *Socrates and the Jews*.

51. See Gilman, *Freud, Race and Gender*, especially 12–93.

52. See Levine, *Amateur and Professional* and the works cited in n. 12.

53. 'There were only three in the whole of our class to take up medicine, and we scribbled our names on a skeleton which we bought together': Letter from Sigmund, Freud to Martha Bernays, 22 August 1883: Freud, *Letters of Freud*, 41–4.

54. Thanks to Mary Beard and Michael Ledger-Lomas for comments on an early draft of this chapter, and especially to Clare Pettitt and David Gange who read and commented on it.

2 When things matter

1. Stevenson, *Child's Garden of Verses*, poem xxiv, 'Happy Thought'.
2. Berg, *Luxury and Pleasure* is excellent on how the 'product revolution' (5) began in the eighteenth century; Cohen, *Household Gods* is also excellent on how the true explosion of domestic stuff starts only from the 1860s.
3. See especially Brown, 'Rise and Function', Brown, *Society and the Holy* and Brown, *Body and Society*. The Resurrection of the body is an integral article of faith in the Nicene Crede, whose place in the daily prayers was wrangled about by Victorians at length.
4. See Brown, *Body and Society* and *Eye of a Needle* for the ancient background; Janes, *Victorian Reformation* for an interesting slant on a major aspect of the Victorian response.
5. A huge bibliography could be given: good starting points for the evangelical revival are Bradley, *Call to Seriousness*; Bebbington, *Evangelicalism*; Ward, *Evangelical Awakening*; on Tractarianism, Chadwick, *Spirit of the Oxford Movement*; Nockles, *Oxford Movement*; and for a full bibliography Crumb, *Oxford Movement*; in general for the politics see Paz, *Anti-Catholicism*; Parry, *Democracy and Religion*; Machin, *Politics and the Churches*; Reed, *Glorious Battle*.
6. Hall, *Civilizing Subjects* emphasizes well the political control involved in both projects.
7. And abroad, see now Bremner, *Imperial Gothic*.
8. Renan, *Recollections*, 224.
9. Fleming, *Memoir and Select Letters* is the fullest biography, though resolutely uncritical. See also now Scott, 'Britain in the Classical World'.
10. Fleming, *Memoir and Select Letters*, 48.
11. See Levine, *Boundaries of Fiction*; Hingley, *Recovery of Roman Britain*.
12. Fleming, *Memoir and Select Letters*, 7. On the figure of the antiquary, see Brown, *Hobby-Horsical* and the discussion above, pp. 23–4.
13. The scheme of images has been much discussed: see for a representative sample, each with further bibliography: Huskinson, 'Pagan Mythological Figures'; Black, 'Christian and Pagan Hopes'; Henig, *Religion in Roman Britain*, 175–7; Scott, *Villa Mosaics*, 155–66; Perring, 'Frampton Mosaics', who sees a fully gnostic ideology at work. Barrett, 'A Virgilian Scene' identified one figure as an image of Aeneas with reference to Virgil's *Aeneid*.
14. Fleming, *Memoir and Select Letters*, 25.
15. See Hingley, *Imperial Origins*; *Recovery of Roman Britain*; Bell, 'Ancient to Modern'; *Greater Britain*; Vance, *Victorians and Ancient Rome*; 'Anxieties of Empire'; Hoselitz, *Imagining Roman Britain*; Bradley ed., *Classics and Imperialism*; Butler, *Shadow of Rome*; Vasunia, *Colonial India*; and for the American case see Winterer, *Culture of Classicism*. See now on Lysons' nationalism, Scott, 'Britain in the Classical World'.

16. Hingley, *Recovery of Roman Britain*, 259. Koditschek, *Nineteenth-Century Visions* is particularly useful here.
17. Wright, *Early Inhabitants*, 120. Wright will play a significant role in what follows.
18. See Todd, 'Rediscovery'.
19. See Goldhill, *Victorian Culture*, 154–244, with further bibliography.
20. Martin Tupper, the Royal Family's favourite, in 1850, and much cited since, most tellingly in Appiah, *My Father's House*, 47.
21. Wright, *Early Inhabitants*, 296.
22. *Ibid.*, 298.
23. *Ibid.*, 299.
24. Lysons, *Romans of Gloucestershire*, 6. See Poste, *Britannia Antiqua* for a further contemporary attack on Wright. R.W. Morgan, a liberal Anglican, in his *St Paul in Britain* argued that St Paul stayed at Pudens' house – an argument that became part of a case for the disestablishment of the Welsh Church: see Garnett and Bush, 'Rome', 290.
25. Lysons, *Romans of Gloucestershire*, 10.
26. *Ibid.*, 20.
27. Martial XI 53 (cf. VIII 60 where a Claudia, maybe the same woman, is described as being very tall); Martial IV 13 for the wedding; several of Martial's poems seem to be addressed to this Pudens (I 31; IV 29; V 48; VI 58; VII 11; VII 97; XIII 69, and an Aulus is addressed in V 28; VI 78; VII 14; XI 38; XII 51 (though none of the Christian writers mention his apparent passion for young men).
28. The fact that the names of Claudia and Pudens are separated by the name Linus is explained by e.g. Guest, *Origines Celticae* following Ussher, on the grounds that Linus is the son of Claudia and Pudens and to be identified as Linus, bishop of Rome, whose mother's name is given as Claudia [*Apostolic Constitutions* 7.4].
29. Lysons, *Romans of Gloucestershire*, 20.
30. *Ibid.*, 23.
31. Williams, *Ecclesiastical Antiquities*. Lysons owned the book as we can see from Sotheby's sale of his library: *Catalogue of the Valuable Library of the late Rev Samuel Lysons to be sold 12th July 1880*, Sotheby, Wilkinson and Hodge, London, 1880.
32. Pudentiana is supposed to be the daughter of Pudens in Rome, but her cult was suppressed in 1969 because of lack of evidence of her existence. Morgan, *St Paul in Britain*, 109–10 disconcertingly asserts that the 'children of Claudia and Pudens. . . .were brought up on [St Paul's] knees'.
33. Wiseman, *Fabiola*, 186; Wiseman, *Lady Morgan's Statements*, 9–10; Lady Morgan replied to Wiseman only in 1851, a delay best explained by the prominence of Wiseman's appointment in 1850 and the so-called Papal Aggression.
34. Grover, 'Pre-Augustinian Christianity', 224.

35. *Ibid.*, 225. Hesketh, *Making the Past Speak*, shows that historical positivism is being established at the cutting edge of professional historiography in the 1860s.
36. Grover, 'Pre-Augustinian Christianity', 225.
37. *Ibid.*, 225.
38. *Ibid.*, 223.
39. *Ibid.*, 221.
40. See Poste, *Britannic Researches*, 393–5, also attacking Wright.
41. Lysons, *Romans of Gloucestershire*, 15.
42. Lysons, *Claudia and Pudens*. By 1865, his most popular book (Lysons, *British Ancestors*), which went into four editions, was attempting to prove the connection between the language of early Britain and Mesopotamia, in what he calls 'Chaldaeo-British names' – one of the forerunners of Anglo-Israelite ideas.
43. Mercier, *Mother Church*, 6, 39. Mercier, more surprisingly, also wrote an essay comparing *Oedipus* and *Lear* as tragedies.
44. Farrar, *Darkness and Dawn*, 101.
45. Church, *Burning of Rome*; see also de Mille, *Helena's Household*; Webb, *Pomponia*. The Italian poet, Giovanni Pascoli, in 1909 also wrote a long hexameter poem in Latin called *Pomponia Grecina*.
46. Renan, *Anti-Christ*, 3.
47. Ruskin, *Verona*, 108–9.
48. Conybeare, *Roman Britain*, 257, my italics.
49. Von Harnack, 'Christianity and Christians', 263.
50. Lampe, *Christians in Rome*, 196.
51. Alexander, *Ancient British Churches*, 105–7 – for the Religious Tract Society.
52. See Giles, *Ancient Britons*, 194–6.
53. *Morning Post* 5 February (1844).
54. On Salvin, see Allibone, *Anthony Salvin*.
55. Neale, *Letters*, 14 – a letter from Boyce.
56. Boyce, *Memorial*, 10.
57. Neale, *History of Pues*, 3; (first edition 1841). The spelling 'Pues', for the third edition, is designed to be insulting. See also Bowden, *Remarks on Pews*; Cambridge Camden Society, *Twenty-Three Reasons*; *Twenty-Four Reasons*.
58. Barry, 'Modern Architects', 127.
59. Opposition: Anon., *Wooden Walls*; novel: Paget, *Milford Malvoisin*; see also Stuart, *Pew System*; general discussion White, *Cambridge Movement*, 106–9.
60. Bloom, *Shakespeare's Church*, 20.
61. *The Handbook for Visitors to Stratford-upon-Avon* (Stratford, 1851) 25, 26.
62. Cambridge Camden Society, *Round Church*, 1. Their objections to the church had in fact been long anticipated by the *Cambridge Guide, or Description of the University and Town of Cambridge*, which was reprinted several times, and which stated (1830: 224): 'Its primary form has been much disfigured by subsequent buildings, and in its present state appears under many disadvantages.'

63. *Times*,1, January (1845), 4.
64. Ibid.
65. Robertson ed., *Judgment*.
66. *Ecclesiologist* 4 (1845), 194.
67. Faulkner, *Appeal*, 1, 2.
68. See Bentley, *Ritualism and Politics*; White, *Cambridge Movement*; Yates, *Anglican Ritualism* and, in most detail for the Round Church, Rose, 'Stone Table'. The secretary of the Cambridge Camden Society, the classicist F. A. Paley, did go over to Rome, was expelled from college rooms for encouraging another student in the same direction, and his career suffered greatly on account of his Catholicism: see Collard, 'Victorian Outsider', Collard, 'F. A. Paley'.
69. See, for example, Wightwick, 'Gothic Architecture', especially 11.
70. Close, *Restoration of Churches*, 17.
71. The case has been considered in full detail by Rose, 'Stone Table'. See also White, *Cambridge Movement*, 131–44, 161–4.
72. Rose, 'Stone Table', 130.
73. Wiseman, *Fabiola*, 186–7 points out that Pope Evaristus, the fourth successor to Peter, on the basis of Genesis 28, determined that only stone altars should be erected – a piece of historical evidence whose polemical thrust can now be appreciated.
74. See Scholefield, *Christian Altar*; Collison, *Remarks on a Sermon*; Collison, *Further Remarks*; Warren, *Lord's Table*; Collison, *Stone Altars*; Goode, *Altars Prohibited*; Blackburne, *Historical Inquiry*; and the fuller scale argument of Close, *Church Architecture*; Close, *Restoration of Churches*; Close, *Reply*.
75. *Ecclesiologist* 1 (1841), 30.
76. Collison, *Further Remarks*, 15.
77. Warren, *Lord's Table*, 15.
78. Dykes, *Eucharistic Truth*, 11, 12, 15.
79. Robertson, *Judgment*, 61.
80. *Ecclesiologist* 4 (1845), 218.
81. He had already done a stone altar for the Beresfords (Allibone, *Salvin*, 115–16) and similarly ritualist designs for Egerton-Warburton (Yates, *Anglican Ritualism*, 166). Salvin was dropped by the Cambridge Camden Society and roundly criticized in his later work: see Allibone, *Salvin*, 119–21.
82. Newman, *Apologia*, 120.
83. The marked spread of ritualist worship, one explanation of such suspicion, is enumerated by Yates, *Anglican Ritualism*, 70–149; see also Janes, *Victorian Reformation*.
84. Chadwick, *Victorian Church*, i 499.
85. Arnold, *Miscellaneous Works*, 140–1; Stanley, *Life and Correspondence*, 257.
86. See Bentley, *Ritualism and Politics*, 36.
87. Trollope, *Barchester Towers*, 22.

88. A previous attempt at regulation, the Church Discipline Act (1840), had proved unworkable: see Yates, *Anglican Ritualism*, especially 213–45.

89. Bentley, *Ritualism and Politics*, 54 – summarizing a detailed account of the infighting.

90. Mossman, *Relations that Exist*, 32. See also Cooper, 'Eucharist'; Cooper, 'Holy Spirit'; Carey, *Ritualism*.

91. See Gavazzi, *Priest in Absolution*; Wainwright, *Secrets of Ritualism*; Ashley, *Sequel*.

92. Ashley, *Sequel*, 11.

93. A Suburban Vicar, 'Ecclesiastical Deadlock', 24; see Wrightson, *Four Sermons*; Gillmor, *Public Worship* who is anti-Ritualist but still worries about the loss of a bishop's authority.

94. For an exemplary sampling of such broadsides, see Hobson, *Public Worship*; Shipley, *Ought We to Obey?*; Lendrum, *Judicial Committee*; Dykes, *Eucharistic Truth*.

95. Wolley, *Impending Crisis*, 14.

96. Cox, *Church of England*, 93.

97. Pananglican Synod, *Pananglican Synod*, 31.

98. Church, *Church and State*.

99. Denison, *Archdeacon of Taunton*, 15; see also Denison, *Notes of my Life*.

100. See Reynolds, *Martyr of Ritualism* on Mackonochie.

101. *Guardian*, 26 November (1890); see the discussion of Bentley, *Ritualism and Politics*, 120.

102. E.W. Benson, unpublished diary, 8 March 1891, Trinity College, Cambridge.

103. See Yates, *Anglican Ritualism* with extensive further bibliography; Bentley, *Ritualism and Politics*; Graber, *Ritual Legislation*; Janes, *Victorian Reformation*.

104. On Watts and Co. see Lepine, 'On the Founding'. I had my attention drawn to this chasuble by Ayla Lepine – for which much thanks. Her forthcoming work on this and other such items is eagerly awaited. On the subversive possibilities of stitching in this era see the seminal Parker, *Subversive Stitch* and on the use of such embroidery in politics see Tickner, *Spectacle of Women*.

105. So the Society itself claims. But religious houses of a monastic nature had been set up by Newman at Littlemore in 1840; by J.W. Faber at Elton in 1843; by Robert Aitken at St James, Leeds also in 1843.

106. See McDannell, *Material Christianity*, 122–3, and e.g. Olive Whitney's 'Cross of Flowers' (1875) published by L. Prang and Co. and online at the Boston Public Library: http://commons.wikimedia.org/wiki/File:Cross_of_Flowers_ (Boston_Public_Library).jpg. There is a nineteenth-century chasuble, made apparently out of her mother's dress, and painted by St Thérèse of Lisieux (known as 'Little Flower'), which decorates a cross with a picture of the face of Jesus surrounded by a climbing rose, where each flower represents one of her family members; but images of this did not circulate until well into the twentieth century.

107. Proverbs 3.18, 11.30, 15.4. This may be represented as early as the synagogue of Dura Europos, probably 3rd century CE: see Levine, *Visual Judaism*, 365, following Herbert Kessler (Weitzman and Kessler, *Frescoes*, 153–83).
108. Carruthers, *Book of Memory*, 123.

3 Imperial landscapes, the biblical gaze, and techniques of the photo album

1. The *locus classicus* for this sentiment is Baxandall, *Patterns of Intention*, 107: 'Viewing [is] theory-laden.'
2. See especially Bar-Yosef, *Holy Land*; with the background of Ben-Arieh, *Jerusalem*; *Jerusalem*; *Jerusalem*; Ben-Arieh and Davis, *Jerusalem*; Çizgen, *Photographs*; Nir, *Bible and the Image*; Howe, *Revealing the Holy Land*; Long, *Imagining the Holy Land*; Nassar, *Photographing Jerusalem*; Onne, *Photographic Heritage*; with Davis, *Landscape of Belief* and the rather more superficial Vogel, *A Promised Land* for the American case; with the pictures in Gibson, *Jerusalem*; Schiller, *First Photographs*.
3. See Bar-Yosef, *Holy Land*; and for general background Buzard, *Beaten Track*, Urry, *Tourist Gaze*.
4. Said, *Orientalism*; *Question of Palestine*; *Culture and Imperialism*. Onne, *Photographic Heritage*; Nir, *Bible and the Image*; Howe, *Revealing the Holy Land*; Ryan, *Picturing Empire* are particularly relevant to this chapter, as is the general work of e.g. Banks and Ruby eds., *Made to Be Seen* (with further bibliography).
5. This is not the place for a full doxography of so extensively debated an issue. Suffice to say that Said's work on orientalist scholarship has been profoundly criticised by Irwin, *Lust of Knowing* and especially by Marchand, *German Orientalism*; on the boundaries of East and West, important developments have been made by Bhabha, *Location of Culture* and Young, *White Mythologies* – with the comments of Lockman, *Contending Visions*, and on gender from several angles including most relevantly here, Melman, *Women's Orients*, Lewis, *Rethinking Orientalism*, Micklewright, *Victorian Traveller*, Roberts, *Intimate Outsiders*. In general, most recently, see Netton ed., *Orientalism Revisited* which unaccountably does not cite Marchand, *German Orientalism*. Deringil, '"Nomadism and Savagery"' is especially sharp on the politics of Said's treatment of the Ottoman Empire. The battle over photographic images as a dynamic of East–West relations is notably absent from most general books on orientalism, for example, McFie, *Orientalism*, McKenzie, *Orientalism*. The initial work on Ottoman photography has been undertaken mainly by Turkish and Arab scholars, especially Çizgen, Oztuncay, Özendes, Çelik, Alloula, Erdogdu. For exceptions see below n.113.
6. Hourani, 'How Should We Write'.

7. See Khalidi, *Palestinian Identity*, though even he underplays the affiliation of the inhabitants of Palestine to a Syrian national ideal.

8. See now for a general survey Masters, *Arabs of the Ottoman Empire*, especially 130–224, with further bibliography.

9. On the railways see Schöllgen, *Imperialismus*, 38–49; McMurray, *Distant Ties*; Pick, 'Meissner Pasha'; and Norris, *Land of Progress*. McMeekin, *Berlin-Baghdad Express* is lively but unreliable. On the pipelines, the forthcoming work of Rachel Havrelock is eagerly awaited. See already Havrelock, *River Jordan* for the geopolitics of boundaries in the region; and Norris, *Land of Progress* for the politics of industrial development in Haifa and the Dead Sea in particular.

10. On Montefiore and his contribution, see Green, *Moses Montefiore*.

11. *Palestine Exploration Fund Quarterly* 7.3 (1875): 115.

12. See Larsen, 'Thomas Cook'.

13. See, for example, Peters, *Jerusalem*; Rosovsky, *City of the Great King*; Goldhill, *Jerusalem*.

14. See Röhricht, *Bibliotheca geographica*.

15. Martineau, *Eastern Life*, 408, 407.

16. *Ibid.*, 407.

17. Kinglake, *Eothen*, 116.

18. *Ibid.*, 147.

19. Mott, *Stones of Palestine*, 62. Cf. 24 'I think the Song of Deborah one of the most sublime of hymns, especially when read on the very spot, amid all its striking associations' (though striking is perhaps not the most apt word to have chosen for the Deborah story).

20. Graham, *Russian Pilgrims*, 123.

21. See Silberman, *Digging for God*; Bar-Yosef, *Holy Land*; Goren, 'Nineteenth-century Surveys'.

22. Fergusson, *Palaces of Ninevah*, 9.

23. Fox Talbot, one of the prime inventors of photography, was a founder member and helped fund the Society of Biblical Archaeology (Robson, 'Deciphering Cuneiform', 202), and was also involved with extensive Assyriological research (Robson, 'Deciphering Cuneiform'; Brusius, 'Talbot and Decipherment').

24. *Art Chronicle*, January 1890: 21.

25. *Illustrated London News*, 1890: xxx.

26. On the technology of the camera as culturally significant see Crary, *Techniques*; Tagg, *Burden of Representation*; and for its development as a social medium in Britain see Edwards, *British Photography*; more generally, Otter, *Victorian Eye*, and, from a different angle, Downing, *After Images*, 87–166; or with regard to the history of science, the outstanding work of Daston and Galison, *Objectivity*. On its use in anthropology, see Banks and Ruby, *Made to Be Seen* for an overview, with extensive bibliography. Particularly relevant here are Edwards, *Anthropology* and Pinney and Peterson, *Other Histories*.

27. For collections of images, see in particular, Chevedden, 'Photographic Heritage'; Çizgen, *Photographs*; Gavin ed., 'Imperial Self-Portrait'; Gibson, *Jerusalem*; Khalidi, *Before their Diaspora*; Landau, *Abdul-Hamid's Palestine*; Lyons, Papadopoulou, Stewart and Szegedy-Maszak eds., *Early Views*; Nir, *Bible and the Image*; Onne, *Photographic Heritage*; Schiller, *First Photographs*; and for more general discussion, often with many photographs, see Gavin ed., 'Imperial Self-Portrait'; Howe, *Revealing the Holy Land*; Howe, 'Sacred Geography'; Lyons, 'Art and Science'; Nassar, *Photographing Jerusalem*; Nir, *Bible and the Image*; Onne, *Photographic Heritage*; Schwartz and Ryan eds., *Picturing Place*; Silver-Brody, *Documentors*; Solomon-Godeau, 'Photographer in Jerusalem'. I would never travel in this region without Barthes, *Camera Lucida*. The most recent contribution to the general area of debate is Bohrer, *Photography and Archaeology*, though his comments on Jerusalem, 147–50, are not developed.

28. See Onne, *Photographic Heritage*, 1–20.

29. *British Journal of Photography* 3 April (1868): 158–9.

30. Lerebours, *Excursions Daguerriennes*, i. For the impact of this distinction in science see the brilliant study of Daston and Galison, *Objectivity*.

31. See Solomon-Godeau, 'Photographer in Jerusalem'; Howe, *Revealing the Holy Land*, 20–5.

32. Frith, *Egypt and Palestine* cited by Armstrong, *Scenes in a Library*, 285, and discussed by her 277–359; see also Nir, *Bible and the Image*, 61–84.

33. Figures from Onne, *Photographic Heritage*. On Robertson, see Öztuncay, *James Robertson*.

34. For a detailed history of photographic theory's contested relation to art especially in the 1860s see Edwards, *British Photography*, 119–64, 205–46.

35. See Howe, *Revealing the Holy Land*, 'Sacred Geography'.

36. See the discussion of Lyons, 'Art and Science'.

37. Conder, *Modern Traveller*, 74; see also Brown, *Encyclopedia*, 682 (a much used encyclopedia); Bannister, *Survey of the Holy Land*, 274–5; Kelly, *New System*, 19; Walk, *Visit to Jerusalem*, 19; *The Christian Penny Magazine* 22 (3 November 1832) 170; *The Portfolio* 3 (1824): 38; Carpenter, *Scripture*, 363.

38. Chateaubriand, *Travels*, 391.

39. There are many nineteenth-century paintings and drawings of Ruth and Naomi, of which perhaps those of Watts and Calchéron are the best known.

40. Qureshi, *Peoples on Parade* is particularly good on this.

41. For Don Quixote see Edwards, *British Photography*, 143.

42. Smith, *Historical Geography*, 99. For Smith's life see Smith, *George Adam Smith*; Campbell, *Fixing the Indemnity*, especially 77–104; and for his intellectual place, the rather unsatisfactory discussions of Butlin, (1988) 'George Adam Smith'; Aiken, *Scriptural Geography*, 132–85. As the preface to the 25th edition (1931) makes clear, Allenby used Smith as a field guide, and Smith responded by adding an appendix on Allenby's campaigns: see also Gardner, *Allenby*, 114.

43. Stanley, *Sinai and Palestine*. On Stanley see now Witheridge, *Dr Stanley*, which, for a biography of a writer, has surprisingly little to say about the writing.

44. Bedford, *Photographic Pictures*. On Bedford, see Spencer, *Francis Bedford*. Prothero, *Life and Letters*, 311, with an acute sense of the class divisions, does not include Bedford as 'one of the party' – a snobbery followed by Witheridge, *Dr Stanley*, 223–31.

45. Stanley, *Sermons*, 31.

46. *Ibid.*, 32.

47. Prothero, *Life and Letters*, 238, 240 – speaking of Stanley, *Sinai and Palestine*.

48. McCallum ed., *Holy Bible*.

49. Stead, *Studies*, 20 gives a vivid account of how this painting 'struck the imagination of the common people ... Rude coalheavers ... used to tell over and over again how the Queen had given the Book of Books ... to the heathen far away who sought to know what it was that made England great': the image of Empire revels in the dissemination from high art and high culture to the 'rude coalheavers'.

50. See Armstrong, *Scenes in a Library*, 302; and Roberts, 'Cultural Crossing'.

51. See Roberts, *Intimate Outsiders* for a good analysis of such cultural cross-dressing, especially 23–37 with the case of the painter Lewis in Cairo; and from the other side, Lewis, *Rethinking Orientalism*, especially 243–51. For Indian examples, see Low, *White Skins*, 191–237.

52. Howe, *Revealing the Holy Land*, 28; Vogel, *A Promised Land* – a term coined in 1965 by John Kirkland Wright.

53. On Bonfils, see Gavin, *Image of the East*; Woodward, 'Photographic Practice'; with the background of Çizgen, *Photographs*; Gigord and Beaugé, *Images d'Empire*.

54. On the American Colony, see Vester, *Our Jerusalem*; and the barely fictional Lagerlöf, *Jerusalem*; with occasional comments in Blyth, *Jerusalem*.

55. Alloula, *Colonial Harem*, 4. See also Slyomovics, 'Visual Ethnography'.

56. See in particular di Bello, *Women's Albums*, and Micklewright, *Victorian Traveller*. On the carte-de-visite and its inventor Disdéri, see McCauley, *Disdéri* and in a more developed social context Edwards, *British Photography*, 67–117. On photographs in the household, see Osborne, *Travelling Light*, 52–68. On the home as a stage see Cohen, *Household Gods*, 122–44, for 'the power of a settting to communicate a person's essence' (124).

57. Ledger-Lomas, 'Illustrated Bibles' (unpublished lecture).

58. Silver-Brody, *Documentors*; in general see Bal, *Double Exposures*, 195–224; Karp and Lavine eds., *Exhibiting Cultures*.

59. See Micklewright, *Victorian Traveller*, especially 139–80; di Bello, *Women's Albums*, both with further bibliography. For the complexities of class and photography see especially Edwards, *British Photography*.

60. Very well discussed by Micklewright, *Victorian Traveller*, especially, on the history of such albums, 139–80, along with di Bello, *Women's Albums*.

61. Micklewright, *Victorian Traveller*, 143–50 discusses and illustrates Blyth's albums now in the British Museum.

62. By contrast there has been some exceptional work on private albums, especially women's collections: see Micklewright, *Victorian Traveller*, especially 139–80; di Bello, *Women's Albums* – each with further bibliography. The background supplied by Melman, *Women's Orients* is fundamental here. See also Lewis, *Rethinking Orientalism*.

63. Compare the failures of the American attempts at mapping: see Hallote, *Bible, Map and Spade*; Hallote, Cobbing and Spurr, *Photographs*.

64. Daston and Galison, *Objectivity*, 22, 42.

65. Good background in Wharton, *Selling Jerusalem*, 97–144.

66. Graham, *Russian Pilgrims* is the most vivid account of this pilgrimage.

67. See Finn, *Stirring Times*; Besant, *Twenty-One Years' Work*; Bliss, *Palestine Exploration*; Blyth, *Jerusalem* for a selection of first-hand accounts; for later discussion see the seminal Tibawi, *British Interests* and also Eliav, *Britain and the Holy Land*; Greaves, 'The Jerusalem Bishopric'; Moscrop, *Measuring Jerusalem*; Perry, *British Mission*; Vereté, 'British Consulate'; Welch, 'Anglican Churchmen'.

68. Fortna, *Imperial Classroom*, 87.

69. *Ibid.*, 41; see also Deringil, 'Invention of Tradition', 13–21.

70. Fortna, *Imperial Classroom*, 50–60, 94–5; Deringil, 'Invention of Tradition', 13–21. As Fortna's excellent discussion also points out, article 129 of the 1869 Education Regulation which denied a licence to any private school teaching 'contrary to custom and [state] policy and ideology' was largely ignored.

71. Translated and cited in Deringil, 'Invention of Tradition', 15.

72. Their credulousness may by gauged by the critical eye of Miss Eliza Platt, for example, who already in 1842, when shown the rock which Moses struck, wrote (*Journal of a Tour* I: 165): 'the possibility even of this place being the scene of the miracle alluded to has scarcely ever been admitted by any, but the monks themselves; the Arabs, who pay it no less honour; and pilgrims, of equal ignorance and superstition'.

73. See Davis, *Landscape of Belief*, 77–87 for a discussion of the Orientalism of this volume.

74. See Long, *Imagining the Holy Land*; Rieser, *Chautauqua Movement*; Davis, *Landscape of Belief*, 89–97; Hurlbut, *Chautauqua*; Vincent, *Heyl Vincent*.

75. Rieser, *Chautauqua Movement*, 97.

76. Vincent, *Chautauqua Movement*, 264.

77. Prothero, *Life and Letters*, 204.

78. Vincent, *Chautauqua Movement*, 264.

79. *Ibid.*, 50.

80. Vogel, *A Promised Land*, 2–3 notes that Palestine Park 'inspired praise and merriment': so Kipling was extremely sniffy about its 'elaborately arranged mass of artificial hillocks surrounding a mud puddle and wormy streak of

slime connecting it with another mud puddle'; Roosevelt called it 'the most American thing about America'.

81. They can most conveniently be viewed now through the Pitts Theological Library website at Emory University, which has usefully digitized the complete series.

82. Stanley, *Sermons*, 1.

83. For the (contemporary) history of the invention see Brewster, *Stereoscope* (and on Brewster himself see Morrison-Low and Christie eds., *'Martyr of Science'*); Holmes, 'Stereoscope'; for the craze and dip in sales see Osborne, *Stereograph*, whose title alone indicates his evangelical commitment to the stereoscope's moral purpose. See also Schiavo, 'From Phantom Image', with further bibliography.

84. Herman Vogel cited in Wajda, 'Room with a Viewer', 112.

85. Figures from Wajda, 'Room with a Viewer'. On its popularity see Schiavo, 'From Phantom Image' and in a more general context of its technology the seminal Crary, *Techniques*; also Long, *Imagining the Holy Land*, 89–130.

86. Breasted, *Egypt*, 53. Baldwin, *Touring the Holy Land* and Kent, *Bible Lands* are duller and less successful tours of Palestine than Hurlbut's, which was reprinted several times and translated into German.

87. Quoted as part of the puffery of Forbush, *Methods and Advantages*, 7.

88. Forbush, *Methods and Advantages*, 3. Forbush cites Vincent specifically as an inspiration.

89. Osborne, *Stereograph*.

90. Thomson, *Biblical Illustrations*, 27. The first publication was in 1859, and it was reprinted often in the USA and England. I cite from the popular American edition; all editions had a set of lithographs, not photographs. On Thomson, see Murre-van den Berg, 'Pilgrimage and Mission'; Varisco, 'Framing the Holy Land'.

91. Cited from other citations by Dolkart ed., *James Tissot*, 13.

92. Dolkart ed., *James Tissot*, 13.

93. See *ibid.* for all the information in this paragraph, with further discussion and bibliography.

94. Tissot, *Life of Our Saviour*, ix. On the importance of the vocabulary of 'restore' here, see chapter 6 below.

95. Compare the huge popular success and critical disdain for Marie Corelli's biblical novel, *Barabbas* (1893): see Goldhill, *Victorian Culture*, 237–42.

96. Bohrer, 'Sweet Waters', 121–38. These albums are listed in Gigord and Beaugé, *Images d'Empire*, 194–7. On Abdullah Frères see Özendes, *Abdullah Frères*, Öztuncay, *Photographers of Constantinople*, 176–233; as well as Gigord and Beaugé, *Images d'Empire*. On Berrgren see Öztuncay, *Photographers of Constantinople*, 291–301. On Kargopoulu, see Öztuncay, *Vassiliaki Kargopoulo*. Özendes, *Orientalism and Photography* 166 *et passim* also notes collections of post-cards and other travel collections as albums.

97. See Özendes, *Orientalism and Photography*. Sébah's photographs were also used in the illustrated travel albums of C. Clément, *The City of the Sultan* (1895); H. Barth, *Konstantinopel* (1913); F. Endes, *Die Turkie* (1916). On European exhibitions of Ottoman photographs see Öztuncay, *Vassiliaki Kargopoulo*, 98–195, though Lewis, *Rethinking Orientalism* is more conceptually adept with such cultural interchanges.

98. Makdisi, 'Ottoman Orientalism'. See also the insightful Deringil, 'Nomadism and Savagery' and (the more clunky) Herzog, 'Nineteenth-Century Baghdad'.

99. Makdisi, 'Rethinking Ottoman Imperialism', 40.

100. *Ibid.*, 43.

101. See Gigord and Beaugé, *Images d'Empire*, 203–7. For an excellent discussion of how modernity, the city and visual technology are interrelated see Otter, *Victorian Eye*.

102. On the railways see Schöllgen, *Imperialismus*, 38–49; McMurray, *Distant Ties*; Norris, *Land of Progress*. The British Embassy in Constantinople was well aware of the strategic importance of the railway, see Smith, *Embassy of Sir William White* on Sir William White's diplomacy.

103. See Gavin ed., 'Imperial Self-Portrait'; and more generally Deringil, *Well-Protected Domains*, especially 135–65.

104. Cited by Deringil, *Well-Protected Domains*, 136.

105. See Landau, *Abdul-Hamid's Palestine*.

106. Typical is Jacobson, *Orientalist Photography*, 20: 'The image of the Orient in the 19th century was defined almost exclusively by foreigners and resident Christian photographers . . . Though in theory it would indeed be illuminating to see if the East might have been portrayed differently through the eyes of the Muslim majority, this is not possible.' For a typical and less strident silence see Perez, *Focus East*, who mentions Abdul-Hamid only once just to list him as a patron of the Abdullah Frères Studio. The list of books that did not discuss Muslim photographers or the Abdul-Hamid collection, even when relevant to an argument, would be long; but, for a more positive bibliography, see Landau, *Abdul-Hamid's Palestine*, written before the discovery of the London albums; Çizgen, *Photographs*; Gigord and Beaugé, *Images d'Empire*, especially 191ff; Gavin, 'Imperial Self-Portrait'; Allen, 'Collection'; Allen, 'Analysis'; Çelik, 'Speaking Back' (1992); reprised briefly in Çelik, 'Speaking Back' (2002). Woodward, 'Photographic Practice'; Shaw, 'Ottoman Photography'. See also Gonzalez, *Local Portraiture*; Nassar, 'Local Photography'. Slyomovics, 'Visual Ethnography' building on Alloula, *Colonial Harem* is a good example of the insightful analysis of colonial photography without adequate treatment of Ottoman photographers.

107. See Cox, *Diversions of a Diplomat*, 36–46. The modernization of the Ottoman Empire, especially after the Tanzimat reforms, has become in recent years a lively topic of analysis: see Makdisi, 'Rethinking Ottoman Imperialism'; Deringil, 'Mapping the Orient', each with further bibliographies, and below. For the period after 1908, see Watenpaugh, *Being Modern*.

108. Allen, 'Analysis', 34. See also Çelik, 'Speaking Back', who calls the images 'corrective'.
109. The story of this grotesque shopping expedition is told with the quotation in Deringil, *Well-Protected Domains*, 151.
110. Makdisi, 'Rethinking Ottoman Imperialism', 38.
111. For the fez as an 'invention of tradition' re-defining modern Ottoman dress see Deringil, 'Invention of Tradition', 8–9.
112. See in general Graham-Brown, *Images of Women*; Gigord and Beaugé, *Images d'Empire*, 137–45. For male stereotyped images see Erdogdu, 'Picturing Alterity'. On the Harem, see in particular Roberts, *Intimate Outsiders*, and Lewis, *Rethinking Orientalism*, both with extensive further bibliography, with the important background of Melman, *Women's Orients*.
113. See Landau, *Abdul-Hamid's Palestine* – there are also pictures of Armenians and some women. For what the album leaves out see also the brief comments of Allen, 'Analysis'. This material sadly does not seem to have been considered at length by Western scholars since its first notice in Gavin ed., 'Imperial Self-Portrait', though see for typical and sensible brief comments Woodward, 'Photographic Practice'; Shaw, 'Ottoman Photography'. For the World's Fair, see Katz, *Jordanian Jerusalem*, 8–10; Çelik, 'Speaking Back' (2002), and Long, *Imagining the Holy Land*, and especially for the representation of Jerusalem at the St Louis World's Fair see Kirschenblatt-Gimblett, 'Place in the World'.
114. Halidé Edib, an educated and sophisticated Turkish woman, paradigmatically writes of Jerusalem: 'there was a hot and unwholesome atmosphere, mixed with religious passion verging on hysteria. The Turk alone had a calm, impartial and quiet look' (Adivar, *Memoirs* 426, discussed by Makdisi, 'Rethinking Ottoman Imperialism', 46) – a remark which echoes so many Protestant comments, though, of course, for them the Turk would be included in the hot and unwholesome.
115. See Çelik, 'Speaking Back', 89–96. Fatme Aliye Hanim, a woman from the Ottoman Empire, also wrote counteractive texts that were made much of at Chicago. For Ottoman responses see Cohen, *Becoming Ottomans*, 62–73.
116. On Iranian representations of Western women see Tavakoli-Targhi, *Refashioning Iran*, 54–76. On Ottoman modernization there is a massive bibliography back even beyond the arguments of Bernard Lewis and Albert Hourani. See, for example, the standard Davison, *Reform*, and, with a different sense of the politics of representation, Çelik, *Displaying the Orient*; Fleming, *Muslim Bonaparte*; Makdisi, 'Ottoman Orientalism'; Makdisi, 'Rethinking Ottoman Imperialism'; Watenpaugh, *Being Modern*. Gerber, *Ottoman Rule*, followed by Mazza, *Jerusalem*; Jacobson, *Empire to Empire*, and, most shrilly for a broader Palestine, Norris, *Land of Progress*, attempt to show, in aggressive contrast to the story of the Israeli miracle, how significant material modernization took place throughout the nineteenth century under Ottoman rule. But despite undoubted administrative changes, the infrastructure of

Jerusalem, especially in comparison with European cities, remained deeply undeveloped (for example, in terms of water supply, roads, facilities and, later, electricity). Perhaps most importantly, Jerusalem was repeatedly represented by all parties primarily as a city of historical import. For the Ottoman reception of the Jews as a sign of civilization in contrast with the West see Cohen, *Becoming Ottomans*.

117. See the *World's Fair Souvenir Album of Jerusalem* published by the Jerusalem Exhibit Co. (St Louis, 1904) – and in general Rydell, *Visions of Empire*.
118. See Kirschenblatt-Gimblett, 'Place in the World'.
119. See *ibid*.
120. *Prospectus*, Jerusalem Exhibit Company (St Louis, 1903) 14.
121. As reported in Gavin ed., 'Imperial Self-Portrait'.

4 Building history

1. Warren, *Underground Jerusalem*, 559; cf. 363, 458–9.
2. See Hyamson, *British Projects*; and especially Bar-Yosef, *Holy Land*; and, more generally, Brown, *Providence and Empire*.
3. See Ben-Arieh, *Jerusalem* (1986); Ben-Arieh, *Jerusalem* (1984); Kroyanker, *Adrikhalut*; Goldhill, *Jerusalem*, 227–77.
4. See Garrigan, *Ruskin on Architecture*; Helsinger, *Ruskin and the Art of the Beholder*; Brooks, *John Ruskin*; Swenerton, *Artisans and Architects*; Wheeler and Whiteley eds., *Lamp of Memory*; Daniels and Brandwood eds., *Ruskin and Architecture*.
5. Ruskin, *Works* VII. intro; ch. 7.
6. Ruskin, *Works* V. 333.
7. On labour, see Hanson, '*Labor*', with further bibliography.
8. Brooks, 'Ruskin', 176.
9. Eastlake, *History of the Gothic Revival*, 266.
10. Letter to W. S. Williams (31 July 1848): Smith, *Letters of Charlotte Brontë*, 94. She is referring to the first volume of *Modern Painters*. On Ruskin's influence see Garrigan, *Ruskin on Architecture*; Brooks, *John Ruskin*; Chitty, 'Ruskin's Architectural Heritage'; Casteras *et al.*, *Victorian Eye*; Hanley and Walton eds., *Constructing Cultural Tourism*.
11. For Ruskin on religion see in particular Wheeler, *Ruskin's God*; also Brooks, *John Ruskin*, 33–60.
12. For Ruskin's ambivalent relation to photography, see Harvey, 'Ruskin and Photography'; Solomon-Godeau, 'Photography and Industrialization'; and for a detailed exploration of the relation between art and photography, Edwards, *British Photography*, 119–64, 205–46.
13. See Wheeler, *Ruskin's God*.
14. This and subsequent quotations from Forster, *Room with a View*, ch. 2.

15. On the life of Ashbee see Crawford, *C. R. Ashbee*, and Ashbee, *Janet Ashbee*; on Henry Ashbee, see Marcus, *Other Victorians*, especially 34–76; Gibson, *Erotomaniac*. 'Pisanus Fraxi' is an anagram of 'fraxinus' and 'apis', pseudonyms under which Ashbee *père* published learned notes, and which in Latin mean 'Ash' and 'Bee'.

16. See Brooks, *John Ruskin*, 313–19; Crawford, *C. R. Ashbee* is seminal.

17. See MacCarthy, *Simple Life*. Janet Ashbee describes in mocking terms a tea party with Lady Elcho, Mrs Patrick Campbell, two Mitford daughters of Lord Redesdale, and Sidney and Beatrice Webb (MacCarthy, *Simple Life*, 80–2), as well as the visit of the just retired Prime Minister, Balfour (*ibid.*, 143).

18. See Ashbee, *American Sheaves*: he went as a representative of the newly formed National Trust.

19. See Ashbee, *American Sheaves*, 90–109, quotation from 108–9; the story of the row, with the cartoons from the Press, is told in Crawford, *C.R. Ashbee*, 96–8.

20. Ashbee, *Study of the New Civics*, 22.

21. Ashbee, *American Sheaves*, 26.

22. *Ibid.*

23. *Ibid.*

24. See Field, *Evangelist of Race.*

25. Ashbee, *Palestine Notebook*, especially 105–15 on Zionism.

26. See Ashbee, *Survey of London.*

27. See Ashbee, *Trinity Hospital*, for the campaign.

28. See Ashbee, *Study of the New Civics*, plate 55.

29. See in particular Ashbee, *Study of the New Civics*, his fullest statement.

30. See Ashbee, *Transactions of the Guild*, and Ashbee, *Workshop Re-construction.*

31. Ashbee, *Workshop Re-construction*, 125.

32. Ashbee, *American Sheaves*, 95.

33. Crawford, *C.R. Ashbee* is best; see also MacCarthy, *Simple Life*, for the Cotswold years.

34. The estrangement is unexplained, but possibly associated with the divorce of Henry Ashbee: his wife and unmarried daughters moved in with the son, Charlie. The estrangement was total and lasted until death. Henry Ashbee's will with scandalous malice left money to his daughters only if they could prove to trustees that they could not earn a living and if they were not living with Charlie. The Press were horrified and fascinated. See Gibson, *Erotomaniac*, 150–1.

35. Letter, 2 September 1897, cited Ashbee, *Janet Ashbee*, 25, and, more fully, Crawford, *C. R. Ashbee*, 75.

36. See Ashbee, *Janet Ashbee*, 34.

37. See *ibid.*, 133–6.

38. Volume v of Ashbee's unpublished memoirs, 'Fantasia in Egypt', records his experiences and reactions, which he sums up as 'a sense of impotent rage and humiliation', a 'sourness' (10), and (110) as the 'fantastic irrelevance' of his

work there. He submitted a report to Lord Milner's commission, parts of which are included in an appendix to the same volume. He was involved with education, and maintained an interest in preservation, but had little outlet for his broader architectural interests.

39. Storrs, *Orientations*, 323.
40. General account in Ben-Arieh, *Jerusalem* (1986); Ben-Arieh, *Jerusalem* (1984); see also Jaffe, *Yemin Moshe*; Kark, *Jerusalem Neighbourhoods*; Zoin-Goshen, *Beyond the Wall*. Woodward, *Hell in the Holy Land* is useful on the military background. On contemporary arguments about modernization, and the state of Jerusalem in these years, see Gerber, *Ottoman Rule*; *Jerusalem*; Jacobson, *Empire to Empire*.
41. This first report is unpublished, and Ashbee's copy is now in the Ashbee papers in the library of King's College, Cambridge. He used the same language in Ashbee, *Palestine Notebook*, 3, 18.
42. See Biger, *Empire in the Holy Land*.
43. Ashbee, *Palestine Notebook*, 146–8.
44. Ibid., 167.
45. Ibid., 167.
46. See Biger, *Empire in the Holy Land* for the broader context of the reconstruction of Palestine.
47. Ashbee, *Palestine Notebook*, 61–77. By 1922, however, plans under the name of the High Commissioner, Herbert Samuel, for the development of Palestinian arts and crafts, inaugurated by an exhibition, were shelved by order of the Colonial Office.
48. Ashbee, *Palestine Notebook*, 78–9.
49. Ibid., 81. See n. 47 above.
50. Ashbee, *Jerusalem*, 21. That Europe is the frame is typical of Ashbee's vision. Later architects, notably St Austen Barbe Harrison and Clifford Holliday, strove to integrate Eastern/local elements into their new designs: see Fuchs and Herbert, 'Representing Mandatory Palestine', 281–333, and Cormack, 'Unity out of Diversity?'
51. Unpublished; also in the Ashbee papers in the library of King's College, Cambridge. Interestingly, an article in the Egyptian newspaper *The Sphinx* (15 February 1919), which undoubtedly reflects official policy, is a card-carrying rejection of restoration in Morris' terms: 'There is no question of restoration. The aim of the authorities is rather to discover and to preserve all that remains of the past, and to undo as far as possible, the evil that has been done.' The gap between rhetoric and practice, and the shiftiness of the language of preservation/restoration is strongly marked here.
52. See Silberman, *Digging for God*; Marcus, *View from Nebo*; and, with equally transparent agendas, Abu El-Haj, *Facts on the Ground*; Ricca, *Reinventing Jerusalem*.
53. See Ben-Arieh, 'Jerusalem Travel Literature'; and for the photography see the previous chapter of this book.

54. Masters, *Arabs of the Ottoman Empire*, 195.
55. Deringil, '"Nomadism and Savagery"', 320.
56. Ashbee himself was prevented from seeing through this part of his plan though it was completed just after he left the city: see Ashbee, *Palestine Notebook*.
57. Ashbee, *Jerusalem*, 21.
58. It was explicitly based on the principles of the National Trust, for which Ashbee had lectured in America (Ashbee, *Palestine Notebook*, 139). Like so many imperial committees, it invited representatives of the major concerned parties, while maintaining a majority of the ruling administration. Included in the 32-strong committee here were the Mayor of Jerusalem, the Presidents of the Jewish Community, Franciscan Community and the Dominican Community, the Mufti, the Greek and Armenian Patriarchs, Chairman of the Zionist Commission, as well as distinguished academics, Geddes, Vincent and Abel. This was a committee of considerable distinction.
59. Vol. v of the unpublished memoirs, 'Fantasia in Egypt', 98–9. He writes also (121): 'The more I think about it the more it seems to me that the Guild – Guild socialism (we haven't got the right name yet) "the Guild Spirit" – is the practical way out of the bureaucratic impasse.' This reflects the more heated remarks in the unedited diaries, e.g. 27 April (1917). He amusingly describes his attempts to get glass-blowing going again in Hebron in Ashbee, *Palestine Notebook*, 153–7.
60. The most vivid description is Graham, *Russian Pilgrims*.
61. See Kroyanker, *Adrikhalut*.
62. Ashbee, *Palestine Notebook*: 'quite furiously angry' is the description of Richmond, Ashbee's friend and replacement (from the Ashbee journals, 24 January 1924).
63. Ashbee, *Jerusalem*, 4.
64. Ashbee, *Palestine Notebook*, 77.
65. Ashbee, *Study of the New Civics*, 152; *Palestine Notebook*, 164–88.
66. Ashbee, *Palestine Notebook*, 31.
67. *Ibid.*, 167.
68. Thanks especially to Peter Mandler and Astrid Swenson for helpful comments on the draft of this chapter. Versions of this piece were delivered first at the 'Plunder and Preservation' conference in Cambridge; then as the Schaffner Lecture, in my role as the Schaffner Professor in British Studies at Chicago, and finally as the Maccabaean Lecture at King's College London. Thanks to the audiences in each place for questions which helped me make my arguments more precise.

5 Restoration

1. For the history, see Biddle ed., *Church*; Goldhill, *Jerusalem*, 1–45.
2. Siberry, *New Crusaders* is an intellectually dull start for this topic; more generally on the chivalric urge, see Girouard, *Return to Camelot*.

3. See Goldhill, 'Discovery of Victorian Jerusalem'.
4. For different aspects of this issue see Bar-Yosef, *Holy Land*; Schöllgen, *Imperialismus*; Silberman, *Digging for God*; Stanley, *Protestant Missions*; Porter, *Religion versus Empire?*
5. Disraeli, *Tancred*, 70.
6. See White, *Cambridge Movement*; Webster and Elliott eds., '*A Church As It Should Be*'.
7. Delafons, *Politics and Preservation*, 12. See Brooks 'Introduction'; Brooks, 'Building the Rural Church'; Cherry, 'Patronage'; Saint, 'Church Building'.
8. Freeman, *Church Restoration*, 14. As we saw in chapter 2, there was indeed a severe objection to the restoration of the altar: see above pp. 48–51. For Freeman's later historical rows see Hesketh, *Making the Past Speak*, 86–92, and especially Koditschek, *Nineteenth-Century Visions*, 240–50.
9. Brooks, 'Introduction', 20.
10. See Swenson, 'Conceptualizing Heritage' redrafted into the excellent Swenson, *Rise of Heritage*, building on Tschudi-Madsen, *Restoration*; Lowenthal and Binney eds., *Our Past Before Us*; Wohlleben ed., *Konservieren*; Miele, 'Conservation Militants'; Hunter ed., *Preserving the Past*; Lowenthal, *Heritage Crusade*; Miele ed., *From William Morris*.
11. Scott, 'Opening Address', 9. For the repeated ambiguities in Scott's statements of principle see Pevsner, *Architectural Writers*, 168–82.
12. See especially Lowenthal, *Heritage Crusade*; Swenson, *Rise of Heritage*.
13. Stevenson, 'Architectural Restoration', 219.
14. Beckett, *Church Restoration*, 5.
15. Viollet-le-Duc, *Dictionnaire raisonnée*, viii, 14.
16. See for more detailed explication White, *Cambridge Movement*; Webster and Elliott eds., '*A Church As It Should Be*'.
17. Ferrey, *Recollections*, 85.
18. Wightwick, 'Present Conditions', 10. On Wightwick see Reid, 'George Wightwick'. In general on this religious ferment, see Hilton, *Age of Atonement*; Larsen, *Contested Christianity*.
19. Close, 'Restoration'. The accusations of popery, as with the Oxford Movement, were swift and violent: see Brandwood, '"Mummeries"'.
20. Barry, 'Modern Architects', 127.
21. Scott, *Plea for the Faithful Restoration*, 114, 54. On Scott and the Camdenites see Stamp, 'George Gilbert Scott'.
22. *Ecclesiologist* 3 (1844): 113.
23. *Builder* 14 Dec. (1878): 1312.
24. Cambridge Camden Society, *A Few Words*, 19.
25. Freeman, *Church Restoration*, 5.
26. A Looker On, 'Theory of Restoration' 650.
27. Viollet-le-Duc, *Dictionnaire raisonée*, viii, 14.

28. Renan, *Life of Jesus*, 25. The translator, in the manner of a generous anti-restorationist, describes Renan's own work as 'an exquisitely conceived and executed romance rather loosely or remotely based upon history', xvii.

29. *Sessional Papers of the Royal Institute of British Architects 1876–7* 27, 1877: 263.

30. Beckett, *Church Restoration*, 27.

31. Scott, 'Opening Address' 6.

32. See Brooks, 'Building the Rural Church'.

33. Scott, 'Opening Address', 8.

34. Scott, '"Architectural Restoration"', 250.

35. Beckett, *Church Restoration*, 11.

36. Street, *Memoirs*, 62.

37. Stevenson, 'Architectural Restoration', 219–20.

38. Bodley, 'Church Restoration', 70.

39. Stevenson, 'Anti-Restorers', 362.

40. Ruskin, *Seven Lamps*, 161 – sections xviii–xx contain some of Ruskin's most high-flown rhetoric of obloquy ('Of more wanton or ignorant ravage it is vain to speak . . .'). Dishon, 'Three Men' notes the indebtedness of the Cambridge Camden Society to Ruskin's aesthetics, but does not discuss Ruskin's deep antipathy to restoration.

41. Huggins, 'Restoration', 728. Huggins, 'Chester Cathedral Restoration' likens restorers to the hooliganism of Elgin.

42. X. Y., *Yorkshire Gazette* 6 November (1830); see Denslagen, *Architectural Restoration*, 55–60.

43. Stevenson, 'Architectural Restoration', 224.

44. Loftie, 'Thorough Restoration', 140.

45. Stevenson, 'Architectural Restoration', 221.

46. See Hardy, *Memories*.

47. Scott, *Plea for the Faithful Restoration*, 26.

48. Aitchison, 'Imitated Architecture', 358.

49. Miele, 'Morris and Conservation', 61; see also Hall, 'Affirming Community Life'.

50. Froude, *Nemesis of Faith*, 24–5.

51. These different senses and valuations of the old are explored throughout Froude's text in a remarkably intricate manner. On Froude and his sense of the past see Brady, *James Anthony Froude*; Hesketh, *Making the Past Speak*, 64–72; 86–93; Koditschek, *Nineteenth-Century Visions*, 151–204.

52. Ruskin, *Seven Lamps*, 163.

53. Huggins, 'Restoration', 728. See also Huggins, 'Chester Cathedral Restoration' 280.

54. Stevenson, 'Anti-Restorers', 361. See Fawcett, 'A Restoration Tragedy'.

55. Brooks, 'Building the Rural Church', 51. See Mandler, 'Nationalizing the Country House'; *Fall and Rise*.

56. Trollope's Barchester novels are the most obvious example.

57. White, '"Restoration"', 115.
58. *Builder* (1878): 661.
59. Barry, 'Modern Architects', 127.
60. Beckett, *Church Restoration*, 27.
61. *Sessional Papers of the Royal Institute of British Architects 1876–77* 27: 230, 232. On Beresford Hope see Brooks, '"Stuff of a Heresiarch"'.
62. See Miele, 'Morris and Conservation'.
63. See Aarsleff, *From Locke to Saussure*; Lincoln, *Theorizing Myth*; van Hulle and Leerssen eds., *Editing the Nation's Memory*.
64. Leerssen, *National Thought*, 200.
65. On Tacitus see the fine study of Krebs, *Dangerous Book*.
66. See the excellent Marchand, *German Orientalism* for the orientalist aspect of this.
67. Wagner, *Prose Works* I 53. See Goldhill, *Victorian Culture*, 125–50.
68. Wagner, *Prose Works* I 136.
69. *Ibid.*, 32.
70. Leerssen, 'Introduction'. See also Dentith, *Epic and Empire*.
71. Tucker, *Epic*, 512.
72. Macaulay, *Lays of Ancient Rome*, preface to 'Horatius'. On Macaulay, see in general Clive, *Macaulay*; Hall, *Macaulay and Son* (especially 250–3); Edwards, 'Macaulay's Rome'; Levine, *Boundaries of Fiction*; and in particular McKelvey, 'Primitive Ballads', and Koditschek, *Nineteenth-Century Visions*, who both also argue for the connection of Macaulay's writing with biblical criticism and liberal historicism.
73. Macaulay, *Lays of Ancient Rome*, preface.
74. *Ibid.*, preface.
75. Disraeli, *Sybil*, 14.
76. Whibley, *Lord John Manners*, I 131.
77. *Ibid.*, 153.
78. Disraeli, *Sybil*, 422, 421–2.
79. See Goldhill, *Victorian Culture*, 153–244; also e.g. Chandler, *Dream of Order*; Fleischman, *Historical Novel*; Sanders, *Victorian Historical Novel*; Shaw, *Historical Fiction*; Chapman, *Sense of the Past*; Orel, *Changing Attitudes*; Maitzen, *Victorian Historical Writing*; McCaw, *Victorian Historiography* – all indebted to Lukács, *Historical Novel*.
80. Bulwer Lytton, *Last Days of Pompeii*, 23.
81. *Ibid.*, 24.
82. *Ibid.*, 24.
83. *Ibid.*, 25–6.
84. *Ibid.*, 542.
85. *Ibid.*, 542–3.
86. Beard, *Parthenon*, 82.
87. See Auerbach, *Great Exhibition*; Davies, *Great Exhibition*; Purbrick ed., *Great Exhibition*; Hobhouse, *Crystal Palace*; Buzard, Childers and Gillooly

eds., *Victorian Prism*; Moser, *Designing Antiquity*; and Nichols, *Greece and Rome*.

88. Hardy, *Fiddler of the Reels*, 191.
89. Fergusson, *Topography of Jerusalem*; *Holy Sepulchre*; *Temple of the Jews*.
90. Layard, *Nineveh Court*; see Layard, *Nineveh*. On Layard see especially the superb Larsen, *Conquest of Assyria*; and on the reception of the work see the fine study of Bohrer, *Orientalism* 98–223; also Malley, *From Archaeology to Spectacle*, 45–126.
91. Phillips, *Crystal Palace and Park*, 44.
92. *Ibid.*, 57.
93. Layard, *Nineveh Court*, 52.
94. *Ibid.*, 48.
95. *Ibid.*, 57; see Malley, *From Archaeology to Spectacle*, 149–55.
96. Jebb, *Bacchylides*, 121.
97. Sayce, '*Higher Criticism*', 24. He aimed to find a middle ground between the higher critics and their extreme theological opponents, neither of whom, according to Sayce, could take proper account of archaeology's discoveries, because of their extremism. The photographic pioneer Fox Talbot forms a link between Assyriology and the new technology discussed in chapter 3: see Robson, 'Deciphering Cuneiform'; Brusius, 'Talbot and Decipherment'.
98. *Times*, 9 February (1849): 5 – the importance of this review for the reception of Layard's work is stressed by Bohrer, *Orientalism*, 153–4.
99. Layard, *Nineveh Court*, 7. Larsen, 'Nineveh' notes that Layard himself was not a religiously motivated scholar.
100. See e.g. the particularly relevant study of Bilsel, *Antiquity on Display*.
101. Watkin, *C. R. Cockerell*, 12.
102. Dalloway, *Statuary and Sculpture*, 366.
103. Cockerell, *Temples of Jupiter*, ix.
104. *Ibid.*, 44.
105. A problem very smartly analysed by Bilsel, *Antiquity on Display*, 1–28 for the Pergamon Museum in Berlin.
106. Beard and Henderson, *Classics*, 80.
107. Cockerell, *Temples of Jupiter*, 65.
108. See Bilsel, *Antiquity on Display*.
109. Waterfield, *Layard of Nineveh*, 171.
110. See Gere, *Prophets of Modernism*.
111. Munich, *Queen Victoria's Secrets*, 27.
112. Planché, *Souvenir*, preface (n.n.). This is a beautiful folio volume with hand-tinted lithographs of the major participants at the ball in costume. For a further description of the aristocratic anxiety about the event see Planché, *Recollections*, 275–8.
113. Planché, *Souvenir*.
114. *Art Union* (1842): 140.

115. Eastlake, *Art of Dress*, 68 – the reprint in book form from the *Quarterly Review* 1847.
116. Carlyle, *Sartor Resartus*, 45.
117. Leerssen, *National Thought*, 127.
118. See Girouard, *Return to Camelot*; Mandler, '"In the Olden Time"'; Mandler, *Fall and Rise*, 21–70. Lord John Manners' contribution to this movement (Manners, *A Plea*) is mercilessly mocked by Monckton Milnes, quoted as the epigraph to this chapter.
119. Tooley, *Queen Victoria*, 128.
120. Richardson, *Eglinton Tournament* (n.n.) On Eglinton, see Poinke, 'Ritual Failure'.
121. *Literary Gazette* (1831): 90.
122. Aikman, *Account of the Tournament*, 7.
123. Fitzgerald, *Euphranor*, 8. The hero suitably loves Kenholm Digby's *Broadstone of Honour*, the 'breviary of Young England' (Whibley, *Lord John Manners* I: 133).
124. Aikman, *Account of the Tournament*, xvi, 9, 13.
125. Patterson, *Reminiscences*, 181.
126. Hare, *Two Noble Lives*, 208.
127. Aikman, *Account of the Tournament*, 16.
128. Fitzgerald, *Euphranor*, 8.
129. [Richardson], 'The Tournament', 5.
130. Mackay, *Through the Long Day*, 73.
131. Disraeli, *Endymion*, ch. lix.
132. Girouard, *Return to Camelot*, 93.
133. Owen, 'To the Right Hon.'
134. See Buddemeier, *Panorama, Diorama, Photographie*; Altick, *Shows of London*; Oettermann, *Panorama*.
135. Altick, *Shows of London*, 149; Bar-Yosef, *Holy Land*, 145.
136. Altick, *Shows of London*, 150.
137. *Times* 27 Dec. (1861): 6.
138. *Pall Mall Gazette* 5 Sept. (1889). For a good general discussion see Bar-Yosef, *Holy Land*, 105–81.
139. Bar-Yosef, *Holy Land*, 105–81: 'It was the Sunday school which stood at the heart of this biblical culture', 180.
140. Long, *Imagining the Holy Land*. See above chapter 3.
141. Çelik, *Displaying the Orient*.
142. Deringil, *Well-Protected Domains*, 136.
143. See the excellent Qureshi, *Peoples on Parade*.
144. See Bar-Yosef, *Holy Land*, 149–61; Rubinstein and Rubinstein, *Philosemitism*; and in general Stanley, *Protestant Missions*, Thorne, *Congregational Missions*, and Porter, *Religion versus Empire?*; for contemporary histories of the London Society for Promoting Christianity among the Jews see Halsted, *Our Missions*; Gidney, *History of the London Society*.

145. See Lewis, *Origins of Christian Zionism* which transcends Hyamson, *British Projects*.

146. Warren, *Underground Jerusalem*, 559; cf 363, 458–9. See above ch. 4 pp. 109–10.

147. Eliot, *Daniel Deronda*, 875; see Anderson, 'George Eliot' with further bibliography.

148. See e.g. the seminal Levine, *Boundaries of Fiction*.

149. See Mitchell, *Picturing the Past*; Melman, *Culture of History*; Qureshi, *Peoples on Parade*.

Coda: A final dig

1. Benson, *Edward White Benson*, made slightly more palatable in Benson, *Edward White Benson* (abridged); Palmer and Lloyd, *Father of the Bensons* lacks sophistication.

2. See Bolt, *As Good as God*.

3. Benson, *Edward White Benson*, 180.

4. Abroad in the Empire cathedrals had been constructed at a far lesser scale and with many problems of climate and local conditions: see Bremner, *Imperial Gothic*.

5. Harrison, *Victorian Stained Glass* is one of the few monographs even aiming at a synoptic view, though Morris and Burne-Jones have, of course, been more frequently discussed: see e.g. the fine study of MacCarthy, *Last Pre-Raphaelite*.

6. Larkworthy, *Clayton and Bell* is a lecture for the Ecclesiological Society; see also Harrison, *Victorian Stained Glass*, 29–33.

7. *Truro Cathedral Guide* (1949) 14th edition, 12. Stubbs *et al.*, *The Cornish See*, 44–50 gives a full explanatory description of the plan, and regrets that most churches show 'a total lack of sequence of thought' in their glass.

8. See Blair, *Form and Faith*; Blair ed., *John Keble* is less satisfying.

9. See the seminal study of Morris, *F. D. Maurice*.

10. Sargent, *Henry Martyn*; less hagiographically, but without great flair: Martyn, *Henry Martyn*. It is hard not to recall that Benson's beloved and idealized son, who died aged only 17 during Benson's first year at Truro, and who had been named for Benson's patron at Cambridge, was called Martin.

11. Sargent's biography went to ten editions (Sargent, *Henry Martyn*).

12. Hylson-Smith, *Evangelicals*, 21.

13. Benson, *Edward White Benson*, i: 470.

14. There is also a marble memorial to the Wesleys in Westminster Abbey, unveiled by Stanley in 1876, a gesture bringing the Methodists into the embrace of Stanley's liberal, broad Anglicanism.

15. See most recently Koditschek, *Nineteenth-Century Visions*, 99–150, and Hall, *Macaulay and Son*, 258–329.

16. Clayton and Bell also made the roof of the chapel of St John's College, Cambridge, which has painted individual worthies across the ages.

17. Benson, *Sermon*, 15; the mayor in welcoming Benson similarly celebrated the 'Restoration of our ancient rites', Benson, *Sermon*, 9, a phrase to be understood in the light of chapter 5 of this book.

18. At Camborne there is an extraordinary window from 1863, commissioned by the Oddfellows, which includes a red banner of 'Widows and Orphans' Fund, and the gaunt allegorical figure of Want strides over the grave of the dead father. Such a politically aggressive window is hard to parallel elsewhere in the nineteenth century. Thanks to Michael Swift for pointing me to this window: see Swift, 'Anglican Stained Glass', 14–15.

19. Arnold, *Adventures of Phra*, 57, 242. Phra comments (340): 'Vague fantasies began to form within my mind and . . . began to egg me on *to write myself*': a fine expression of the desire for self-formation through writing.

20. See e.g. Xenophon, *Memorabilia* 3. 9, discussed by Goldhill, 'Seductions of the Gaze' and, especially, Rouveret, *Histoire et imaginaire*.

Bibliography

Aarsleff, H., *From Locke to Saussure: Essays on the Study of Language and Intellectual History*, London, 1982.

  The Study of Language in England, Princeton, 1967.

Abu El-Haj, N., *Facts on the Ground: Archaeological Practice and Territorial Self-fashioning in Israeli Society*, Chicago, 2001.

Adivar, Halide Edib, *Memoirs of Halidé Edib: with Illustrations*, London, 1926.

Aiken, E., *Scriptural Geography: Portraying the Holy Land*, London, 2010.

Aikman, J., *An Account of the Tournament at Eglinton, Revised and Corrected by Several of the Knights*, Edinburgh, 1839.

Aitchison, G., 'Ancient Buildings: What Principles Should Govern Their Restoration or their Preservation as Memorials', *The Builder* 35, 1877: 983–5.

  'Imitated Architecture', *The Builder* 36, 1878: 358–9.

Aker, J., *Sight-Seeing: Photography of the Middle East and Its Audiences, 1840–1940*, Cambridge, Mass, 2000.

Alexander, W., *The Ancient British Churches, being an Enquiry into the History of Christianity in Britain Prior to the Establishment of the Heptarchy*, London, 1853.

Allen, W., 'The Abdul Hamid II Collection', *History of Photography* 8, 1984: 119–45.

  'Analysis of Abdul-Hamid's Albums', in Gavin ed., 'Imperial Self-Portrait', 1988, 33–7.

Allibone, J., *Anthony Salvin: Pioneer of Gothic Revival Architecture 1799–1881*, Cambridge, 1987.

Alloula, M., *The Colonial Harem*, trans. B. Harlo, Minneapolis, 1986.

Altick, R., *The Shows of London*, Cambridge, Mass., 1978.

Anderson, A., 'George Eliot and the Jewish Question', *Yale Journal of Criticism* 10, 1997: 39–61.

Anon., *The Wooden Walls of England in Danger: A Defence of Church Pews*, London, 1844.

  'Debate on French Restoration', *The Ecclesiologist* 22, 1861: 213–15.

Anstruther, I., *The Knight and the Umbrella: an Account of the Eglinton Tournament 1839*, London, 1963.

Appadurai, A. ed., *The Social Life of Things: Commodities in Cultural Perspective*, Cambridge, 1986.

Appiah, A., *In My Father's House: Africa in the Philosophy of Culture*, London, 1992.

Armstrong, C., *Scenes in a Library: Reading the Photograph in the Book 1843–1875*, Cambridge, Mass., 1998.

Armstrong, I., *Victorian Glassworlds: Glass Culture and the Imagination 1830–1880*, Oxford, 2008.

Armstrong, K., *Holy War: The Crusades and their Impact on Today's World*, London, 1988.

Armstrong, R., *A Compulsion for Antiquity: Freud and the Ancient World*, Ithaca, NY, 2005.

Arnold, E., *The Wonderful Adventures of Phra the Phoenician*, London, 1890.

Arnold, T., *The Miscellaneous Works of Thomas Arnold*, New York, 1845.

Ashbee, C., *American Sheaves and English Seed Corn: Being a Series of Addresses Mainly Delivered in the United States*, London and New York, 1901.

Chapters in Workshop Re-construction and Citizenship, London, 1894.

Jerusalem 1918–1920, Being the Records of the Pro-Jerusalem Council during the Period of the British Military Administration, London, 1921.

Jerusalem 1920–22, Being the Records of the Pro-Jerusalem Council during the First Two Years of the Civil Administration, London, 1924.

A Palestine Notebook 1918–1923, London, 1923.

The Survey of London: Being the First Volume of the Register of the Committee for the Survey of the Monuments of Greater London Containing the Parish of Bromley-by-Bow, London, 1900.

Transactions of the Guild and School of Handicraft, London, 1890.

The Trinity Hospital in Mile End: An Object Lesson in National History, London, 1896.

Where the Great City Stands: A Study of the New Civics, London, 1917.

Ashbee, F., *Janet Ashbee: Love, Marriage and the Arts and Crafts Movement*, Syracuse, NY, 2002.

Ashley, J., *Sequel to the 'Church of the Period' with the Author's Reasons for Leaving the Church of England*, London, 1878.

Auerbach, J., *The Great Exhibition of 1851: A Nation on Display*, New Haven, 1999.

Auldjo, J., *Journal of a Visit to Constantinople and Some of the Greek Islands in the Spring and Summer of 1833*, London, 1835.

Narrative of an Ascent to the Summit of Mont Blanc, London, 1828.

Sketches of Vesuvius with Short Accounts of the Principal Eruptions, London, 1833.

Bal, M., *Double Exposures: The Subject of Cultural Analysis*, London and New York, 1996.

Baldwin, E., *Touring the Holy Land through the Stereoscope*, New York and London, 1905.

Banks, M. and Ruby, J. eds., *Made to Be Seen: Perspectives on the History of Visual Anthropology*, Chicago, 2011.

Bannister, J., *A Survey of the Holy Land, its Geography, History and Destiny*, Bath and London, 1844.

Bar-Yosef, E., *The Holy Land in English Culture 1799–1917*, Oxford, 1998.

Barker, S. ed., *Excavations and Their Objects: Freud's Collection of Antiquity*, Albany, 1996.

Barrett, A., 'A Virgilian Scene from the Frampton Roman Villa, Dorset', *The Antiquaries Journal* 57, 1977: 312–14.

Barry, E., 'Position of Modern Architects in respect of Architectural Restoration', *The Builder* 36, 1878: 126–9.

Barthes, R., *Camera Lucida: Reflections on Photography*, trans. R. Howard, New York, 1981.

Baxandall, M., *Patterns of Intention: On the Historical Explanation of Pictures*, New Haven, 1985.

Beard, M., *The Parthenon*, London, 2002.

  Pompeii: The Life of a Roman Town, London, 2008.

Beard, M. and Henderson, J., *Classics: A Very Short Introduction*, Oxford, 1995.

Beaulieu, J. and Roberts, M. eds., *Orientalism's Interlocutors: Painting, Architecture, Photography*, Durham and London, 2002.

Bebbington, D., *Evangelicalism in Modern Britain: A History from the 1730s to the 1980s*, London, 1989.

Beckett, E., *A Book on Building, Civil and Ecclesiastical: With the Theory of Domes, and of the Great Pyramid; and a Catalogue of Sizes of Churches and Other Large Buildings*, London, 1876.

  Church Restoration, London, 1876.

Bedford, F., *Mr F. Bedford's Photographic Pictures Taken During the Tour in the East in which, by Command, he Accompanied His Royal Highness, the Prince of Wales*, London, 1863.

Bell, D., 'From Ancient to Modern in Victorian Imperial Thought', *The Historical Journal* 49.3, 2006: 1–25.

  The Idea of Greater Britain: Empire and the Future of World Order, Princeton, 2007.

Bell, E. G., *Introduction to the Prose Romances, Plays and Comedies of Edward Bulwer Lytton*, Chicago, 1910.

Ben-Arieh, Y., *Jerusalem in the Nineteenth Century*, Tel Aviv, 1989.

  Jerusalem in the 19th Century: Emergence of the New City, Jerusalem and New York, 1986.

  Jerusalem in the 19th Century: The Old City, New York, 1984.

  'Jerusalem travel literature as historical source and cultural phenomenon', in Ben-Arieh and Davis eds., *Jerusalem*, 1997: 25–46.

  Painting the Holy Land in the Nineteenth Century, Jerusalem, 1997.

  The Rediscovery of the Holy Land in the Nineteenth Century, Jerusalem, 1979.

Ben-Arieh, Y. and Davis, M., eds., *Jerusalem in the Minds of the Western World 1800–1948*, Westport and London, 1997.

Benson, A. C., *The Life of Edward White Benson*, 2 vols. London, 1899.

  The Life of Edward White Benson, abridged version, London, 1901.

Benson, E. W., *Sermon Preached in Truro Cathedral, on his Enthronement, by the Bishop of Truro, on the 1st May, 1877: with an Account of the Proceedings at his Public Reception in the Town Hall, Truro*, Truro, 1877.

Bentley, J., *Ritualism and Politics in Victorian Britain: The Attempt to Legislate for Belief*, Oxford, 1978.

Beresford Hope, A., *The English Cathedral in the Nineteenth Century*, London, 1861.

Berg, M., *Luxury and Pleasure in Eighteenth-Century Britain*, New Haven, 2005.

Bernal, M., *Black Athena: The Afro-Asiatic Roots of Classical Civilization*, 3 vols. New Brunswick, 1987–2006.

Besant, W., *Twenty-One Years' Work in the Holy Land*, London, 1886.

Bhabha, H., *The Location of Culture*, London, 1994.

Biddle, M. ed., *The Church of the Holy Sepulchre*, New York, 2000.

Biger, G., *An Empire in the Holy Land: The Historical Geography of the British Administration in Palestine 1917–1929*, Jerusalem, 1994.

Bilsel, C., *Antiquity on Display: Regimes of the Authentic in Berlin's Pergamon Museum*, Oxford, 2012.

Black, E., 'Christian and Pagan Hopes of Salvation in Romano-British Mosaics', in Henig and King eds., *Pagan Kings*, 1986: 147–58.

Black, J., *Maps and Politics*, London, 1997.

Blackburne, J., *A Brief Historical Inquiry into the Introduction of Stone Altars into the Christian Church; with Remarks upon the Probable Effects of the Altar and its Ornaments upon Church Architecture in General*, Cambridge, 1844.

Blair, K., *Form and Faith in Victorian Poetry*, Oxford, 2012.

Blair, K. ed., *John Keble in Context*, London, 2004.

Bliss, F., *The History of Palestine Exploration*, New York, 1906.

Bloom, J., *Shakespeare's Church: Otherwise the Collegiate Church of the Holy Trinity of Stratford-upon-Avon*, London, 1902.

Blyth, E., *When We Lived in Jerusalem*, London, 1927.

Boak, R., *Sacred Stitches: Ecclesiastical Textiles in the Rothschild Collection at Waddesdon Manor*, Aylesbury, 2013.

Bodley, G., 'Church Restoration in France', *The Ecclesiologist* 22, 1861: 70–8.

Bohrer, F., *Orientalism and Visual Culture: Imagining Mesopotamia in Nineteenth-Century Europe*, Cambridge, 2003.

Photography and Archaeology, London, 2011.

'The Sweet Waters of Asia: Representing Difference/Differencing Representation in Nineteenth-Century Istanbul', in Hackforth-Jones and Roberts, *Edges of Empire*, 2005: 121–38.

Boivin, N., *Material Culture, Material Minds: The Impact of Things on Human Thoughts, Society and Evolution*, Cambridge, 2008.

Bolt, R., *As Good as God as Clever as the Devil: The Impossible Life of Mary Benson*, London, 2011.

Bourke, R., *Romantic Discourse and Political Modernity: Wordsworth, the Intellectual and Cultural Critique*, New York, London, Toronto, 1997.

Bowden, J., *A Few Remarks on Pews*, London, 1843.

Bowles, W., *Pudens and Claudia of St Paul; or, the Earliest Introduction of the Christian Faith to These Islands through Claudia, Certainly a British Lady, supposed daughter of Caractacus*, Bristol, 1839.

Boyce, E. J., *A Memorial of the Cambridge Camden Society, Instituted May 1839 and the Ecclesiological (late Cambridge Camden) Society, May 1846*, London, 1888.

Bradley, I., *The Call to Seriousness: The Evangelical Impact on the Victorians*, London, 1976.

Bradley, M. ed., *Classics and Imperialism in the British Empire*, Oxford, 2010.

Brady, C., *James Anthony Froude: An Intellectual Biography of a Victorian Prophet*, London, 2013.

Brand, V. ed., *The Study of the Past in the Victorian Age*, Oxford, 1998.

Brandwood, G., '"Mummeries of a Popish Character": The Camdenians and Early Victorian Worship', in Webster and Elliott eds., 'A Church', 2000: 62–97.

Breasted, J. H., *Egypt through the Stereoscope*, New York and London, 1909.

Bremner, G., *Imperial Gothic: Religious Architecture and High Anglican Culture in the British Empire c1840–1870*, New Haven, 2013.

Brewster, D., *The Stereoscope: Its History, Theory, and Contribution*, London, 1856.

Bridel, P., *Palestine Illustrated: A Collection of Views Obtained in the Holy Land by Messrs F. Thévoz and Co., Geneva*, London, 1892.

Briggs, A., *Victorian Things*, London, 1988.

Brockliss, L. and Eastwood, D. eds., *A Union of Multiple Identities: The British Isles, c. 1750–c. 1850*, New York and Manchester, 1996.

Brooks, C., 'Building the Rural Church: Money, Power and the Country Parish', in Brooks and Saint eds., *Victorian Church*, 1995: 51–81.

   'Introduction' in Brooks and Saint eds., *Victorian Church*, 1995: 1–29.

   'Ruskin and the Politics of Gothic', in Daniels and Brandwood eds., *Ruskin and Architecture*, 2003: 165–87.

   '"The Stuff of a Heresiarch": William Butterfield, Beresford Hope, and the Ecclesiological Vanguard', in Webster and Elliott eds., 'A Church', 2000: 121–48.

Brooks, C. and Saint, A. eds., *The Victorian Church: Architecture and Society*, Manchester, 1995.

Brooks, M. *John Ruskin and Victorian Architecture*, New Brunswick and London, 1987.

Brown, B., *A Sense of Things: the Object Matter of American Literature*, Chicago, 2003.

   'Thing Theory', *Critical Inquiry* 28, 2001: 1–22.

Brown, B. ed., *Things*, Chicago, 2004.

Brown, I., *The Hobby-Horsical Antiquary: A Scottish Character 1640–1830*, Edinburgh, 1980.

Brown, J., *The Encyclopedia of Religious Knowledge*, Brattleboro, Vt., 1844.

Brown, P., *The Body and Society: Men, Women and Sexual Renunciation in Early Christianity*, New York, 1988.

'The Rise and Function of the Holy Man in Late Antiquity', *JRS* 61, 1971: 80–101.

Society and the Holy in Late Antiquity, London, 1982.

Through the Eye of a Needle: Wealth, the Fall of Rome and the Making of Christianity in the West, 350–550 A.D., Princeton, 2013.

Brown, S., *Providence and Empire: Religion, Politics and Society in the United Kingdom 1815–1914*, Harlow, 2008.

Brusius, M., 'From Photographic Science to Scientific Photography: Talbot and Decipherment at the British Museum around 1850', in Brusius, Dean and Ramalingam eds., *William Henry Fox Talbot*, 2013: 219–44.

Brusius, M., Dean, K. and Ramalingam, C. eds. *William Henry Fox Talbot: Beyond Photography*, New Haven, 2013.

Buddemeier, H., *Panorama, Diorama, Photographie: Entstehung und Wirkung neuer Medien im 19. Jahrhundert*, Munich, 1970.

Bulloch, J., 'The Family of Auldjo', *Scottish Notes and Queries* 12.8, 1934: 113–15.

'John Auldjo FRS', *N&Q* 166, 1934: 327–32.

Bulwer Lytton, E., *The Last Days of Pompeii*, London, 1834.

Burke, J., *Lingard's History of England, abridged*, London, 1855.

Butler, S., *Britain and its Empire in the Shadow of Rome: The Reception of Rome in Socio-Political Debate from the 1850s to the 1920s*, London, 2012.

Butlin, R., 'George Adam Smith and the Historical Geography of the Holy Land', *Journal of Historical Geography* 4, 1988: 381–404.

Buzard, J., *The Beaten Track: European Tourism, Literature and the Ways to 'Culture' 1800–1918*, Oxford, 1993.

Buzard, J., Childers, J. and Gillooly, E. eds., *Victorian Prism: Refractions of the Crystal Palace*, Charlottesville and London, 2008.

Cambridge Camden Society, *The Church of the Holy Sepulchre or the Round Church, Cambridge*, Cambridge, 1842.

The Church of the Holy Sepulchre, Cambridge, 1844.

A Few Words to Church Builders, Cambridge, 1848.

Hieriurgia Anglicana or Documents and Extracts Illustrative of the Rituals of the Church of England after the Reformation, London, 1848.

The Round Church, circular dated 13 March 1844.

Twenty-Three Reasons for Getting Rid of Church Pews – or Pues, Cambridge, 1846.

Twenty-Four Reasons for Getting Rid of Church Pews – or Pues, Cambridge, 1846.

Camden, W., *Britain, or, a Chorographicall Description of the Most Flourishing Kingdomes, England, Scotland, and Ireland*, trans P. Holland, London, 1610.

Cameron Lyons, M. and Jackson, D., *Saladin: The Politics of Holy War*, Cambridge, 1982.

Campbell, I. D., *Fixing the Indemnity: The Life and Work of Sir George Adam Smith (1856–1942)*, Carlisle, 2004.

Carey, S., *Ritualism: A Sermon*, London, 1885.

Carlyle, T., *Sartor Resartus*, Boston and London, 1897.

Carpenter, W., *Scripture Natural History*, Boston, Lincs, 1833.

Carruthers, M., *The Book of Memory*, Cambridge, 1990.

Cartledge, P., Millett, P. and Von Reden, S. eds., *Kosmos: Essays in Order, Conflict and Community in Classical Athens*, Cambridge, 2002.

Casteras, S. *et al.*, *John Ruskin and the Victorian Eye*, New York, 1993.

Çelik, Z., *Displaying the Orient: Architecture of Islam at Nineteenth-Century World's Fairs*, Berkeley, 1992.

'Speaking Back to Orientalist Discourse at the World's Columbian Fair', in Edwards ed., *Anthropology and Photography*, 1992: 77–97.

'Speaking Back to Orientalist Discourse', in Beaulieu and Roberts eds., *Orientalism's Interlocutors*, 2002: 19–42.

Chadwick, W. O., *The Spirit of the Oxford Movement*, Cambridge, 1990.

The Victorian Church, 2 vols., London, 1966–70.

Challis, D., *From the Harpy Tombs to the Wonders of Ephesus: British Archaeologists in the Ottoman Empire 1840–1880*, London, 2008.

Champion, T. 'Protecting the Monuments: Archaeological Legislation from the 1882 Act to *PPG 16*', in Hunter ed., *Preserving the Past*, 1996: 38–56.

Chandler, A., *A Dream of Order: The Medieval Idea in Nineteenth-Century English Literature*, London, 1970.

Chapman, R., *The Sense of the Past in Victorian Literature*, London and Sydney, 1986.

Chareyron, N., *Pilgrims to Jerusalem in the Middle Ages*, trans. W. D. Wilson, New York, 2005.

Chateaubriand, F. de, *Travels in Greece, Palestine, Egypt, and Barbary, during the years 1806 and 1807*, trans. F. Shoberl, New York, 1814.

Cherry, M., 'Patronage: The Anglican Church and the Local Architect in Victorian England', in Brooks and Saint eds., *The Victorian Church*, 1995: 173–91.

Chevedden, P., 'The Photographic Heritage of the Middle East: An Exhibition of Early Photographs of Egypt, Palestine, Syria, Turkey, Greece, & Iran, 1849–1893', *Occasional Papers on the Near East* 1.3, 1979–82: 67–106.

Chitty, G., 'Ruskin's Architectural Heritage: *The Seven Lamps of Architecture* – Reception and Legacy', in Daniels and Brandwood eds., *Ruskin and Architecture*, 2003: 25–54.

Christensen, A. ed., *The Subverting Vision of Bulwer Lytton*, Newark, 2004.

Church, A. J., *The Burning of Rome*, London, 1903.

Church, R. W., *On the Relations Between Church and State*, London, 1881.

Çizgen, E., *Photographs of the Ottoman Empire 1839–1919*, Istanbul, 1987.

Clark, A. and Chalmers, D., 'The Extended Mind', *Analysis* 58, 1998: 7–19.

Clark, V., *Holy Fire: The Battle for Christ's Tomb*, San Francisco, 2005.

Cline, E., *Jerusalem Besieged: From Ancient Canaan to Modern Israel*, Ann Arbor, 2004.

Clive, J., *Thomas Babington Macaulay: The Shaping of the Historian*, London, 1973.

Close, F., *Church Architecture Scripturally Considered, from the Earliest Ages to the Present Time*, London, 1844.

　A Reply to the 'Remarks' of the Rev. T.K. Arnold, M.A. on Close's 'Church Architecture', London, 1844.

　The Restoration of Churches is the Restoration of Popery: Proved and Illustrated from the Authenticated Publications of 'Cambridge Camden Society', London, 1844.

Cockerell, C. R., *The Temples of Jupiter Panhellenicus at Aegina and Apollo Epikourius at Bassae near Phigaleia in Arcadia*, London, 1860.

Cohen, A., *Economic Life in Ottoman Jerusalem*, Cambridge, 1989.

Cohen, D., *Household Gods: The British and their Possessions*, New Haven, 2006.

Cohen, J. P., *Becoming Ottomans: Sephardi Jews and Imperial Citizenship in the Modern Era*, Oxford, 2014.

Cohen, R., *Saving the Holy Sepulchre: How Rival Christians Came Together to Rescue their Holiest Shrine*, Oxford, 2008.

Colbert, C., *A Measure of Perfection: Phrenology and the Fine Arts in America*, Chapel Hill and London, 1997.

Collard, C., 'F. A. Paley', in Jocelyn ed., *Aspects*, 1996: 67–80.

　'A Victorian Outsider: F. A. Paley (1816–88)' in Jocelyn and Hurt eds., *Tria Lustra*, 1993: 329–41.

Collison, F., *On the History of Christian Altars: a Paper Read before the Cambridge Camden Society Nov. 28, 1844*, Cambridge, 1845.

　Remarks on a Sermon by Professor Scholefield, Entitled the Christian Altar: Being a Vindication of the Catholic Doctrines Therein Impugned, Cambridge, 1842.

　Some Further Remarks on the Christian Altar and Eucharistic Sacrifice: with Strictures on Vedilius and Williams, Cambridge, 1843.

Colvin, S., 'Restoration and Anti-Restoration', *The Nineteenth Century* 6: 446–70, 1877.

Combe, G., *Constitution of Man*, Edinburgh, 1828.

　Elements of Phrenology, Edinburgh, 1824.

　Essays on Phrenology; or, An Enquiry into the principles and utility of the system of Drs. Gall and Spurzheim, and into the objections made to it, Edinburgh, 1819.

　System of Phrenology, Edinburgh, 1836.

Conder, C., *City of Jerusalem*, London, 1909.

Conder, J., *The Modern Traveller*, vol. i, London, 1830.

Conybeare, J., *Roman Britain*, London, 1903.

Conybeare, W. and Howson, J., *The Life and Epistles of St Paul*, 7th edition, 2 vols., London, 1860 [1852].

Cooper, A., *'The Eucharist Not a True and Propitiatory Sacrifice' or 'Vestments and the Eastward Position Unnecessary and Illegal'*, London and Brighton, 1875.

　'The Real Presence of the Holy Spirit', or 'Close Communion with God', London and Brighton, 1875.

Cooper, F., *The Temple of Apollo Bassitas*, vol. ii, prepared by C. Madigan, Baltimore, 1992.

Cooter, R., *The Cultural Meaning of Popular Science: Phrenology and the Organization of Consent in Nineteenth-Century Britain*, Cambridge, 1984.

Cormack, R., 'Unity out of Diversity? The Making of a Modern Christian Monument in Anglo-Egyptian Sudan', in Swenson and Mandler eds., *Plunder and Preservation*, 2013.

Cox, H., *Is the Church of England Protestant?*, 3rd edn, London, 1890 [1874].

Cox, S., *Diversions of a Diplomat in Turkey*, New York, 1887.

Crary, J., *Techniques of the Observer: On Vision and Modernity in the Nineteenth Century*, Cambridge, Mass., 1990.

Crawford, A., *C.R. Ashbee: Architect, Designer and Romantic Socialist*, New Haven, 1985.

Crockett, W., *Abbotsford*, London, 1905.
  The Scott Country, London, 1905.

Crumb, L., *The Oxford Movement and its Leaders: A Bibliography of Secondary and Lesser Primary Sources*, Lanham, 2009.

Cuno, J., *Who Owns Antiquity? Museums and the Battle over our Ancient Heritage*, Princeton, 2008.

Dalloway, J., *Of Statuary and Sculpture Among the Ancients*, London, 1816.

Daniels, R. and Brandwood, G. eds., *Ruskin and Architecture*, Reading, 2003.

Daston, L. ed., *Things that Talk: Object Lessons from Art and Science*, New York, 2004.

Daston, L. and Galison, P., *Objectivity*, New York, 2007.

Davies, J., *The Great Exhibition*, Stroud, 1999.
  Phrenology, Fad and Science: A 19th-Century American Crusade, New Haven, 1955.

Davis, J., *The Landscape of Belief: Encountering the Holy Land in Nineteenth-Century American Art and Culture*, Princeton, 1996.

Davison, R., *Reform in the Ottoman Empire 1856–1876*, Princeton, 1963.

Delafons, J., *Politics and Preservation: A Policy History of the Built Heritage 1882–1996*, London, 1997.

De Mille, J., *Helena's Household: A Tale of Rome in the First Century*, London, 1867.

Denison, G., *A Charge of the Archdeacon of Taunton at his Visitation, April 1877*, London, 1877.
  Notes of my Life, 1805–1878, Oxford, 1878.

Denslagen, W., *Architectural Restoration in Western Europe: Controversy and Continuity*, Amsterdam, 1994.

Dentith, S., *Epic and Empire in Nineteenth-Century Britain*, Cambridge, 2006.

Deringil, S., 'The Invention of Tradition as Public Image in the Late Ottoman Empire, 1808–1908', *Comparative Studies in Society and History* 35, 1993: 3–29.

'"They Live in a State of Nomadism and Savagery": The Late Ottoman Empire and the Post-Colonial Debate', *Comparative Studies in Society and History* 45, 2003: 311–42.

The Well-Protected Domains: Ideology and the Legitimation of Power in the Ottoman Empire, 1876–1909, London and New York, 1998.

Descoeudres, J.-P. ed., *Pompeii Revisited: The Life and Death of a Roman Town*, Sydney, 1994.

Di Bello, P., *Women's Albums and Photography in Victorian England: Ladies, Mothers and Flirts*, Aldershot, 2007.

Dinsmoor, F., 'The Sculptured Frieze from Bassae (a revised sequence)', *AJA* 60, 1956: 401–52.

Dishon, D., 'Three Men in a Gondola: Ruskin, Webb and Street', in Webster and Elliott eds., *A Church*, 2000: 190–210.

Disraeli, B., *Endymion*, London, 1880.

Sybil, London, 1845.

Tancred, or the New Crusade, London, 1847.

Dolkart, J. ed., *James Tissot: The Life of Christ*, London and New York, 2009.

Douglas, M. and Isherwood, B., *The World of Goods: Towards an Anthropology of Consumption*, Harmondsworth, 1978.

Downing, E., *After Images: Photography, Archaeology and Psychoanalysis, and the Tradition of Bildung*, Detroit, 2006.

Dykes, J., *Eucharistic Truth and Ritual: a Letter to the Right Reverend The Lord Bishop of Durham*, 2nd edn, London and Durham, 1874.

Eastlake, C., *A History of the Gothic Revival*, London, 1872.

Eastlake, Lady E., *Music and the Art of Dress*, London, 1852.

'Physiognomy', *Quarterly Review* 90, 1851–2: 62–91.

Edmondson, G., *The Church in Rome in the First Century*, London, 1913.

Edwards, C., 'Translating Empire? Macaulay's Rome', in Edwards ed., *Roman Presences*, 1999: 70–87.

Edwards, C. ed., *Roman Presences: Receptions of Rome in European Culture 1789–1945*, Cambridge, 1999.

Edwards, E. ed., *Anthropology and Photography 1860–1920*, New Haven, 1992.

Edwards, S., *The Making of British Photography: Allegories*, University Park, Pa., 2006.

Eliav, M., *Britain and the Holy Land 1838–1914: Selected Documents from the British Consulate in Jerusalem*, Jerusalem, 1997.

Eliot, G., *Daniel Deronda*, London, 2012.

Elsner, J. and Cardinal, R. eds., *The Cultures of Collecting*, London, 1994.

Erdogdu, A., 'Picturing Alterity: Representational Strategies in Victorian Type Photography of Ottoman Men', in Hight and Sampson, *Colonialist Photography*, 2002: 107–25.

Farrar, F., *Darkness and Dawn*, London, 1892.

Faulkner, R., *An Appeal to the Protestant Public Respecting the Popish Abominations of a Stone Altar and Credence Table, in St Sepulchre's Church*, Cambridge, 1844, n.p.

Fawcett, J., 'A Restoration Tragedy: Cathedrals in the Eighteenth and Nineteenth Centuries', in Fawcett ed., *The Future of the Past*, 1976: 75–116.

Fawcett, J. ed., *The Future of the Past: Attitudes to Conservation 1174–1974*, London, 1976.

Fergusson, J. *Essay on the Ancient Topography of Jerusalem, with Restored Plans of the Temple &c. and Plans, Sections, and Details of the Church Built by Constantine the Great over the Holy Sepulchre, now Known as the Mosque of Omar*, London, 1847.

   The Holy Sepulchre and the Temple at Jerusalem, London, 1865.

   The Palaces of Nineveh and Persepolis Restored: An Essay on Ancient Assyrian Art and Persian Architecture, London, 1851.

   The Temple of the Jews and Other Buildings in the Haram Area of Jerusalem, London, 1878.

Ferrey, B., *Recollections of A. Welby Pugin and his Father, Augustus Pugin*, London, 1861.

Ferris, I., *The Achievement of Literary Authority: Gender, History and the Waverley Novel*, Ithaca, N.Y., 1991.

Field, G., *Evangelist of Race: The Germanic Vision of Houston Stewart Chamberlain*, New York, 1981.

Finn, J., *Stirring Times*, 2 vols., London, 1878.

Fitzgerald, E., *Euphranor: A Dialogue on Youth*, London, 1851.

Fleischman, A., *The Historical Novel: Walter Scott to Virginia Woolf*, Baltimore, 1971.

Fleming, K., *The Muslim Bonaparte: Diplomacy and Orientalism in Ali Pasha's Greece*, Princeton, 1999.

Fleming, L., *Memoir and Select Letters of Samuel Lysons V.P.R.S., V.P.S.A. 1763–1819*, Oxford, 1934.

Forbush, W. B., *The Methods and Advantages of the Travel Lesson of the Old Testament*, New York and London, 1904.

Forrester, J., 'Mille e tre: Freud and Collecting', in Elsner and Cardinal eds., *Cultures of Collecting*, 1994: 224–51.

Forster, E. M., *A Room with a View*, London, 1908.

Fortna, B., *Imperial Classroom: Islam, the State and Education in the Late Ottoman Empire*, Oxford, 2002.

Fraser, R., *Charlotte Brontë*, London, 1985.

Freedgood, D., *The Ideas in Things: Fugitive Meaning in the Victorian Novel*, Chicago, 2006.

Freeman, E. A., *Principles of Church Restoration*, London, 1846.

Freud, E. ed., *Letters of Sigmund Freud 1873–1939*, trans. T. Stern and J. Stern London, 1963.

Freud, S., *The Standard Edition of the Complete Psychological Works of Sigmund Freud*, trans. J. Strachey, 24 vols., London, 1956–74.

Frith, F., *Egypt and Palestine*, 2 vols., London, 1859.

Fritzsche, P., *Stranded in the Present: Modern Time and the Melancholy of History*, Cambridge, Mass., 2004.

Froude, J., *The Nemesis of Faith*, London, 1849.

Fuchs, R. and Herbert, G., 'Representing Mandatory Palestine: Austen St Barbe Harrison and the Representational Buildings of the British Mandate in Palestine, 1922–37', *Architectural History* 43, 2000: 281–333.

Fuss, D., *The Sense of an Interior: Four Writers and the Rooms that Shaped Them*, New York and London, 2004.

Gamwell, L. and Wells, R. eds., *Sigmund Freud and Art: His Personal Collection of Antiquities*, London, 1989.

Gange, D. and Ledger-Lomas, M. eds., *Cities of God: Archaeology and the Bible in Nineteenth-Century Britain*, Cambridge, 2013.

Gardner, B., *Allenby*, London, 1965.

Garnett, J. and Bush, A., 'Rome', in Gange and Ledger-Lomas eds., *Cities of God*, 2013: 285–314.

Garrigan, K., *Ruskin on Architecture: His Thought and Influence*, Madison, 1973.

Gaskell, E., *The Life of Charlotte Brontë*, London, 1857.
  North and South, London, 1855.

Gavazzi, A., *The Priest in Absolution: An Exposure*, London, 1877.

Gavin, C., *The Image of The East: Nineteenth-Century Photography by Bonfils*, Chicago, 1982.

Gavin, C. ed., 'Imperial Self-Portrait: The Ottoman Empire as Revealed in the Sultan Abdul-Hamid II's Photographic Album', *Journal of Turkish Studies* 12, 1988.

Gell, A., *Art and Agency: An Anthropological Approach*, Oxford and New York, 1998.

Gell, W., *Sir William Gell in Italy. Letters to the Society of Dilettanti*, ed E. Clay with M. Frederiksen, London.

Gerber, H., *Ottoman Rule in Jerusalem 1800–1914*, Berlin, 1985.

Gere, C., *Knossos and the Prophets of Modernism*, Chicago, 2009.

Gérin, W., *Charlotte Brontë: The Evolution of Genius*, Oxford, 1967.

Gibson, I., *The Erotomaniac: The Secret Life of Henry Spencer Ashbee*, London, 2001.

Gibson, S., *Jerusalem in Original Photographs 1850–1920*, London, 2003.

Gidney, W., *The History of the London Society for Promoting Christianity Amongst the Jews*, London, 1908.

Gigord, P. de and Beaugé, G., *Images d'Empire: aux origines de la photographie en Turquie*, trans. Y. Bener, Istanbul, 1993.

Gilbar, G. ed., *Ottoman Palestine 1800–1914*, Leiden, 1990.

Giles, J., *History of the Ancient Britons from the Earliest Period to the Invasion of the Saxons*, London, 1847.

Gill, C., *Wordsworth and the Victorians*, Oxford, 1998.

Gillmor, W., *The Public Worship Regulation Act: Two Sermons Preached at Illingworth, Yorkshire*, London and Halifax, 1875.

Gilman, S., *Freud, Race and Gender*, Princeton, 1993.

Girouard, M., *The Return to Camelot: Chivalry and the English Gentleman*, New Haven, 1981.

Gitelman, L and Pingree, G. eds., *New Media 1740–1915*, Boston, 2003.

Goldhill, S., 'The Cotswolds in Jerusalem: Restoration and Empire', in Mandler and Swenson eds., *From Plunder to Preservation*, 2013: 115–45.

   'The Discovery of Victorian Jerusalem', in Gange and Ledger-Lomas eds., *Cities of God*, 2013: 71–110.

   Jerusalem: City of Longing, Cambridge, Mass., 2008.

   'The Seductions of the Gaze: Socrates and his Girlfriends', in Cartledge, Millett and von Reden eds. *Kosmos*, 2002: 105–24.

   The Temple of Jerusalem, London, 2004.

   Victorian Culture and Classical Antiquity: Art, Opera, Fiction and the Proclamation of Modernity, Princeton, 2011.

Gonzalez, C., *Local Portraiture: Through the Lens of the 19th-Century Iranian Photographers*, Leiden, 2012.

Goode, M., 'Dryasdust Antiquarianism and Soppy Masculinity: the Waverley Novels and the Gender of History', *Representations* 82, 2003.

Goode, W., *Altars Prohibited by the Church of England*, London, 1844.

Gordon, L., *Charlotte Brontë: A Passionate Life*, London, 2008.

Goren, H., '"Sacred but not surveyed": Nineteenth-century Surveys of Palestine', *Imago Mundi* 54, 2002: 87–110.

Graber, G., *Ritual Legislation in the Victorian Church of England: Antecedents and Passage of the Public Worship Regulation Act, 1874*, Lewiston, NY, 1993.

Graham, S., *With the Russian Pilgrims to Jerusalem*, London, 1913.

Graham-Brown, S., *Images of Women: The Portrayal of Women in Photography of the Middle East 1850–1950*, London, 1988.

Greaves, R. W., "The Jerusalem Bishopric, 1841", *English Historical Review* 64, 1949: 328–52.

Green, A., *Moses Montefiore: Jewish Liberator, Imperial Hero*, Cambridge, Mass, 2010.

Grover, J. W., 'On a Roman Villa at Chedworth', *Journal of the British Archaeological Association* 24, 1868: 129–35.

   'Pre-Augustinian Christianity in Britain: as Indicated by the Discovery of Christian Symbols', *Journal of the British Archaeological Association* 23, 1867: 221–30.

Grover, K. ed., *Hard at Play: Leisure in America 1840–1940*, Rochester, NY, 1992.

Guest, E., *Origines Celticae*, London, 1883.

Hackforth-Jones, J. and Roberts, M. eds., *Edges of Empire: Orientalism and Visual Culture*, Oxford, 2005.

Hales, S. and Paul, J. eds., *Pompeii in the Public Imagination from its Rediscovery to Today*, Oxford, 2011.

Hall, C., *Civilizing Subjects: Metropole and Colony in the English Imagination 1830–1867*, Cambridge, 2002.

Macaulay and Son: Architects of Imperial Britain, New Haven, 2012.

Hall, M., 'Affirming Community Life: Preservation, National Identity and the State, 1900', in Miele ed., *From William Morris*, 2005: 129–58.

Hallote, R., *Bible, Map and Spade: The American Palestine Exploration Society, Frederick Jones Bliss and the Forgotten Story of Early American Biblical Archaeology*, Piscataway, 2006.

Hallote, R., Cobbing, F. and Spurr, J., *The Photographs of the American Palestine Exploration Society*, Boston, 2012.

Halsted, T., *Our Missions, being a History of the Principal Missionary Transactions of the London Society for Promoting Christianity amongst the Jews from its Foundation in 1809 to the Present Year*, London, 1866

Hanley, K. and Walton, J., *Constructing Cultural Tourism: John Ruskin and the Tourist Gaze*, Bristol, Buffalo, Toronto, 2010.

Hanson, B., '*Labor ipse Voluptas*: Scott, Street, Ruskin and the value of Work', in Daniels and Brandwood eds., *Ruskin and Architecture*, 2003: 123–61.

Hanssen, J, Philipp, T. and Weber, S. eds., *The Empire in the City: Arab Provincial Capitals in the Late Ottoman Empire*, Beirut, 2002.

Hardy, T., *The Fiddler of the Reels and Other Short Stories*, eds. K. Wilson, K. Brady and P. Ingham, London, 2003.

Memories of Church Restoration, ed. A. Whitworth, Whitby, 2002.

Hare, A., *The Story of Two Noble Lives: Being Memorials of Charlotte, Countess Canning and Louisa, Marchioness of Waterford*, London, 1893.

Harrison, M., *Victorian Stained Glass*, London, 1980.

Hartley, L., *Physiognomy and the Meaning of Expression in Nineteenth-Century Culture*, Cambridge, 2001.

Harvey, M., 'Ruskin and Photography', *Oxford Art Journal* 7, 1985: 25–33.

Hassell, J., *From Pole to Pole, being the History of Christian Missions in All Countries of the World*, 2nd edn, London, 1872.

Havrelock, R., *River Jordan: The Mythology of a Dividing Line*, Chicago, 2011.

Helsinger, E., *Ruskin and the Art of the Beholder*, Cambridge, Mass., 1982.

Hendrix, H., *Writers' Houses and the Making of Memory*, London, 2007.

Henig, M., *Religion in Roman Britain*, 2nd edn, London, 1995.

Henig, M. and King, A. eds., *Pagan Gods and Shrines of the Roman Empire*, Oxford, 1986.

Henry, R., *The History of Great Britain from the First Invasion of it by the Romans under Julius Caesar*, 2nd edn, Dublin, 1789.

Herzog, C., 'Nineteenth-Century Baghdad through Ottoman Eyes', in Hanssen, Philipp and Weber eds., *The Empire in the City*, 2002: 311–28.

Hesketh, I., *The Science of History in Victorian Britain: Making the Past Speak*, London, 2011.

Higgins, C., *Under Another Sky: Journeys in Roman Britain*, London, 2013.

Hight, E. and Sampson, G. eds., *Colonialist Photography: Imag(in)ing Race and Place*, London and New York, 2002.

Hillenbrand, C., *Crusades: Islamic Perspectives*, New York, 1999.

Hilton, B., *The Age of Atonement: The Influence of Evangelicalism on Social and Economic Thought 1785–1865*, Oxford, 1986.

Hingley, R., *The Recovery of Roman Britain 1586–1906*, Oxford, 2008.

  Roman Officers and English Gentlemen: The Imperial Origins of Roman Archaeology, London and New York, 2000.

Hobhouse, H., *Crystal Palace and the Great Exhibition: A History of the Royal Commission for the Exhibition of 1851*, London, 2002.

Hobson, W., *Public Worship Regulation Act: Letter to the Right Hon. Mountague Bernard*, London, 1877.

Holmes, O. W., 'The Stereoscope and the Stereograph', *Atlantic Monthly* 3, 1850: 738–48.

Hoselitz, V., *Imagining Roman Britain: Victorian Responses to a Roman Past*, Woodbridge, 2007.

Hourani, A., 'How Should We Write the History of the Middle East', *International Journal of Middle Eastern Studies* 23, 1991: 125–36.

Howe, K., *Revealing the Holy Land: The Photographic Exploration of Palestine*, Santa Barbara, 1997.

  'Mapping a Sacred Geography: Photographic Surveys by the Royal Engineers in the Holy Land, 1864–1868', in Schwartz and Ryan eds., *Picturing Place*, 2003: 226–42.

Howorth, H., 'Christianity in Roman Britain', *Transactions of the Royal Historical Society* 2, 1885: 117–72.

Huggins, S., 'Chester Cathedral Restoration', *Athenaeum* 2548, 26 August 1876: 279–80.

  'The Restoration of our Cathedrals and Abbey Churches', *Athenaeum* 2276, 10 June 1871: 728.

Hunter, M. ed., *Preserving the Past: the Rise of Heritage in Modern Britain*, Stroud, 1996.

Hurlbut, J., *The Story of Chautauqua*, New York, 1921.

  Travelling in the Holy Land through the Stereoscope, New York and London, 1900.

Huskinson, J, 'Some Pagan Mythological Figures and their Significance in Early Christian Art', *Papers of the British School at Rome* 42, 1974: 68–97.

Hyamson, H., *British Projects for the Restoration of the Jews*, Leeds, 1971.

Hylson-Smith, K., *Evangelicals in the Church of England, 1734–1984*, Edinburgh, 1989.

Irving, W., *Miscellanies*, London, 1835.

Irwin, R., *For Lust of Knowing: The Orientalists and their Enemies*, London, 2006.

Jacobson, A., *From Empire to Empire: Jerusalem between Ottoman and British Rule*, Syracuse, NY, 2011.

Jacobson, K., *Odalisques and Arabesques: Orientalist Photography*, London, 2007.

Jaffe, E., *Yemin Moshe: The Story of a Jerusalem Neighbourhood*, Westport, Conn., 1988.

Jamieson, P., *Auldjo: A Life of John Auldjo 1805–1886*, Wilby, Norwich, 2009.

Janes, D., *Victorian Reformation: The Fight over Idolatry in the Church of England, 1840–60*, Oxford and New York, 2009.

Jebb, R., *Bacchylides: The Poems and Fragments*, Cambridge, 1905.

Jenkyns, R., 'Late Antiquity in English Novels of the Nineteenth Century', *Arion* 3, 1995: 141–66.

Jocelyn, H. ed., *Aspects of Nineteenth-Century British Classical Scholarship: Eleven Essays*, Liverpool, 1996.

Jocelyn, H. and Hurt, H. eds., *Tria Lustra*, Liverpool, 1993.

Jokhileto, J., *A History of Architectural Conservation*, Oxford, 1999.

Kark, R., *Jerusalem Neighbourhoods: Planning and By-laws (1855–1930)*, Jerusalem, 1991.

Karp, I. and Lavine, S. eds., *Exhibiting Cultures: The Poetics and Politics of Museum Display*, Washington, D.C., 1991.

Katz, K., *Jordanian Jerusalem: Holy Places and National Spaces*, Gainesville, 2005.

Kelly, C., *Kelly's New System of Universal Geography*, London, 1819.

Kent, C., *Description of One Hundred and Forty Places in Bible Lands, to be Seen Through the Stereoscope or by Means of Stereoticon Slides*, New York and London, 1911.

Khalidi, W., *Before their Diaspora: A Photographic History of Palestinians 1876–1948*, Washington, 1984.

   Palestinian Identity: The Construction of Modern National Consciousness, New York, 1997.

Kinglake, A. W., *Eothen*, London, 1900 [1844].

[Kingsley, C.], 'Sir E. B. Lytton and Mrs Grundy', *Fraser's* 41, 1850: 98–111.

Kirschenblatt-Gimblett, B., 'A Place in the World: Jews, the Holy Land and the World's Fairs', in Shandler and Wenger eds., *Encounters*, 1998: 60–82.

Knoepflmacher, U. and Tennyson, G. eds. *Nature and the Victorian Imagination*, Berkeley, 1978.

Koditschek, T., *Liberalism, Imperialism, and the Historical Imagination: Nineteenth-Century Visions of a Greater Britain*, Cambridge, 2011.

Koselleck, R., *Futures Past: On the Semantics of Historical Time*, trans. K. Tribe, Cambridge, Mass., 1985.

   The Practice of Conceptual History: Timing History, Spacing Concepts, trans. T. Presner, K. Behnke and J. Welge, Stanford, 2002.

Krebs, C., *A Most Dangerous Book: Tacitus' Germania from the Roman Empire to the Third Reich*, New York, 2011.

Kroyanker, D., *Adrikhalut bi-Yerushalayim* [in Hebrew], 6 vols., Jerusalem, 1985–1993.

Kühnel, B., 'Geography and Geometry of Jerusalem', in Rosovsky ed., *City of the Great King*, 1996: 288–332.

Lager, E., 'Interview', in Descoeudres ed., *Pompeii Revisited*, 1994.

Lagerlöf, S., *Jerusalem*, 2 vols., London, 1901–2.

Lamb, J., *The Things Things Say*, Princeton, 2011.

Lampe, P., *From Paul to Valentinus: Christians in Rome in the First Two Centuries*, Philadelphia, 2004.

Landau, J., *Abdul-Hamid's Palestine*, Jerusalem and London, 1979.

Larkworthy, P., *Clayton and Bell: Stained Glass Artists and Decorators*, London, 1984.

Larsen, M., *The Conquest of Assyria: Excavations in an Antique Land*, London, 1996.

Larsen, T., *Contested Christianity: The Political and Social Contexts of Victorian Theology*, Waco, Tex., 2004.

'Nineveh', in Gange and Ledger-Lomas eds., *Cities of God*, 2013: 111–35.

'Thomas Cook, Holy Land Pilgrims and the Dawn of the Modern Tourist Industry', in Swanson ed., *The Holy Land*, 2000: 329–42.

Layard, A., *Nineveh and its Remains*, 2 vols., London, 1849.

The Nineveh Court in the Crystal Palace, London, 1854.

Leerssen, J., 'Introduction', in van Hulle and Leerssen eds., *Editing*, 2008: 13–27.

National Thought in Europe: A Cultural History, Amsterdam, 2006.

Leland, C. G., *Memoirs*, London, 1893.

Lendrum, A., *The Judicial Committee, the Misgovernment of the Church and the Remedy*, London, 1882.

Leonard, M., *Socrates and the Jews: Hellenism and Hebraism from Moses Mendelssohn to Sigmund Freud*, Chicago, 2012.

Lepine, Ayla, 'On the Founding of Watts and Co., 1874', in *BRANCH: Britain, Representation and Nineteenth-Century History*, ed. Dino Franco Felluga, 2013 Extension of Romanticism and Victorianism on the Net. Accessed 29.7.13.

Leppman, W., *Pompeii in Fact and Fiction*, London, 1968.

Lerebours, N., *Excursions Daguerriennes*, Paris, 1842.

Le Strange, G., (1965) *Palestine under the Moslems 650–1500*, Beirut, 1965.

Levine, G., *The Boundaries of Fiction: Carlyle, Macaulay, Newman*, Princeton, 1968.

Levine, L., *Visual Judaism in Late Antiquity: Historical Contexts of Jewish Art*, New Haven, 2012.

Levine, P., *Amateur and Professional: Antiquarians, Historians and Archaeologists in Victorian England, 1838–1886*, Cambridge, 1986.

Levy-Rubin, M and Rubin, R., 'The Image of the Holy City in Maps and mapping', in Rosovsky ed., *City of the Great King*, 1996: 352–79.

Lewin, T., *Life and Epistles of St Paul*, 5th edn, 2 vols., London, 1860 [1851].

Lewis, D., *The Origins of Christian Zionism: Lord Shaftesbury and Evangelical Support for a Jewish Homeland*, Cambridge, 2010.

Lewis, R., *Rethinking Orientalism: Women, Travel and the Ottoman Harem*, London, 2002.

Lincoln, B., *Theorizing Myth: Narrative, Ideology and Scholarship*, Chicago, 1999.

Lockman, Z., *Contending Visions of the Middle East: The History and Politics of Orientalism*, Cambridge, 2010.

Loftie, W., 'Thorough Restoration', *Macmillan's Magazine* 36, 1877: 136–42.

Long. B., *Imagining the Holy Land: Maps, Models and Fantasy Travels*, Bloomington, 2003.

A Looker On, 'Theory of Restoration', *The Builder* 28, 1870: 649–50.

Low, G., *White Skins/Black Masks: Representation and Colonialism*, London, 1996.

Lowenthal, D., *The Heritage Crusade and the Spoils of History*, London, 1996.

Lowenthal, D. and Binney, M. eds., *Our Past Before Us: Why Do We Save it?*, London, 1981.

Lukács, G., *The Historical Novel*, trans H. and S. Mitchell, Harmondsworth, 1969.

Lyons, C., 'The Art and Science of Antiquity in Nineteenth-Century Photography', in Lyons, Papadopoulou, Stewart and Szegedy-Maszak eds., *Early Views*, 2005: 22–65.

Lyons, C, Papadopoulou, J., Stewart, L. and Szegedy-Maszak, A. eds., *Early Views of Ancient Mediterranean Sites*, London, 2005.

Lysons, S., *Reliquiae Britannico-Romanae*, 3 vols., London, 1813–17.

Lysons, S. (jun.), *Claudia and Pudens: or, The Early Christians in Gloucester*, London, 1861.

   Our British Ancestors: Who and What Were They?, Oxford and London, 1865.

   The Romans of Gloucestershire, London, 1860.

Lytton, V., *The Life of Edward Bulwer*, 2 vols., London, 1913.

M. K. R., *Public Worship Act, illustrated by M.K.R.*, London, 1877.

M. U., 'Moderation in Restoration', *The Builder* 28, 1870: 202–3.

Macaulay, T., *Lays of Ancient Rome*, London, 1842.

MacCarthy, F., *The Last Pre-Raphaelite: Edward Burne-Jones and the Victorian Imagination*, London, 2011.

   The Simple Life: C.R. Ashbee in the Cotswolds, London, 1981.

Machin, G., *Politics and the Churches in Great Britain 1869–1921*, 2nd edn, Oxford, 1987.

Mackay, C., *Through the Long Day*, London, 1887.

Maggiolini, P., 'Studies and Souvenirs of Palestine and Transjordan: The Revival of the Latin Patriarchate of Jerusalem and the Rediscovery of the Holy Land during the Nineteenth Century', in Netton ed., *Orientalism Revisited*, 2013: 165–75.

Maitzen, R., *Gender, Genre and Victorian Historical Writing*, New York and London, 1998.

Makdisi, U., 'Mapping the Orient: Non-Western Modernization, Imperialism, and the End of Romanticism', in Michie and Thomas eds., *Nineteenth-Century Geographies*, 2003: 40–54.

   'Ottoman Orientalism', *American Historical Review* 107, 2002: 768–96.

   'Rethinking Ottoman Imperialism: Modernity, Violence and the Cultural Logic of Ottoman Reform', in Hanssen, Philipp and Weber eds., *The Empire in the City* (2002): 29–48.

Malley, S., *From Archaeology to Spectacle in Victorian Britain: The Case of Assyria, 1845–1854*, Farnham, 2012.

Mandler, P., *The Fall and Rise of the Stately Home*, New Haven, 1997.

'"In the Olden Time": Romantic History and the English National Identity', in Brockliss and Eastwood eds., *A Union*, 1996: 78–92.

'Nationalizing the Country House', in Hunter ed., *Preserving the Past*, 1996: 99–114.

Mandler, P. and Swenson, A. eds., *From Plunder to Preservation: Britain and the Heritage of Empire, c1800–1940. Proceedings of the British Academy 187*, London, 2013.

Manners, J., *A Plea for National Holy Days*, London, Oxford, Cambridge, Durham, 1843.

Marchand, S., *Down from Olympus: Archaeology and Philhellenism in Germany, 1750–1070*, Princeton, 1996.

German Orientalism in the Age of Empire, Cambridge, 2009.

Marcus, A., *The View from Nebo: How Archaeology is Rewriting the Bible and Reshaping the Middle East*, Boston, New York and London, 2000.

Marcus, S., *The Other Victorians: A Study of Sexuality and Pornography in Mid-nineteenth-century England*, New York, 1964.

Marsh, P., *The Victorian Church in Decline: Archbishop Tait and the Church of England 1868–1882*, London, 1969.

Martineau, H., *Eastern Life, Past and Present*, 3 vols., London, 1848.

Martyn, J., *Henry Martyn 1781–1812: Scholar and Missionary to India and Persia: A Biography, Studies in the History of Missions* 18, Lewiston, 1999.

Massin, B., 'From Virchow to Fischer: Physical Anthropology and "Modern Race Theories" in Wilhelmine Germany', in Stocking ed., *Volksgeist*, 1996.

Masters, B., *The Arabs of the Ottoman Empire, 1516–1918*, Cambridge, 2013.

Maxwell-Scott, M. M., *Abbotsford: The Personal Relics and Antiquarian Treasures of Sir Walter Scott*, London, 1893.

Mazza, R., *Jerusalem: From the Ottomans to the British*, London and New York, 2009.

McCallum, G. ed., *The Holy Bible Containing the Old and New Testaments: translated out of the original tongues, and with the former translations diligently compared and revised by His Majesty's special command: with introductory remarks to each book, parallel passages, critical, explanatory, and practical notes; illustrated with photographs by Frith*, London, Glasgow, Edinburgh, 1862.

McCauley, E., *A.E.E. Disdéri and the Carte de Visite Photograph*, New Haven, 1985.

McCaw, N., *George Eliot and Victorian Historiography: Imagining the National Past*, Basingstoke, 2000.

McDannell, C., *Material Christianity: Religion and Popular Culture in America*, New Haven and London 1995.

McFie, A., *Orientalism*, London, 2002.

McKelvey, W., 'Primitive Ballads, Modern Criticism, Ancient Skepticism: Macaulay's "Lays of Ancient Rome"', *Victorian Literature and Culture* 28, 2000: 287–309.

McKenzie, J., *Orientalism: History, Theory and the Arts*, Manchester, 1995.

McMeekin, S., *The Berlin-Baghdad Express: The Ottoman Empire and Germany's Bid for World Empire*, Cambridge, Mass., 2010.

McMurray, J., *Distant Ties: Germany, the Ottoman Empire and the Construction of the Baghdad Railway*, Westport, CT, 2001.

Melman, B., *The Culture of History: English Uses of the Past 1800–1953*, Oxford, 2006.

   Women's Orients: English Women and the Middle East, 1718–1918. Sexuality, Religion and Work, London, 1992.

Mercier, Mrs. J., *By the King and Queen: A Story of the Dawn of Religion in Britain*, London, 1886.

   Our Mother Church: Simple Talk on High Topics, London, 1886.

Meskell, L. ed., *Archaeologies of Materiality*, Oxford, 2005.

Michie, H. and Thomas, R. eds., *Nineteenth-Century Geographies: The Transformation of Space from the Victorian Age to the American Century*, New Brunswick, NJ and London, 2003.

Micklewright, N., *A Victorian Traveller in the Middle East: The Photography and Travel Writing of Annie, Lady Brassey*, Aldershot, 2003.

Miele, C., '"Their Interest and Habit": Professionalism and the Restoration of Medieval Churches, 1837–77', in Brooks and Saint eds., *The Victorian Church*, 1995: 151–72.

   'Conservation and the Enemies of Progress', in Miele ed., *From William Morris*, 2005: 1–29.

   'The First Conservation Militants: William Morris and the Society for the Protection of Ancient Buildings', in Hunter ed., *Preserving the Past*, 1996: 17–37.

   'Morris and Conservation', in Miele ed., *From William Morris*, 2005: 31–65.

   'Re-Presenting the Church Militant: The Camden Society, Church Restoration, and the Gothic Sign', in Webster and Elliott eds., *A Church*, 2000: 257–94.

Miele, C. ed., *From William Morris: Building Conservation and the Art and Craft Cult of Authenticity 1877–1939*, New Haven, 2005.

Miller, A. H., *Novels Behind Glass: Commodity Culture and Victorian Narrative*, Cambridge, 1995.

Miller, L., *The Brontë Myth*, London, 2001.

Mitchell, L., *Bulwer Lytton: The Rise and Fall of a Victorian Man of Letters*, London and New York, 2003.

Mitchell, R., *Picturing the Past: English History in Text and Image, 1830–1870*, Oxford, 2000.

Mitchell, T., *Colonizing Egypt*, Berkeley, 1988.

Mole, T. ed., *Romanticism and Celebrity Culture 1750–1850*, Cambridge, 2010.

Morgan, R. W., *St Paul in Britain; or, The Origin of the British as Opposed to Papal Christianity*, London, 1861.

Morris, B., *The First Arab-Israeli War*, New Haven, 2008.

Morris, J., *F. D. Maurice and the Crisis of Christian Authority*, Oxford, 2005.

Morris, W., 'Restoration', *Athenaeum* 2591, 23 June 1877: 807.

Morrison-Low, A., and Christie, J. R. eds., *'Martyr of Science': Sir David Brewster 1781–1868*, Edinburgh, 1984.

Morton, S., *Crania Aegyptiaca or Observations on Egyptian Ethnography Derived from Anatomy, History and the Monuments*, Philadelphia and London, 1844.

Moscrop, J. J., *Measuring Jerusalem: The Palestine Exploration Fund and British Interests in the Holy Land*, London, 2000.

Moser, S., *Designing Antiquity: Owen Jones, Ancient Egypt and the Crystal Palace*, New Haven, 2012.

Mossman, T., *The Relations that Exist at Present between the Church and the State in England: A Letter addressed to the Right Hon. W.E. Gladstone MP*, London, 1883.

Mott, A., *The Stones of Palestine: Notes of a Ramble Through the Holy Land*, London, 1865.

Mulvey-Roberts, M., 'Edward Bulwer Lytton (1803–1873)', in Thomson, Voller and Frank, eds., *Gothic Writers*, 2002.

Munich, A., *Queen Victoria's Secrets*, New York, 1996.

Murre-van den Berg, H., 'William McClure Thomson's *The Land and the Book* (1859): Pilgrimage and Mission in Palestine', in Murre-van den Berg ed. *New Faith*, 2006: 43–63.

Murre-van den Berg, H. ed., *New Faith in Ancient Lands. Western Missions in the Middle East in the Nineteenth and Early Twentieth Centuries [Studies in Christian Missions 32]*, Leiden, 2006.

Nassar, I., 'Early Local Photography in Jerusalem: From the Imaginary to the Social Landscape', *History of Photography* 27, 2003: 320–32.

   Photographing Jerusalem: The Image of the City in Nineteenth-Century Photography, Boulder, Col., 1997.

Natseh, Y., *Ottoman Jerusalem: The Living City 1517–1917*, ed. S. Auld and R. Hillenbrand, 2 vols., London, 2000.

[Neale, J. M.]. *The History of Pews: A Paper Read Before the Cambridge Camden Society on Monday, November 22nd, 1841*, Cambridge, 1841.

Neale, J. M., *History of Pues*, 3rd edn, Cambridge, 1843.

   Letters of John Mason Neale DD, Selected and Edited by his Daughter, London, 1910.

   The Place Where Prayer Was Wont To Be Made, Rugeley, 1844.

Netton, I. ed., *Orientalism Revisited: Art, Land and Voyage*, London and New York, 2013.

Newman, J., *Apologia Pro Vita Sua*, London, 1864.

Nichols, K., *Greece and Rome at the Crystal Palace*, Oxford, 2015.

Nir, Y., *The Bible and the Image: The History of Photography in the Holy Land, 1839–1899*, Pennsylvania, 1985.

Nixon, J. and Richardson, R., *The Eglinton Tournament*, London, 1843.

Nockles, P., *The Oxford Movement in Context: Anglican High Churchmanship 1760–1857*, Cambridge, 1994.

Norris, J., *Land of Progress: Palestine in the Age of Colonial Development, 1905–1948*, Oxford, 2013.

O'Donnell, R., '"Blink by [him] in Silence": The Cambridge Camden Society and A. W. N. Pugin', in Webster and Elliott, *A Church*, 2000: 98–120.

Oettermann, S., *The Panorama*, Boston, 1997.

Oliphant, M., 'Bulwer', *Blackwood's Edinburgh Magazine* 77, 1855: 223.

Onne, E., *Photographic Heritage of the Holy Land, 1839–1914*, Manchester, 1980.

Orel, H., *The Historical Novel from Scott to Sabatini – Changing Attitudes to a Literary Genre 1814–1920*, Aldershot, 1995.

Oren, M., *Six Days of War: June 1967 and the Making of the Modern Middle East*, Oxford, 2002.

Orrells, D., 'Rocks, Ghosts and Footprints: Freudian Archaeology', in Hales and Paul eds. *Pompeii*, 2011: 185–98.

Orrells, D., Bhambra, G. and Roynon, T. eds., *African Athena: New Agendas*, Oxford, 2011.

Osborne, A. E., *The Stereograph and the Stereoscope with Special Maps and Books Forming a Travel System. What They Mean for Individual Development. What they Promise for the Spread of Civilization*, London, 1909.

Osborne, P. D., *Travelling Light: Photography, Travel and Visual Culture*, Manchester, 2000.

Osborne, R. and Tanner, J. eds., *Art's Agency and Art History*, Malden and Oxford, 2007.

Otter, C., *The Victorian Eye: A Political History of Light and Vision, 1800–1900*, Chicago, 2008.

Ousby, I., *The Englishman's England: Taste, Travel and the Use of Tourism*, Cambridge, 1990.

Owen, R., 'To the Right Hon. the Earl of Eglinton, Eglinton Castle, Ayrshire', *The Northern Star and Leeds General Advertiser*, 21 September 1839: 1.

Özendes, E., *Abdullah Frères: Ottoman Court Photographers*, trans. P. M. Isin, Istanbul, 1998.

   From Sébah & Joaillier to Foto Sébah: Orientalism and Photography, trans. P. M. Isin, Istanbul, 1999.

Öztuncay, B., *James Robertson: Pioneer of Photography in the Ottoman Empire*, Istanbul, 1992.

   The Photographers of Constantinople: Pioneers, Studios, and Artists from Nineteenth-Century Istanbul, Istanbul, 2003.

   Vassiliaki Kargopoulo: Photographer to His Majesty the Sultan, Istanbul, 2000.

Paget, F., *Milford Malvoisin, or Pews and Pewholders*, London, 1842.

Palmer, G. and Lloyd, N., *Father of the Bensons: The Life of Edward White Benson, Sometime Archbishop of Canterbury*, Harpenden, 1998.

Pananglican Synod, *The Pananglican Synod before 'St. Augustine's Chair' or the Venerable Bede's Account of the Christianity that Came from Rome*, London, 1878.

Parker, R., *The Subversive Stitch: Embroidery and the Making of the Feminine*, revised edn, London, 1996.

Parry, J., *Democracy and Religion: Gladstone and the Liberal Party, 1867–1875*, Cambridge, 1986.

Patterson, J., *Autobiographical Reminiscences*, Glasgow, 1871.

Paz, G., *Popular Anti-Catholicism in Mid-Victorian Britain*, Stanford, 1992.

Pearl, S., *About Faces: Physiognomics in Nineteenth-Century Britain*, Cambridge, Mass., 2010.

Perez, N., *Focus East: Early Photography in the Near East, 1839–1885*, New York, 1988.

Perring, D., '"Gnosticism" in Fourth-Century Britain: the Frampton Mosaics Reconsidered', *Britannia* 34, 2003: 97–127.

Perry, Y., *British Mission to the Jews in Nineteenth-century Palestine* London and Portland, Ore., 2003.

Peters, F. E., *Jerusalem: The Holy City in the Eyes of Chroniclers, Visitors, Pilgrims and Prophets from the Days of Abraham to the Beginnings of Modern Times*, Princeton, 1985.

Jerusalem and Mecca: The Typology of the Holy City in the Near East, New York, 1986.

Pevsner, N., 'Scrape and Anti-Scrape', in Fawcett ed. *The Future*, 1976: 35–54.

Some Architectural Writers of the Nineteenth Century, Oxford, 1972.

Phillips, S., *Guide to the Crystal Palace and Park*, London, 1854.

Pick, W., 'Meissner Pasha and the Construction of Railways in Palestine and Neighbouring Countries', in Gilbar ed., *Ottoman Palestine*, 1990: 179–218.

Piggott, J., *The Palace of the People: The Crystal Palace at Sydenham 1854–1936*, London, 2004.

Pinney, C. and Peterson, N., *Photography's Other Histories*, Durham, NC, 2003.

Planché, J. R., *Recollections and Reflections*, London, 1901.

Souvenir of the Bal Costumé, Given By Her Most Gracious Majesty, Queen Victoria, at Buckingham Palace, March 12th, 1842. The Drawings from the Original Dresses by Mr Coke Smith. The Descriptive Letter Press by J. R. Planché ESQ, FRS, London, 1843.

Platt, E., *Journal of a Tour through Egypt, the Peninsula of Sinai, and the Holy Land, in 1838, 1839*, 2 vols., London, 1842.

Plotz, J., *Portable Property: Victorian Culture on the Move*, Princeton, 2008.

Poinke, A., 'A Ritual Failure: The Eglinton Tournament, the Victorian Medieval Revival, and Victorian Ritual Culture', *Studies in Medievalism* 16, 2008: 25–45.

Pope-Hennessy, U., *The Laird of Abbotsford: An Informal Presentation of Sir Walter Scott*, London and New York, 1932.

Porter, A., *Religion versus Empire? British Protestant Missionaries and Overseas Expansion 1700–1914*, Manchester, 2004.

Poste, B., *Britannia Antiqua: Ancient Britain*, London, 1857.

  Britannic Researches or New Facts and Rectifications of Ancient British History, London, 1853.

Price, L., *How To Do Things With Books in Victorian Britain*, Princeton, 2012.

Prichard, T., *The Heroines of Welsh History*, London, 1854.

Prothero, R., *The Life and Letters of Dean Stanley*, London and New York, 1910.

Purbrick, L. ed., *The Great Exhibition of 1851. New Interdisciplinary Essays*, Manchester, 2001.

Pusey, E., *Remarks on the Prospective and Past Benefits of Cathedral Institutions*, London, 1833.

Quigley, C., *Skulls and Skeletons*, North Carolina, 2001.

Qureshi, S., *Peoples on Parade: Exhibitions, Empire and Anthropology in Nineteenth-century Britain*, Chicago, 2011.

Ray, G. ed., *The Letters and Private Papers of William Makepeace Thackeray*, 4 vols., Cambridge, Mass., 1945–6.

Reed, J., *Glorious Battle: The Cultural Politics of Victorian Anglo-Catholicism*, Nashville, 1996.

Reid, R., 'George Wightwick: A Thorn in the Side of the Ecclesiologists', in Webster and Elliott eds. '*A Church*', 2000: 239–57.

Reinhard, K., 'The Freudian Things: Construction and the Archaeological Metaphor', in Barker ed., *Excavations*, 1996: 57–79.

Renan, E., *Anti-Christ*, trans. W. G. Hutchinson, London, 1899 [1876].

  The Life of Jesus, trans C. Gore, London, 1927 [1864].

  Recollections of my Youth, 3rd edn, London, 1897.

Reynolds, M., *Martyr of Ritualism: Father Mackonochie of St Alban's Holburn*, London, 1965.

Rhodes, R., *The Lion and the Cross: Early Christianity in Victorian Novels*, Columbus, OH, 1995.

Ricca, S., *Reinventing Jerusalem: Israel's Reconstruction of the Jewish Quarter after 1967*, London, 2007.

Richardson, E., *Classical Victorians: Scholars, Scoundrels and Generals in Pursuit of Antiquity*, Cambridge, 2013.

Richardson, J., *The Eglinton Tournament*, London, 1843.

[Richardson, J.], 'The Tournament', *The Times*, 2 September 1839: 5.

Richardson, W.H., 'The Ravages of Restoration', *Athenaeum* 2607, 13 October 1877: 472.

Rieser, A., *The Chautauqua Movement: Protestants, Progressives and the Culture of Modern Liberalism*, New York, 2003.

Riley-Smith, J., *The Crusades, Christianity and Islam*, New York, 2008.

Riley-Smith, J. ed., *The Oxford History of the Crusades*, Oxford, 1999.

Roberts, M., 'Cultural Crossing: Sartorial Adventures, Satiric Narratives, and the Question of Indigenous Agency in Nineteenth-Century Europe and the Middle East', in Hackforth-Jones and Roberts, *Edges of Empire*, 2005: 70–94.

   Intimate Outsiders: The Harem in Ottoman and Orientalist Art and Travel Literature, Durham and London, 2007.

Robertson, D., 'Mid-Victorians amongst the Alps', in Knoepflmacher and Tennyson eds. *Nature*, 1978: 113–36.

Robertson, J. ed., *The Judgment of the Rt Hon Sir Herbert Jenner Fust, Kt. Dean of the Arches &c. &c. &c. in the Case of Faulkner v. Litchfield and Stearn, on the 31st January 1845*, London, 1845.

Robson, E., 'Restoration in France', *The Ecclesiologist* 22, 1861: 311–12.

Robson, Eleanor, 'Bel and the Dragons: Deciphering Cuneiform before Decipherment', in Brusius, Dean and Ramalingam eds., *William Henry Fox Talbot*, (2013): 193–218.

Röhricht, R., *Bibliotheca geographica Palaestinae: chronologisches Verzeichnis der von 333 bis 1878 verfassten Literatur über das Heilige Land*, London, 1989.

Rose, E., 'The Stone Table in the Round Church and the Crisis of the Cambridge Camden Society', *Victorian Studies* 10, 1966: 119–44.

Rosovsky, N. ed., *City of the Great King: Jerusalem from David to the Present*, Cambridge, Mass., 1996.

Rouveret, A., *Histoire et imaginaire de la peinture ancienne (Ve siècle av. J.C.-Ier siècle ap. J.C.)*, Paris, 1989.

Rubinstein, W. and Rubinstein, H., *Philosemitism: Admiration and Support in the English-Speaking World for Jews, 1800–1939*, Basingstoke, 1999.

Rudnytsky, P., *Freud and Oedipus*, New York, 1987.

Ruskin, J., *The Seven Lamps of Architecture*, New York, 1857.

   Verona and Other Essays, London, 1894.

   Works, 39 vols., ed. E. T. Cook and J. Wedderburn, London and New York, 1903.

Ryan, J., *Picturing Empire: Photography and the Visualization of the British Empire*, Chicago, 1997.

Rydell, R., *All the World's a Fair: Visions of Empire at American International Expositions, 1876–1916*, Chicago, 1984.

Said, E., *Culture and Imperialism*, London, 1993.

   Orientalism, London, 1978.

   The Question of Palestine, New York, 1979.

Saint, A., 'Anglican Church Building in London 1790–1890', in Brooks and Saint eds., *The Victorian Church*, 1995: 30–50.

Sanders, A., *The Victorian Historical Novel 1840–80*, London, 1978.

Sargent, J., *The Life and Letters of Henry Martyn*, London, 1819.

Sayce, A. H. *The 'Higher Criticism' and the Verdict of the Monuments*, London, 1894.

Schiavo, L. B., 'From Phantom Image to Perfect Vision: Physiological Optics, Commercial Photography and the Popularization of the Stereoscope', in Gitelman and Pingree eds., *New Media*, 2003: 113–38.

Schiller, E., *The First Photographs of Jerusalem: The Old City*, Jerusalem, 1978.

Schnapp, A., *Discovering the Past: A History of Archaeology*, London, 1996.

Scholefield, J., *The Christian Altar: a Sermon Preached before the University of Cambridge, on Sunday Morning Oct 23, 1842*, Cambridge, 1842.

Schöllgen, G., *Imperialismus und Gleichgewicht: Deutschland, England und die orientalische Frage*, Munich, 1984.

Schwartz, J. and Ryan, J. eds., *Picturing Place: Photography and the Geographical Imagination*, London, 2003.

Scodel, R. and Bettenworth, A., *Whither Quo Vadis? Sienkiewicz's Novel in Film and Television*, Oxford, 2009.

Scott, G., 'Opening Address of the President', *Sessional Papers of the Royal Institute of British Architects 1875–6* 26, 1876: 2–11.

   A Plea for the Faithful Restoration of Our Ancient Churches, London, 1850.

   'Reply to Mr Stevenson's Paper on "Architectural Restoration: its principles and practice"', *Sessional Papers of the Royal Institute of British Architects 1876–7* 27, 1877: 242–56.

Scott, S., *Art and Society in Fourth-Century Britain: Villa Mosaics in Context*, Oxford, 2000.

   'Britain in the Classical World: Samuel Lysons and the Art of Roman Britain 1780–1820', *Classical Receptions Journal* 6: 294–337.

Shandler, J. and Wenger, B. eds., *'Encounters with the Holy Land': Place, Past and Future in American Jewish Culture*, Pennsylvania, 1998.

Sharpe, E., 'Against Restoration', *The Builder* 31, 1873: 672.

Shaw, H., *The Forms of Historical Fiction: Walter Scott and his Successors*, Ithaca, NY, 1983.

Shaw, W., 'Ottoman Photography of the Late Nineteenth Century: An "Innocent" Modernism?', *History of Photography* 33, 2009: 80–93.

Shelton Mackenzie, R., *Sir Walter Scott: The Story of his Life*, Boston, 1871.

Shipley, O., *Ought We to Obey the New Court Created by the Public Worship Regulation Act?* 2nd edn, London, 1875.

Siberry, E., *The New Crusaders: Images of the Crusades in the Nineteenth and Early Twentieth Centuries*, Aldershot, 2000.

Sienkiewicz, H., *Quo Vadis?*, trans. S. Binion and S. Malevsky, London, 1897.

Silberman, N., *Digging for God and Country: Exploration, Archaeology and the Secret Struggle for the Holy Land*, New York, 1982.

Silver-Brody, K., *Documentors of the Dream: Pioneer Jewish Photographers in the Land of Israel 1890–1933*, Jerusalem and Philadelphia, 1998.

Slyomovics, S., 'Visual Ethnography, Stereotypes and Photographing Algeria', in Netton ed., *Orientalism Revisited*, 2013: 128–50.

Smith, C., *The Embassy of Sir William White at Constantinople 1866–1891*, Oxford, 1957.

Smith, G. A., *The Historical Geography of the Holy Land: Especially in Relation to the History of Israel and of the early Church*, London, 1894.

Smith, L. A., *George Adam Smith: A Personal Memoir and Family Chronicle*, London, 1944.

Smith, M., *The Letters of Charlotte Brontë 1848–1851*, vol. ii, Oxford, 2000.

Solomon-Godeau, A., 'A Photographer in Jerusalem, 1855: Auguste Salzman and his Time', *October* 18, 1981: 91–107.

'Photography and Industrialization: John Ruskin and the Moral Dimension of Photography', *Exposure* 21, 1983: 10–14.

Spencer, S., *Francis Bedford, Landscape Photography and Nineteenth-Century British Culture*, Farnham, 2011.

Stamp, G., 'George Gilbert Scott and the Cambridge Camden Society', in Webster and Elliott eds., '*A Church*', 2000: 173–89.

Stanley, A., *The Life and Correspondence of Thomas Arnold D.D.*, 2nd edn, Oxford, 1890.

Sermons Preached before His Royal Highness the Prince of Wales, During his Tour in the East, in the Spring of 1862, with Notices of Some of the Localities Visited, London, 1863.

Sinai and Palestine in Connection with their History, London, 1856.

Stanley, B., *The Bible and the Flag: Protestant Missions and British Imperialism in the Nineteenth and Twentieth Centuries*, Leicester, 1990.

Stead, A. W., *Studies of the Sovereign and Her Reign*, London, 1887.

Stevenson, J., 'Architectural Restoration: Its Principles and Practice', *Sessional Papers of the Royal Institute of British Architects 1876–77* 27, 1877: 219–35.

'The View of the Anti-Restorers', *The Builder* 36, 1878: 361–2.

Stevenson, R. L., *A Child's Garden of Verses*, ed. S. Schwartz, London, 1979.

Stiebing, W., *Uncovering the Past: A History of Archaeology*, Oxford and New York, 1993.

Stocking, G. ed., *Volksgeist as Method and Ethic: Essays on Boasian Ethnography and the German Anthropological Tradition*, Madison, 1996.

Storrs, R., *Orientations*, London, 1939.

Stray, C., *Classics Transformed: Schools, Universities and Society in England, 1830–1960*, Oxford, 1998.

Street, A. 'Architectural Notes in France', *The Ecclesiologist* 19, 1859: 362–72.

'Architectural Notes in France', *The Ecclesiologist* 20, 1859: 91–100.

'Destructive Restoration on the Continent', *The Ecclesiologist* 18, 1857: 342–5.

Memoirs of George Edmund Street RA 1824–1881, London, 1888.

Stuart, E., *The Pew System: The Chief Hindrance to the Church's Work in Towns*, London, n.d.

Stubbs, W. *et al.*, *The Cornish See and Cathedral: Historical and Architectural Notes*, London, 1889.

A Suburban Vicar, '*The Ecclesiastical Deadlock': or the Case of Sidney Faithorn Green, Priest, Arrested March 19th 1881, in Prison for Conscience Sake. Four Letters Addressed to the Editor of the 'Standard'*, London, 1881.

Swanson, R. N. ed., *The Holy Land, Holy Lands, and Christian History*, Bury St Edmunds, 2000.

Swenerton, M., *Artisans and Architects: The Ruskinian Tradition in Architectural Thought*, Houndmills and London, 1989.

Swenson, A., 'Conceptualizing Heritage in Nineteenth- and Early Twentieth-century France, Germany and England', Ph.D. thesis, Cambridge University, 2007.

   The Rise of Heritage: Preserving the Past in France, Germany and England, 1789–1914, Cambridge, 2013.

Swenson, A. and Mandler, P. eds., *Plunder and Preservation: Britain and the Heritage of Empire, Proceedings of the British Academy* 187, London, 2013.

Swift, M., 'Anglican Stained Glass in Cornwall and its Social Context', *Journal of the Royal Institution of Cornwall* 19, 2009: 7–26.

Symondson, A., 'Theology, Worship, and the Late Victorian Church', in Brooks and Saint eds., *The Victorian Church*, 1995: 192–222.

Tagg, J., *The Burden of Representation: Essays on Photographies and Histories*, Basingstoke, 1988.

Tavakoli-Targhi, M., *Refashioning Iran: Orientalism, Occidentalism, and Historiography*, Basingstoke and New York, 2001.

Taylor, R., *Diegesis: Being a Discovery of the Origins, Evidences and Early History of Christianity*, London, 1834.

Thackeray, W., 'Highways and Low-Ways: or Ainsworth's Dictionary with Notes by Turpin', *Fraser's* 9, 1834: 724–38.

Thomas, G., 'Indian Courtesans in Cartes-de-Visites', *History of Photography* 8, 1984: 83–7.

Thomson, D., Voller, J. and Frank, F. eds., *Gothic Writers: A Critical and Bibliographical Guide*, Westport and London, 2002.

Thomson, W., *The Land and the Book: Biblical Illustrations drawn from the Manners and Customs, the Scenes and the Scenery of the Holy Land*, New York, 1880.

Thorne, S., *Congregational Missions and the Making of Imperial Culture in Nineteenth-Century England*, Stanford, 1999.

Tibawi, A., *British Interests in Palestine 1800–1901*, Oxford, 1961.

Tickner, L., *The Spectacle of Women: Imagery of the Suffrage Campaign 1907–14*, London, 1988.

Timpson, T., *British Ecclesiastical History Including the Religion of the Druids, the Introduction of Christianity into Britain, and the Rise, Progress and Present State of Every Denomination of Christianity in the British Empire*, 2nd edn, London, 1849.

Tissot, J., *The Life of Our Saviour Jesus Christ*, 4 vols., trans. Mrs Arthur Bell, New York, 1898.

Todd, M., 'The Rediscovery of Roman Britain' in Todd ed., *Companion*, 2004: 443–9.

Todd, M. ed., *A Companion to Roman Britain*, Oxford, 2004.

Tooley, S., *The Personal Life of Queen Victoria*, London, 1896.

Trollope, A., *Barchester Towers*, London, 1857.

Truefit, G., 'Paper Read at Worcester Architectural Society', *The Builder* 13, 1855: 489–90.

Tschudi-Madsen, S., *Restoration and Anti-Restoration: A Study in English Restoration Philosophy*, Oslo, 1976.

Tucker, H., *Epic: Britain's Heroic Muse 1790–1910*, Oxford, 2008.

Tuckerman, H., 'Allusions to Phrenology in *Last Days of Pompeii*', *Annals of Phrenology* 1, 1834: 460–1.

Turner, F., 'Christians and Pagans in Victorian Novels', in Edwards ed., *Roman Presences*, 1999.

    The Greek Heritage in Victorian Britain, New York, 1981.

Tytler, G., *Physiognomy in the European Novel: Faces and Fortunes*, Princeton, 1982.

Ucko, P., 'Unprovenanced Material Culture and Freud's Collection of Antiquities', *Journal of Material Culture* 6.3, 2001: 269–322.

Urry, J., *The Tourist Gaze*, 2nd edn, London, 2002.

Ussher, J., *Britannicarum Ecclesiarum Antiquitates*, Dublin, 1639.

Vaczek, L. and Buckland, L., *Travellers in Ancient Lands*, New York, 1981.

Vance, N., 'Anxieties of Empire and the Moral Tradition: Rome and Britain', *International Journal of the Classical Tradition* 18, 2012: 246–61.

    The Victorians and Ancient Rome, Oxford, 1997.

van Hulle, D. and Leerssen, J. eds., *Editing the Nation's Memory: Textual Scholarship and Nation-Building in 19th-Century Europe*, Amsterdam and New York, 2008.

van Wyhe, J., *Phrenology and the Origins of Victorian Scientific Naturalism*, Aldershot, 2004.

Varisco, D., 'Framing the Holy Land in Nineteenth-Century Protestant Bible Customs Texts', in Netton ed., *Orientalism Revisited*, 2013: 187–204.

Vasunia, P., *The Classics and Colonial India*, Oxford, 2013.

Vaughan, R., *Revolutions in English History. Volume I. Revolutions in Race*, 2nd edn, London, 1867 [1860].

Vereté, M., 'Why was a British Consulate Established in Jerusalem?', *English Historical Review* 85, 1970: 316–45.

Vester, B. S., *Our Jerusalem: An American family in the Holy City, 1881–1949*, Garden City, NY, 1951.

Vincent, J., *The Chautauqua Movement*, Boston, 1886.

Vincent, J., Lee, J. and Bain, R., *Early Footsteps of the Man of Galilee*, New York, 1896.

Vincent, L., *John Heyl Vincent: A Biographical Sketch*, New York, 1925.

Viollet-le-Duc, E.-E., *Dictionnaire raisonnée de l'architecture française du XIe au XVIe siècle*, 10 vols., Paris, 1854–68.

Vogel, L., *To See a Promised Land: Americans and the Holy Land in the Nineteenth Century*, Pennsylvania, 1993.

Von Harnack, A., 'Christianity and Christians at the Court of the Roman Emperors before the Time of Constantine', *Princeton Review* 54, 1878: 239–80.

Wagner, R., *Richard Wagner's Prose Works*, trans. W. Ashton Ellis, London, 1892–9.

Wainwright, C., *The Secrets of Ritualism: A Warning*, 2nd edn, London, 1877.

Wajda, S., '"A Room with a Viewer": The Parlor Stereoscope, Comic Stereographs and the Psychic Role of Play in Victorian America', in Grover ed., *Hard at Play*, 1992: 112–38.

Wakeling, C., 'The Non-Conformist Traditions: Chapels, Change and Continuity', in Brooks and Saint eds., *The Victorian Church*, 1995: 82–97.

Walk, C., *A Visit to Jerusalem and the Holy Places Adjacent*, London, 1826.

Ward, W., *The Protestant Evangelical Awakening*, Cambridge, 1992.

Warren, C., *The Lord's Table the Christian Altar, in Some Remarks upon Professor Scholefield's Late Sermon*, Cambridge, 1843.

Warren, C., Capt., *Underground Jerusalem*, London, 1876.

Watenpaugh, K., *Being Modern in the Middle East: Revolution, Nationalism and the Arab Middle Class*, Princeton, 2006.

Waterfield, G., *Layard of Nineveh*, London, 1963.

Waterhouse, A., 'The Ravages of Restoration', *Athenaeum* 2655, 14 September 1878: 345.

Watkin, D., *The Life and Work of C.R. Cockerell*, London, 1974.

Watson, J., *Literature and Material Culture from Balzac to Proust: The Collection and Consumption of Curiosities*, Cambridge, 2004.

Watson, N., *The Literary Tourist: Readers and Places in Romantic and Victorian Britain*, London, 2006.

Watson, N. ed., *Literary Tourism and Nineteenth-Century Culture*, Basingstoke, 2009.

Webb, J., *Pomponia: or the Gospel in Caesar's Household*, Philadelphia, 1867.

Webster, C. and Elliott, J. eds., *'A Church As It Should Be': The Cambridge Camden Society and its Influence*, Stamford, 2000.

Weitzman, K., and Kessler, H., *The Frescoes of the Dura Synagogue and Christian Art*, Washington, D.C., 1990.

Welch, P. J., 'Anglican Churchmen and the Establishment of the Jerusalem Bishopric', *Journal of Ecclesiastical History* 8, 1957: 193–204.

Wharton, A., *Selling Jerusalem: Relics, Replicas, Theme Parks*, Chicago, 2006.

Wheeler, M., *Ruskin's God*, Cambridge, 1999.

Wheeler, M and Whiteley, N. eds., *The Lamp of Memory: Ruskin, Tradition and Architecture*, Manchester and New York, 1992.

Whibley, C., *Lord John Manners and his Friends*, 2 vols., Edinburgh and London, 1925.

White, J., *The Cambridge Movement: The Ecclesiologists and the Gothic Revival*, Cambridge, 1962.

White, W., 'Church Restoration', *The Ecclesiologist* 25, 1864: 246–66.
'"Restoration" versus "Preservation"', *The Builder* 36, 1878: 115; with discussion 167–70.

Wightwick, G., 'Modern English Gothic Architecture', *Quarterly Papers on Architecture* 3, 1845: 1–18.
'On the Present Conditions and Prospects of Architecture in England', *Quarterly Papers on Architecture* 2, 1844: 1–16.

Williams, J., *Claudia and Pudens: An Attempt to Show How Claudia Mentioned in St Paul's Second Epistle to Timothy Was a British Princess*, London, 1848.
The Ecclesiastical Antiquities of the Cymry; or, the Ancient British Church, its History, Doctrine, and Rites, London, 1844.

Winterer, C., *The Culture of Classicism: Ancient Greece and Rome in American Intellectual Life, 1780–1910*, Baltimore and London, 2002.

Wiseman, N., *Fabiola; or the Church of the Catacombs*, London, 1854.
On Lady Morgan's Statements Regarding St Peter's Chair at Rome, Rome, 1833. [Originally published in *Catholic Magazine and Review* 1, 1831: 194–207.]

Witheridge, J., *The Excellent Dr Stanley: The Life of Dean Stanley of Westminster*, London, 2013.

Wohlleben, M. ed., *Konservieren nicht restaurieren*, Braunschweig, 1988.

Wolley, H., *The Impending Crisis of the Church of England*, London and Bromley, 1875.

Woodward, D., *Hell in the Holy Land: World War 1 in the Middle East*, Lexington, 2006.

Woodward, M., 'Between Orientalist Cliché and Images of Modernization: Photographic Practice in the Late Ottoman Empire', *History of Photography* 27, 2003: 363–74.

Wright, T., *The Celt, the Roman and the Saxon: A History of the Early Inhabitants of Britain, down to the Conversion of the Anglo-Saxons to Christianity*, London, 1852.

Wrightson, W., *Four Sermons on the Christian Church, the Christian Mission and the Public Worship Act*, London, 1875.

Yates, N., *Anglican Ritualism in Victorian Britain 1830–1910*, Oxford, 1999.

Yeager, S., *Jerusalem in Medieval Narrative*, Cambridge, 2008.

Young, R., *White Mythologies: Writing History and the West*, London, 1990.

Zander, W., *Israel and the Holy Places of Christendom*, London, 1971.

Zimmerman, A., *Anthropology and Antihumanism in Imperial Germany*, Chicago, 2001.

Zoin-Goshen, H., *Beyond the Wall: Chapters in Urban Jerusalem*, Jerusalem, 2006.

Index